# Nurse to the Imagination

# *Nurse* TO THE IMAGINATION

## 50 YEARS OF THE ROBERT BURNS FELLOWSHIP

*Edited by* LAWRENCE JONES

OTAGO

Published by Otago University Press
PO Box 56/Level 1, 398 Cumberland Street, Dunedin, New Zealand
Fax: 64 3 479 8385
Email: university.press@otago.ac.nz
Website: www.otago.ac.nz/press

First published 2008

ISBN 978 1 877372 65 0

Front cover: Statue of Robbie Burns in the Octagon, Dunedin. Photo by Alan Dove.
Back cover: Lawrence Jones. Photo by Alan Dove.

Otago University Press
Publisher: Wendy Harrex
Editor: Richard Reeve
Production Editor: Fiona Moffat

Printed in New Zealand by Astra Print Ltd, Wellington

# CONTENTS

# THE BURNS FELLOWSHIP: 'TO ENCOURAGE AND PROMOTE'

THE primary aim of the book is to celebrate the first fifty years of the University of Otago's Burns Fellowship and the writing that it has promoted. In 1968 the literary magazine *Landfall* had a kind of preliminary stocktaking of the Fellowship, with a collection of essays by some of the early Fellows and by Alan Horsman, speaking for the University's English Department. Some of those essays are reprinted in this volume; also included is a short, previously unpublished essay by Warren Dibble on his experience of the Fellowship and its context. In 1998 a fortieth-anniversary celebration was held, with readings, lectures and social gatherings.

The main outcome of the fortieth anniversary, preserved in this book, is the magnificent collection of photo portraits made by the late Reg Graham. He captured most of the Fellows who attended that gathering, and those images comprise the bulk of the images printed here. In the years after 1998 he photographed new Fellows, to complete the record, and in this book those photographs have been augmented by a few others. Reg Graham's photographs of the Fellows have been displayed on a wall of the Central Library of the University, and are now published together for the first time in this first book devoted to the Burns Fellowship.

This celebration of writing undertaken by the Fellows is in the form of a literary wine-tasting: included are works or excerpts of about 1500 words from texts either completed or started during tenure, printed in chronological order. The result is a wonderful sampler of five decades of New Zealand writing. A brief editorial introduction summarises where the writer was in terms of his or her career at the time of the Fellowship, and lists what was achieved during the year; in respect of this, I have drawn from literary-historical records, correspondence, and other writings by the Fellows. In a few cases – such as with Duggan, Frame, Mason and Baxter – the complex matter

of work undertaken is treated in more detail. Early in this project we intended to list major works and honours for each Fellow, but that would have become a book in itself. The writing was what the Fellowship was established to encourage, and this is what the book attempts to foreground.

The official description of the Robert Burns Fellowship is brief and to the point:

The Fellowship was established in 1958 by a group of citizens, who wished to remain Anonymous, to commemorate the bicentenary of the birth of Robert Burns and to perpetuate appreciation of the valuable service rendered to the early settlement of Otago by the Burns family. The general purpose of the Fellowship is to encourage and promote imaginative New Zealand literature and to associate writers thereof with the University. It is attached to the Department of English of the University.

The rather lengthier Conditions of Award spell out the ground rules for how these aims are to be carried out. The Fellowships are to be awarded annually, normally for a one-year term, but the term can be extended for up to one further year, and there can also be awards for less than a year. The Fellowship is open 'to writers of imaginative literature, including poetry, drama, fiction, autobiography, biography, essays or literary criticism'. The writer is normally to be resident in New Zealand, but New Zealand residents temporarily overseas can be appointed. The appointees are to be writers 'who in the opinion of the Selection Committee have established by published work or otherwise that they are a serious writer likely to continue writing and to benefit from the Fellowship'. Such a writer does not need to possess any formal qualification 'nor belong to any association or organisation of writers', but should not normally be a full-time teacher in any

university. There are no age restrictions, but 'As between candidates of comparable merit, preference shall be given to applicants under forty years of age at the time of selection'. No person can be selected more than three times or hold the Fellowship for a total of more than four years. The Fellow shall normally reside in Dunedin for the term of the Fellowship, and shall be supplied an office by the Department of English. The Fellow can be 'requested to undertake a limited amount of lecturing or seminar work in the Department of English during not more than one semester in the University year and/or to deliver a course of not more than six lectures open to the public, provided always that Fellows have sufficient free time in which to pursue their own literary work or studies'.

Looking back on fifty years of the Fellowship, we can see that some of the minor original hopes have not entirely eventuated, but the major aims and means most definitely have been realised. The commemoration of Robert Burns and the New Zealand branch of the Burns family has never figured heavily. Of the writings in this collection, only one, James K Baxter's 'A Small Ode on Mixed Flatting', mentions Robert Burns, and it does so in a way that the Scottish poet probably would have appreciated but that would have aroused his nephew Thomas Burns' disapproval (when Baxter was Burns Fellow, *The Merry Muses of Caledonia* had a prominent place on his bookshelf, next to Robert Lowell's *Life Studies*). As for associating the writer with the University, the option of requesting Fellows to lecture has seldom been exercised, although some Fellows so inclined have given memorable public lectures and readings, and some have profitably taken part in classes. The association has tended to be more informal, with some Fellows very much a part of the life of the Department and others mostly working apart from it. The intended policy of privileging writers under forty has mostly been carried out: a survey of the recipients of the Fellowship shows that five were in their twenties when appointed (with Ian Wedde at twenty-five the youngest), twenty-three were in their thirties, ten in their forties, nine in their fifties. The appointees have all been writers likely to continue (although not all of them did). And of course the primary purpose of promoting

and encouraging imaginative New Zealand literature has been achieved magnificently, as this volume attests. As Charles Brasch had hoped to mark in his *Landfall* note on the inaugural tenure of the Burns Fellowship in 1959, the University of Otago has been a 'nurse to the imagination' for New Zealand writers.

In 1958 the literary infrastructure to encourage, promote, and sustain New Zealand literature was still in its formative stages. The 'first generation' *Phoenix*-Caxton-*Tomorrow* writers of the 1930s had laid the groundwork: among their innovations the Caxton Press remained, while Charles Brasch's *Landfall* had been founded in 1947 to develop more permanently what *Phoenix* had tried to start, and the *New Zealand Listener*, especially after 1949 under Monte Holcroft, continued the tradition of *Tomorrow*, with a stronger literary emphasis and a much wider circulation. The New Zealand Literary Fund was set up in 1947, and from its limited budget established the Hubert Church and Jessie McKay Awards in 1952 (in time to save Janet Frame from a leucotomy), the Scholarship in Letters in 1956, and the Award for Achievement in 1957. The Burns Fellowship added a significant piece to this infrastructure by providing the first and most substantial literary residency.

The provision of a Fellowship for a full year or more has often encouraged writers to take on large projects that would be difficult or impossible for a part-time writer. For Noel Hilliard it meant drafting the third novel of his planned tetralogy that would bring the characters of his first two novels together. For Owen Marshall it meant turning from short fiction to write his first published novel. For Paddy Richardson it meant moving from the short story to a large family novel. For Michael King it meant synthesising three years of research into his biography of Janet Frame. For John Caselberg, the Fellowship was a chance to begin a planned eight-play sequence of historical drama.

However, the project has not always worked out as expected. Ian Cross took the year to write most of the big complex novel he had planned, and succeeded, but he also decided that that would be his swan-song as novelist, for the kind of work he wanted to do could be done only in those not-to-be-repeated conditions. Maurice Shadbolt discovered he could not yet write the extended work he

had intended, and turned instead to a kind of *jeu d'esprit* that developed into his quite different first novel. Maurice Duggan put aside his prospective Jamesian novel, wrote some very different stories in reaction, and ended up with his best work.

Radical changes of directions were sometimes the result of the freedom the Fellowship provided. Baxter had planned, among other things, to edit his grandfather's memoirs, but instead wrote a sequence of plays. R.A.K. Mason had planned to write a biography of Rewi Alley, but moved instead towards a project he would not complete for several years, a large historical drama. Witi Ihimaera completed the project of his early books with a collection of short stories moving his characters from a rural to an urban environment, then decided on a decade of voluntary literary silence before moving on to a more radical phase in his writing. Robert Lord took the Fellowship as a chance to return to New Zealand after many years in the United States, and resume a career here. In his autobiography, Roger Hall entitled the chapter on the Fellowship 'From Glide Time to Full Time', and used the Fellowship as a move towards becoming a full-time dramatist-teacher. Conversely, some writers such as Janet Frame or James Norcliffe did what they had always done, but took the chance to do it more intensively, and had outstandingly productive years.

For some years the Burns offered the only chance for a full year's writing with a decent income, but after a restructuring of state support for the arts in the late 1970s, other such opportunities surfaced, beginning with the Victoria University Writing Fellowship in 1979, and subsequently a number of state-funded and privately-funded residencies, grants, and awards. The difference in the supportive infrastructure can be seen if one compares the career of Cross to that of Catherine Chidgey forty-five years later. Cross, in receiving the Burns, had received almost the only support he could get: there were no other residencies, only one other possible grant (the Scholarshp in Letters), and no substantial awards. Chidgey, on the other hand, received the Best First Book of Fiction Award in the 1998 Montana New Zealand Book Awards and was runner-up for the Deutz Medal for Fiction. She also won the Best First

Book Award in the Southeast Asia/South Pacific Section of the 1999 Commonwealth Writers Prize and a Betty Trask Award in the United Kingdom in 1999. In 1998 she was awarded a Buddle Findlay Sargeson Fellowship and the inaugural Adam Foundation Prize, and in 1999 a Todd New Writers' Bursary. Her second novel was runner-up in the Fiction section of the 2000 Montana New Zealand Book Awards, and in 2001 she was the Meridian Energy Katherine Mansfield Memorial Fellow in Menton. In 2002 she won the inaugural Glenn Schaeffer Prize in Modern Letters, in 2003 she shared the Ursula Bethell Residency at the University of Canterbury, and in 2008 she holds a residency at Cork in Ireland. For Cross in 1959 such support for writing would have been unimaginable.

The proliferation of residencies since 1980 has meant that the Burns Fellowship has inevitably drawn more on Otago writers and less on writers from further afield. Of the twenty-three appointments made before 1980, only three were to writers resident in Dunedin at the time of appointment; of the thirty appointments made since 1980, fifteen have been to writers resident in Dunedin. But if writers from elsewhere in the country, especially from the northern half of North Island, have not been attracted to Dunedin when other options surfaced, a significant number of those who did come south, especially before 1980, stayed on after the Fellowship. For writers such as R.A.K. Mason, Janet Frame, James K. Baxter, Ian Wedde, Roger Hall and Robert Lord, the Fellowship led to important stays of productive years in Otago. For others such as O.E. Middleton or Hone Tuwhare, the shift was permanent.

Certainly, whether its recipients remained in Dunedin or not, the Fellowship helped to forge links between Dunedin cultural institutions and individual writers. The publishing programme of the Bibliography Room of the English Department, initiated by Keith Maslen, printed works by Mason, Caselberg, Ruth Dallas, Baxter and Tuwhare. Otago University Press has produced volumes by Baxter, Dallas, Lord, Cilla McQueen and Middleton and publishes *Landfall*. John McIndoe, especially under the editorship of Brian Turner, published books by Caselberg, Middleton, Noel Hilliard, McQueen, Bill Sewell, Owen Marshall and Turner. Trevor Reeves' Caveman Press

published Tuwhare and Peter Olds. Dunedin journals likewise published much by the Fellows. There were interviews and articles in the University student newspaper *Critic* and in the *Otago Daily Times*, and contributions to the Otago University Students Association *Literary Review* by writers such as Mason, Shadbolt and Noonan. Brasch employed Dallas in the *Landfall* office as assistant from 1961 to 1966, and published much work by the early Fellows: Duggan, Caselberg, Shadbolt, Maurice Gee, Frame, Baxter, Middleton, Graham Billing, Dallas herself. Dunedin's theatres likewise showcased work. The University's Allen Hall Theatre has put on works by Stuart Hoar and Jo Randerson, and the Globe under Patric Carey produced plays by Mason, Baxter, Olds, Warren Dibble and Lord. Roger Hall was among the founders of the Fortune Theatre and his plays remain an economic mainstay; the Fortune has also premiered plays by Renée and Lord.

As the only New Zealand literary award with a continuous fifty-year history, the Fellowship presents a revealing cross-section of literary history, especially in relation to generation, gender, and genre. The Fellowship was established too late to involve many of the first generation of modern New Zealand writers, the *Phoenix*-Caxton-*Tomorrow* group: only R.A.K. Mason among them had a term as Fellow. But the second generation, those born in the decade following World War I who began publishing in the late 1940s, were strongly represented, many having already established themselves before 1958: Cross, Duggan, Caselberg, Frame, Dallas, Baxter, and Middleton. This was also true with the 'third generation', those born between the beginning of the Depression and World War II who began publishing in the later 1950s, with Shadbolt and Gee being appointed early in their careers, and Hilliard and Billing later, after they were more established.

The most strongly represented have been those writers born in the 1940s who began publication in the 1960s and 1970s, with Wedde in 1972 the first, and Michael King and James Norcliffe in 1998–2000 the last. They form a number of distinct groups. There are those associated with *Freed* and/or the new poetry and/or the counter-culture – Wedde, Hunt, Dibble (older – born in 1931), John Dickson, Olds, McQueen. There are the

writers associated with the Maori Literary Renaissance: Ihimaera, Keri Hulme, and their older precursor, Tuwhare (born in 1922, with a first book in 1964). There are writers not associated with a counter-culture and working in more traditional forms: the poets, Turner, Bernadette Hall, and Norcliffe; the fiction writers, Marshall, Elspeth Sandys, and Philip Temple; the dramatists, Hall and Lord; the biographers, Lynley Hood and King. In contrast, writers born in the 1950s or early 1960s have been thinner on the ground, with little but chronology to unite them: Bill Sewell, David Eggleton, Stuart Hoar, Christine Johnston, Paddy Richardson, Dianne Pettis. Since 2001 the Fellowship has been held primarily by the generation born in the 1960s and 1970s. Six have been 'spectacular babies' who participated in Bill Manhire's Victoria University writing programme: Randerson, Alison Wong, Sarah Quigley, Kate Duignan, Chidgey and Laurence Fearnley. The others of their generation, Paula Boock and Nick Ascroft, have been associated more with the Dunedin/Otago scene.

That all-female list of Manhire graduates points to another discernible historic pattern, the recent rise of women writers. If we divide the appointment into decades, we find between 1959 and 1970 ten men and two women, 1971 and 1980 eleven men and one woman, 1981 and 1990 six men and three women, 1991 and 2000 five men and seven women, and between 2001 and 2008 nine women and one man.

There are likewise discernible historical patterns in the genres in which the Fellows have worked. The Fellowship began in the midst of the first real efflorescence of the novel in New Zealand, and the early Fellows were predominantly novelists: Cross, Duggan (frustrated novelist in aim, but writer of short fiction in accomplishment), Shadbolt, Gee, and Frame. After that there was a tapering off in the number of writers of fiction – five in the 1970s but only one in the 1980s, back to five in the 1990s, while all of the Fellows between 2000 and 2007 wrote at least some fiction in their Burns year. Poetry has remained a constant, but the mode has changed considerably, and the distance between Mason's relatively traditional verse in 1962 and Ascroft's postmodernism in 2003 is huge, with a great variety of modes in the years between them.

The history of New Zealand drama is clearly evident in the appointment of the Fellows. Of those appointed before 1976, Caselberg, Mason, and, most spectacularly, Baxter, attempted dramatic works, but they all had been established as poets and wrote clearly literary drama, not designed for the professional theatre (which hardly existed in New Zealand then). Only Dibble wrote within (and against) the conventions of the stage, although radio drama was perhaps his forte. The rise of professional theatre after 1976 is evident in the work of Hall, Lord, Renée and Hoar, who wrote plays that were designed for and received professional production. At the same time, the rise of television drama and film in New Zealand is evident in the work of Michael Noonan and Rawiri Paratene, and writing for those media is important for Sandys, Boock, and Randerson.

Biography and autobiography had been included in the original definition of 'imaginative writing', but only since 1990 have these appeared as genres practised by the Fellows, with Hood, King, and Quigley appointed specifically to carry out biographical projects. Autobiographies and memoirs have not been written during the Fellowship tenure, but, as part of the boom in 'life writing' since 1990, a number have been written by ex-Fellows such as Cross, Shadbolt, Frame, Dallas, Roger Hall and Turner.

These historical patterns and others can be discerned in this book, but they are by-products, and it is hoped that the reader will find this a satisfying celebration of five decades of New Zealand's oldest literary fellowship.

LAWRENCE JONES,
*Dunedin, July 2008*

THE **1960s**

# IAN CROSS 1959

*Ian Cross (b. 1925) has published four novels and two autobiographical works.*

**WHEN** he was appointed as the first Burns Fellow late in 1958, Ian Cross had already published *The God Boy* in the U.S. (1957) and the U.K. (1958). His second novel, *The Backward Sex*, had been accepted for publication in the U.K. and was to appear in 1960. On arrival in Dunedin in March 1959, he started immediately, as he later reported to the Burns Fellowship Committee, 'on a novel that involved work beyond the range of anything I had previously attempted', dealing with four major characters and bringing him into 'a constant struggle with technical problems', but which he was able in his time as Fellow to bring 'to its penultimate stage'.[2] Looking back on the

experience forty-seven years later, he was more sardonic:

In the two-storey wooden building that housed the English Department of the University in a tiny room saved from being claustrophobic by a sash-window, I sat down to write the great New Zealand novel, a project calling for characters whose lives and experiences would span the nation's short history. Nothing to it, really.[3]

The novel, *After Anzac Day*, he completed back in Wellington in 1960, but, he later said, with 'short cuts' that did not 'fulfill the original grand plan for it'.[4] While still Burns Fellow he had said in his answer to a *Landfall* questionnaire that as a family man with three children he could not make an adequate income from writing fiction, and had to turn to the kind of full-time employment that precluded any more novels. Thus 'the novel I'm working on now is likely to be my last'.[5] He did not publish another novel until after his retirement (*The Family Man* in 1993). In the excerpt from *After Anzac Day* below, Jennie Page, one of four main characters, reflects on how she came to be staying in the house of a senior public servant, John Rankin, after her waterside worker father was violently assaulted during the 1951 waterfront strike.

## The Girl
### (FROM *After Anzac Day*)

The fright of her life, as she was standing at the window watching Mrs Rankin leave to catch a bus to the city. A rolling pressure that seemed to be squeezing her body into new shape. But this grand room of green chairs with oval backs and other deep furniture on soft carpet, where the brown wood table and cabinets could shine like mirrors and curtains were thick and rich and even the very air was much more expensive than that which she had breathed in her Newtown home – this grand room was an assurance that nothing really bad could happen to her, for in such extraordinarily soft and luxurious surroundings surely no real pain and trouble could ever touch a person. Not even somebody like herself. The little one was making her sick, that was all: being restless, even though he still had a month or more to wait. She would rather die than let harm come to him. And she would never let anybody take him away from her.

Jimmy would know only when he returned to New Zealand. He would say, 'Hello, Jennie,' in that wonderfully shy manner and for the next few moments it'd be just like he was meeting her for the first time. And then she would tell him. So different it would be from the occasion of Dad's knowing. 'The warehouse says that with the waterfront shutting down and goods not moving there's no sense in keeping me,' Dad had said as he lumbered about the kitchen, all the time looking to her, as though she could help him. 'The whole bloody waterfront all over the country is on strike,' he said. 'They reckon the Government will get the soldiers to work the wharves – too late to save my job, though. That's two jobs now I've lost through the union. Are you listening, girl? Can't you see what it means?'

So she just had to come out with it. 'Dad, I'm going to have a baby.'

But with Jimmy she would be able to just show him the wonder of their child and he would put his arms around both of them, tears in his eyes – he was really soft like that – and all would be so truly happy at last. Telling Dad was trouble and pain, in such a different place from this: though she'd done her best to keep that kitchen decent she could not prevent the grime and smears on the walls, nor the smell of stale cooking that was in the air. The linoleum was worn into scattered pieces and gaps between some of the exposed boards were so wide that it was a mercy that the hard scum of the years of wear and dust and dampness filled the cracks. So very different from this place. All that was in the kitchen was a scrubbed table and a clean tablecloth and clean knives and forks and plates. Right then, looking at Dad, waiting for him to say something, she felt like that kitchen. She could have her lipstick and powder on, but too much about her was run-down and in a mess. And there was Dad, so dulled and swollen now, as though more and more of the beer he'd drunk in the past few years had stayed inside him, bloating out his belly until he was a swollen sponge of flesh.

He looked at her and said, 'I'll try and fix it for you.'

Poor old Dad, she might have known what he'd think of as help for her. But she swallowed the terrible stuff he brought home the next day, choked on it; all the tears streaming from her eyes were not because it was such a powerful drink. She kept on forcing it down until it was all gone and she was dizzy. All the time thinking of Mum, because in the drink was a suggestion of crushed-up mint-leaves.

'That's the girl,' Dad said, and rubbed her head with his hand. She was so dizzy that she put her face against his big stomach and held on to his belt with her hands as he stood beside her. He was not so big and strong and wonderful as she'd thought when she was a little girl, but she did not hold that against him.

He talked to her, more than he'd ever done in his whole life. He'd stood at the gates that morning and watched Air Force vans drive on to the wharves under armed guard, carrying the servicemen who were to unload the ships. 'All those coppers about and soldiers with bayonets,' he said. 'They mean business.'

She coughed again and again; she couldn't help herself.

'Don't worry, Jen, it'll be all right,' he said. 'Don't blame yourself, either. Our sort always get the dirty end of the stick.'

After all these years the photograph of his wonderful first Labour Prime Minister was still on the wall above the mantelpiece, so yellowed and blurred as to be hardly recognisable. She was quite silly in the head, so strong was the stuff she'd taken, and she almost giggled as she said, 'Don't you think it's time we took that picture off the wall?'

But she was truly glad that nothing happened to her baby. And sorry that real harm came to Dad, even though he made her condition an excuse to do what had been on his mind from the day the Government said it was going to break the strike – to go back to work on the wharves with a scab union.

When he told her of his intention she banged the pots around the stove, just the way Mum might have done, and said, 'You know what everybody will say.'

'They'll never call Bill Page a scab,' he said. 'Don't you worry. Anybody else. Not Bill Page. When I go down there people will know that this is not a decent strike. Only a put-up job by the commos.'

He was almost out of his mind at the thought of what he was going to do, yet nothing would stop him, she realised that. He would not sit down and his stumbling about the house was like the blind wanderings of a dazed man. He ranted and raved as though he was already hearing the strikers shouting and jeering at him.

'I don't owe them bastards anything for pushing me out when they didn't want me. They made me like I am and I'll be as good at this as I was before and they'll know they made a mistake about Bill Page. I'm no bloody scab. I can't scab on a union that threw me out a year ago. They scabbed on me.'

The sweating flush of his cheeks was mottled by swollen veins like foul worms burrowing into him.

That last day she was up early and prepared his breakfast without trying to argue with him. The old dungarees, the unbuttoned grey work-shirt and the heavy boots he wore reminded her of how he had looked going off to work when she was a little girl. But now his face was flabby and unshaven and his head like a twisted armour of bone on a neck of crinkled rolls of grey flesh; his bulging stomach made his great chest look weak and the massiveness of his shoulders round and small. He grunted at her as she gave him his lunch in the old tin he had always used.

Because what was in her heart was quite contrary to what she believed in her mind, she told him, 'I'm on your side, Dad, and whatever you do will be all right with me.' That was a lie and the truth at the same time.

He bent his head down at her, like an old bull. 'See here,' he said, running a heavy thumb along the furrow on the side of his head. 'They all know how I got that. They won't call me a scab.'

# MAURICE DUGGAN 1960

*Maurice Duggan (1922–74) published three collections of short stories and a children's book in his lifetime. His* Collected Stories, *a collection of stories for children, and a collection of poems were published after his death.*

**LOOKING** back six years later in his essay 'Beginnings', Maurice Duggan considered that his 'best writing year was 1960, as Burns Fellow at Otago University':

The conditions were wonderful; and it seemed the most natural thing in the world to sit in a room and write. It was a good climate for working. I wrote 'Blues for Miss Laverty', 'Riley's Handbook', a short novel which I am at present revising, and the first draft of 'Along Rideout Road that Summer'. I also wrote much verse of a rather undistinguished kind. And wished the year would never end.[6]

In a brief essay on the Fellowship in 1968, he affirmed that he had taken 'maximum advantage of the opportunity given'.[7] Certainly he achieved in that year what he set out to do. In his application for the Fellowship he had said he wanted to finish a short novel, 'The Burning Miss Bratby', which he had begun in 1959, and work on 'The Wits of Willie Graves', conceived of as a panoramic novel of Northland life, which he had begun in 1956 and then put aside for the more manageable, tightly-focused 'The Burning Miss Bratby'. He partially succeeded in both of these endeavours, in that by August 1960 he had completed a first draft of 'The Burning Miss Bratby' and submitted to the Otago University *Review* 'A Fragment from a Projected Work: The Wits of Willie Graves'.

However, the real accomplishment of the Burns Fellowship year was not the planned 'major' works, both of which turned out to be disappointments. Frank Sargeson for some time had been after Duggan to write the Great New Zealand Novel, and he seemed to hope that 'The Burning Miss Bratby' would be it. When he had completed his first draft, Duggan wrote to the older writer, partly celebrating his feat, but also saying that what he had done was probably 'the frame only', with 'all the denseness, complication, only pencilled in'.[8] More frankly, he wrote to Keith Sinclair the next day, saying that he had read over the draft 'in disgust and despair', and lamented that 'God knows where the draught is coming from but it blows through the holes and gaps in the poor thin story like a blast from the arse-end of a vacuum cleaner'.[9] He finally abandoned his 'poor thin story' in 1973. The much-revised manuscript in the Alexander Turnbull Library reveals an attempt to write a short novel in the fashion of Henry James, an ambition implicit in several articles in *Critic* in April 1960 which were based on a talk given at the Literary Society. In the first, he pointed to *The Golden Bowl* and *The Ambassadors* as models of narrative method, and in the second he cited the Jamesian aesthetic as a critical measuring rod.[10] As for 'The Wits of Willie Graves', when applying for the Fellowship Duggan had admitted that the character of Willie had not yet provided the unifying element for his novel, and he ended up publishing his *Review* 'fragment' and another piece from the projected novel, 'For the Love of Rupert', as separate short stories in *Summer in the Gravel Pit* in 1965.

What made the Burns year Duggan's 'best writing year' was the three unplanned works. The first, 'Blues for Miss Laverty', was written in April 1960. Duggan related to C.K. Stead that the story originated in that talk given to the Literary Society; he had originally created for the talk a hypothetical subject for a story and then decided it was too good to waste, so he had put down the Miss Bratby manuscript to write it. He sent it to Charles Brasch, who accepted it for publication in *Landfall* 56 (December 1960). Then, when Duggan put aside the completed first draft for Miss Bratby in August, he immediately began on a very different kind of short novel which became 'Riley's Handbook'. Freed from the constraints of the Jamesian method, taking his inspiration instead from Beckett and Joyce, he wrote to Sargeson that he had 'burst away down another cul de sac in search of the ineffable' and had written a dozen '"brilliant" but obscure pages as a beginning to something at the moment indescribable, puzzling and strictly non-commercial'.[11] He complained to Sinclair of the Miss Bratby novel that he had never found 'the informing obsession',[12] but in the character of Riley – the rebellious, ranting persona adopted by the artist Fowler when he deserts his wife and respectable career to go live in a disreputable rural pub – he had found his 'obsession' (and in the Captain Cook Hotel, where he had lived for a while during Burns tenure, he had found the model for his fictional milieu). In November, thinking the story complete, he submitted it to Brasch, expecting rejection of this 'lewd & obsessive phantasy', but Brasch enthusiastically accepted it.[13] But, deciding that he had still more to say in the story, Duggan called back the manuscript, worked on the story some more, and added another twenty-two pages to the thirty-six originally submitted, sending it off to Brasch again in August 1961. Brasch quite rightly exclaimed, 'What a triumph it is for your Burns year, and would be if you'd written nothing else then'.[14]

But there was something else written or at least started at the end of the Burns year – 'Along Rideout Road that Summer', perhaps Duggan's finest story. It had its beginning in that talk Duggan gave to the Literary

Society and also in an article that he wrote for *Manuka*, the Auckland Teachers' College annual, in July 1960.[15] That article included a probably fictionalised story of Duggan as an adolescent working on a Maori farm and being unable to connect his New Zealand rural experience with Coleridge's 'Kubla Khan', which he was reading. Again, Duggan found his hypothetical example too good to waste, and turned it into a story which he at least sketched out in his last month on the Burns, but did not finish until September 1962, when he sent it to Brasch, who published it in *Landfall* 65 in March 1963.

The first excerpt below is from those '"brilliant"' but obscure pages' at the beginning of 'Riley's Handbook'. Riley is describing his room at the pub and referring to his sexual encounters there with Myra the barmaid, contrasting his 'Riley' experience to that of his Fowler self in the past, and then entering into the first of his obsessive rants about Pegeen, his dead mother, and his hated father. The second excerpt is the opening of 'Along Rideout Road that Summer', clearly adapted from the 'experience' described in the *Manuka* article. Buster O'Leary, the middle-aged narrator, is reminiscing about his adolescent escapade of running away from his proper small-town Pakeha family to work on the Hohepa farm.

FROM ## Riley's Handbook

A cell? Where else should I look for freedom but in a cell; and neither the first nor the last to seek it there. Self-sufficiency? I wouldn't piss on the idea. A bed, a chair, a table, no mirror, a washhandbasin, paper and pencil for this disgusting purpose, this indecent exposure; a change of clothes. A view of the entrance to the urinal, sometimes an instructive view and never less than diverting, the washing referred to before a constant bunting, the dry replaced by the wet in unending succession, the butts of barrels of various sizes, crates of empty beer bottles. Oh yes and the upended buckets and drying mops; my work. Booze, woman, the daily chores; life is complete. Why interrupt the solemn harmony, the peace, the even rhythm of bladders full and bladders empty, with talk of self-sufficiency? They will come up with failure and selfishness next. The ghouls. Then madness, insanitary habits; and Myra under pressure will admit to being raped four times a week. Out. No honourable failure you may be sure.

Not that it hasn't been in its way a somewhat pathetic strut. I am amazed that it has taken so many in. So many; not least among them assessing committees having at their disposal time and money (time is money) to be spread at mucking-out time for the greater yield in the arts. That horse paddock, no less. So many; critics, art appreciators, acquaintances, friends; and Leah my quondam and still in law my wife. I can't speak for the kids. Yes, I too cunctipotent dad, father and castigator, omnipresent in all jakes, dunnies, single bedrooms at dead of night, under hydrangea bushes and among the manuka scrub behind the beach, the crosseyed widow stripping to bathe, in changing rooms and midnight dormitories. Go to it one and all. Unrebuked. Your sons shall find you out; clayballs. A whole world pulling and poking and why not? A pathetic strut; and a band, not large or even dangerous except in this persistent and irregular interruption, prepared seriously to consider the potential and promise of the

brief mimicry (very dignified in those days of golden weskits and tan beards) of a talent and towering hope. Mine. Let me be honest, I'll enjoy the luxury; there were moments when the imperious flirt of some gesture of my own, such as this perhaps, hoodwinked even me. Until someone helped me to my feet out of the trash on the bar-room floor. Remember that if you will. How superb an irony, the thought is choice, if I had no better view of the whole hysterical affair than those who come to peer on it, keeping their knowledge up to date. And, just to be on the safe side, peer among jars and tubes, shaving lotion, toothpaste, something for my piles, analgesic and perfumed, to reassure themselves that there isn't hidden there a little phial of fatal acid, a shrinking medicine, the key to death. What hope? What hope I mean of their finding it. I did not grow cunning purely by accident. I know my toxicology, don't doubt it. Perhaps when all is said, and there are pages to come yet which make it early for talk of toxicology, perhaps I do deserve and might even claim some credit for having persisted in the role so many years.

Not everything is past remembering. True. Sometimes in the horny night I recollect with an electric and unfamiliar brightness, wincing, some dirndled young female come in summer for instruction in dry point, gouache, impasto, to my elegant even effeminate studio with its couches, lights and locked doors. God, Myra. Tears; for art and the horseshit of experience and a fifteen second jag of the said sad pulsing. And would come again and again. Don't ask me why, though. I can at this stage surely say, without boasting, that I have never understood how it was with women or what they saw in me or why it was that in the face of a moral, emotional and financial bankruptcy, all clearly stated by me from the very first, they were so reluctant to leave and so difficult finally to be rid of, even when told their place was taken. Perhaps it was the total bankruptcy that attracted them; perhaps there was something freakish in so frank a rogue. One or two, two, even stayed to watch a matinée performance and not a few, you name it, were prepared to spend an hour in the silence and stink of the long cupboard among the fag-ends of a promise, paints, turpentine, brushrags, mouldering loaves kept for sentiment that were once kept for still-life but never for nourishment, my wife so excellent a cook. Oh give me credit, even in bankruptcy. But take your talk of self-sufficiency, god, out the back to the gashbucket or the jakes. To give and to receive, the sexual bargain counter where so much changes hands. If I was more successful than some in the matter I was less successful than others, you know, who might be named.

Hardly possible to ask of my melancholy mum in her clay cradle, cunabulum, why it is I have so small a capacity for love where love implies giving; and where, do you say, does it not? How would I know? No. Better leave her in peace, clay to clay and the matter not worth the coffining, to ask the same question of herself. But she has transpired through the leaves, the needles of the reeking pines on

Cemetery Hill, nourishing something for the first time in her life, and the last, her death; spending a few grains of her deadly benefit to the profit of dark trees among whose trunks and on whose fallen needles the ill-begotten living urinate with a lukewarm contempt, that's so, their bladders fuller than their hearts or hers and the relief of expression more exciting. Pegeen. A depression on the surface of the earth, a trough filled with weeds, a mound relapsed on decay, the empty space filled at last and my daddo's intention, somewhat piously expressed because it was never firmly felt, to erect angelic monument to the disremembered darling, never fulfilled. The bitch; let her lie abroad uncemented and unmourned by me and by him who six weeks later was surprised, by me, in the familiar duet with Millie, her younger but no less witless sister. The living comforting the living, lying prone, if that's not too tautological for your taste, moving in the fundamental measure and antique mode of the fuxstrut. They were a long time at it, accepting the validity of the death certificate, I mean. Even as a child I was possessed of enough of the deadly malice to know what I was saying and to tell the detective what it was Millie and dad the agitant had been wrestling over in the darkened room for upwards of a quarter of an hour with not one cry for help in the whole of it. Oh yes. But what would it have served to disinter the melancholy bulk? By her own hand or by his or by the sudden flowering of a mortal tumour, what odds does it make? They took his word while I sat in innocent and religious ecstasy praying they might take his life, innocent or not, for all he'd been guilty of, not least the hate I bore him.

## FROM Along Rideout Road that Summer

I'd walked the length of Rideout Road the night before, following the noise of the river in the darkness, tumbling over ruts and stones, my progress, if you'd call it that, challenged by farmers' dogs and observed by the faintly luminous eyes of wandering stock, steers, cows, stud-bulls or milk-white unicorns or, better, a full quartet of apocalyptic horses browsing the marge. In time and darkness I found Puti Hohepa's farmhouse and lugged my fibre suitcase up to the verandah, after nearly breaking my leg in a cattle-stop. A journey fruitful of one decision – to flog a torch from somewhere. And of course I didn't. And now my feet hurt; but it was daylight and, from memory, I'd say I was almost happy. Almost. Fortunately I am endowed both by nature and later conditioning with a highly developed sense of the absurd; knowing that you can imagine the pleasure I took in this abrupt translation from shop-counter to tractor seat, from town pavements to back-country farm, with all those miles of river-bottom darkness to mark the transition. In fact, and unfortunately there have to be some facts, even fictional ones, I'd removed myself a mere dozen miles from the parental home.

In darkness, as I've said, and with a certain stealth. I didn't consult dad about it, and, needless to say, I didn't tell mum. The moment wasn't propitious; dad was asleep with the *Financial Gazette* threatening to suffocate him and mum was off somewhere moving, as she so often did, that this meeting make public its whole-hearted support for the introduction of flogging and public castration for all sex offenders and hanging, drawing and quartering, for almost everyone else, and as for delinquents (my boy!). … Well, put yourself in my shoes, there's no need to go on. Yes, almost happy, though my feet were so tender I winced every time I tripped the clutch.

Almost happy, shouting Kubla Khan, a bookish lad, from the seat of the clattering old Ferguson tractor, doing a steady five miles an hour in a cloud of seagulls, getting to the bit about the damsel with the dulcimer and looking up to see the reputedly wild Hohepa girl perched on the gate, feet hooked in the bars, ribbons fluttering from her ukulele. A perfect moment of recognition, daring rider, in spite of the belch of carbon monoxide from the tin-can exhaust up front on the bonnet. Don't, however, misunderstand me: I'd not have you think we are here embarked on the trashy clamour of boy meeting girl. No, the problem, you are to understand, was one of connexion. How connect the dulcimer with the ukelele, if you follow. For a boy of my bents this problem of how to cope with the shock of the recognition of a certain discrepancy between the real and the written was rather like watching mum with a shoehorn wedging nines into sevens and suffering merry hell. I'm not blaming old STC for everything, of course. After all, some other imports went wild too; and I've spent too long at the handle of a mattock, a critical function, not to know that. The stench of the exhaust, that's to say, held no redolence of that old hophead's pipe. Let us then be clear and don't for a moment, gentlemen, imagine that I venture the gross unfairness, the patent absurdity, the rank injustice (your turn) of blaming him for spoiling the pasture or fouling the native air. It's just that there was this problem in my mind, this profound, cultural problem affecting dramatically the very nature of my inheritance, nines into sevens in this lovely smiling land. His was the genius as his was the expression which the vast educational brouhaha invited me to praise and emulate, tranquillisers ingested in maturity, the voice of the ring-dove, look up though your feet be in the clay. And read on.

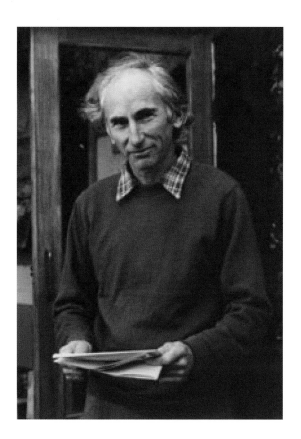

# John Caselberg 1961

*John Caselberg (1924–2004) published four books of verse, one of fictional and non-fictional prose, two volumes of translations of historical Maori writings and a biography of R.A.K. Mason. He completed five of his planned eight verse dramas, but none were published.*

**WHEN** John Caselberg was awarded the Burns Fellowship late in 1960, he had already produced promising and extremely idiosyncratic work in a variety of genres. He had published a volume of poetry in the Pegasus Poets series in 1954, his poetic sequence on Van Gogh from that book had provided the text for his friend Colin McCahon's sequence of lithographs in 1957, his unpublished sequence 'The Wake' had provided the text for McCahon's major work of that title in 1958, and he had published short stories in *Landfall*, including three rhetorical *tours de force* – 'The Halt' (1955), 'Eli Éli Lama Sabachtani' (1957), and 'Earth Water Fire Air' (1959). His major project for 1961

was to begin a planned sequence of eight verse-dramas, 'Crux Australis', that would delineate New Zealand's 'culture-conflict … from 1800–1900, especially the clash between Christianity and Maori religion'.[16]

During the year he completed 'Duaterra King', 'a 4 act verse play concerning Maori-European culture contact and the establishment of Marsden's mission in New Zealand', the first play in the sequence, and gave a private reading of it in Dunedin in October and November 1961.[17] It was given a rehearsed public dramatic reading at the Auckland City Art Gallery by McCahon and Christopher Cathcart's

New Independent Theatre the next year, but it has never been published or given a full dramatic performance. During the year Caselberg also researched some of the Maori historical texts that he was to translate in *Maori is my Name: Maori Historical Writing in Translation* (1975) and compiled the biblical texts for McCahon's major *Second Gate Series*, exhibited in 1962.

The extract below is from the poster printed by the University of Otago Bibliography Room in 1972. McCahon had planned a painting of the speech but it never eventuated.

## William Wilberforce to Everyman

*Lines from a play entitled 'Duaterra King' by John Caselberg in 1961 during tenure of the Robert Burns Fellowship. The play is based on the life of Ruatara, a Maori chief in the Bay of Plenty, who assisted Samuel Marsden to establish the first mission in New Zealand on Christmas Day, 1814.*

*The Rev. Josiah Pratt's drawing room, London. 1807.*

WILBERFORCE:
O Europe, when will the sum of your sins ever be counted?
Will New Zealand in future years also be crippled and blighted
and named for an island of Africa? The wrongs have been already committed.
Mr Marsden, if the Society establishes New Zealand missions
I shall do everything in my power to further your plans.

…

Gentlemen, the trade in blood is not ended.
Greed is too ravenous, and the appetite
of luxury too insatiate.
Despite the Abolition
smuggling from Africa has begun.
Every civilised nation now joins in. Europe
grows fat upon the flesh of Africa. The tearing up
of human beings by their hearts' roots continues unabated.
The horrors on the High Seas of the Middle Passage have not been obliterated.
In America the marketing of naked men and women
as merchandise to be worked to death, or driven, beaten
and bred like captive beasts persists; and,
most terrible of all, the doubly corrupting bond

of servitude and mastery strangles the human mind.
The European's belief in his own thin-lipped superiority
plague-like destroys the marrow of humanity.

Thus Africa is crucified
upon the cross of European pride.
Africa is the name
of European crime.
Africa is a sign
for all the generations yet to come
of European shame.
Legislation
cannot help her or her children
because the crown of iron thorns she wears
impaled upon her bleeding brows
was forged here, inside the brutal foundries
of our European hearts.
We must legislate against our innermost secret thoughts.

The streets
are full. Will those outside
hear me if I speak out loud
enough? You, everyman, coming home from work:
you shouting children playing hide-and-seek
behind the jeweller's: you women, standing on the pavement smiling,
waiting for your lives suddenly to start singing:
you old people praying for your souls: stop! Look up here
at the man whom I would image at my side.
He is Africa.
You notice mostly how his language, looks, gestures, ways
and the colour of his skin are dissimilar from yours;
but after work is over he would sing, entertain himself and others, pray
and await the future just as you do, hopefully.
When then will you learn to come
to shake his hand and look him in the eyes and admit
respect for him, whom God made different?
We dare no longer let ourselves resist Christ's teachings, for while
on earth a single white man's lips can curl to sneer at or taunt
Africa for his colour, pain and death will be the end of it
and every one of us gathered here today will meet again on trial
before our Maker as accomplices in the murder of the human spirit.

# R.A.K. Mason 1962

*R.A.K. Mason (1905–71) published six collections of poetry between 1924 and 1941 but only the* Collected Poems *after that. He also published several plays and two political pamphlets and a history; a collection of short stories was published long after his death.*

**THERE** were thirty-two applicants for the Burns Fellowship in 1962, but the committee seemed to have had no difficulty in selecting Mason. A letter from the Registry to Brash, Thompson and Millar, the solicitors responsible for administering the award, stated that the Committee 'considered Mason to be the foremost living poet' and that they were 'very pleased' with their choice 'and consider it the best appointment made by the Fellowship since it was instituted'.[18] Yet when Mason came to Dunedin as the fourth Burns Fellow, he had not published a book of poetry in twenty-one years. In response to the *Landfall* questionnaire on 'Writers in New

Zealand' in 1960, he had said that his jobs as landscape gardener and trade union officer had kept him 'too busy to leave any spare energy for writing'.[19] When he had been told that he had been awarded the Fellowship, he had replied that his 'first feeling was of reprieve from death'.[20] He had had a bad case of pneumonia and had suffered from depression in the winter of 1961 and was worried about his future, but he told journalists that he hoped 'the award will mark his return to full-time writing'.[21]

In his application and in newspaper interviews Mason said that he planned to focus on writing a book of short stories, 'mainly on Maori themes', and a biography of Rewi Alley.[22] As it turned out, the short stories never eventuated and he barely began the biography (he handed the project on to Willis Airey in 1965). The year was devoted more to the publication of past work than to the writing of new pieces. *The Collected Poems*, a project begun by Denis Glover in 1956, was published during the Burns year and launched in Dunedin in July (it later shared with Allen Curnow's *A Small Room with Large Windows* the 1962 PEN Jessie Mackay Award for Best Book of Poetry). There were also in 1962 two small publications of earlier work – an edition of the 1943 verse drama along with associated China texts, *China Dances*, and a first printing of a revised version of his 1957 radio tribute to A.R.D. Fairburn. He spent time too ordering his literary papers, which he presented to the Hocken Library.

But there was also some new work, and there are in the Mason papers three one-act plays, a 'curtain-raiser' and a sequence of numbered and typed poems which probably came from this time. Mason, when he applied for an extension of the Fellowship on 31 August, said that he had completed during the year 'several one-act plays and poems'.[23] However, the only new works to be published were those reprinted below: 'Tria Carmina ad Miram', which appeared in the University of Otago *Review* in July 1962, and 'Song for Dunedin', probably written in January 1963, which appeared in the *Otago Daily Times* for 27 July 1963. 'Song for Dunedin', he said to Douglas Lilburn in a letter, was written as a song 'in the old Celtic Tradition, with internal rhymes and a muted lilting rhythm', meant to be set to music.[24] Mason also took pride in the appearance of his stanzas, on which basis 'Tria Carmina ad Miram' is presented here in the format in which it first appeared in the 1962 University of Otago *Review*.

He never collected these poems. However, when John Weir planned a brief monograph on him for use in schools (the monograph never eventuated), Mason asked Weir to include in the proposed selection of twenty-five poems the third of the 'Tria Carmina', to be entitled 'Ad Miram' (it was for Mira Szasy, whom he had tutored in the 1930s) and 'Song for Dunedin', which he wished to be the final poem in the selection. 'I would gladly sacrifice some of the earlier stuff for them', he added.[25]

Mason did not receive an extension of the Fellowship, but he remained in Dunedin until 1965 and in these years worked on his intended magnum opus, the historical Otago drama *Strait is the Gate*. He completed a preliminary version of about a thousand lines by May 1963 and an expanded version by August. It was given a public reading by the Otago University Dramatic Society in August, but it was not publicly performed as a full drama until October 1979 at the Globe Theatre in Dunedin, although a truncated version was broadcast as a radio play in 1967, and again in 1974.

## Tria Carmina ad Miram

I
I read somewhere once or was it that Fairburn told
  Me of the man who, falling to death, yet a moment
    clung
To an outcrop where grew a flower, and to it, as his hold
  Weakened, stretched out his mouth for one drop of
    honey on his tongue.

Now into the Pascalian abyss that reveals no end
    It is I have fallen, and clutch clay for a short hopeless
        holding,
And you are that flower on the fall to Hades, but you bend
    Beyond reach at the breach of my mouth, and the
        handhold is yielding.

II
    I died
And you could not so much as ease my pain of passing:
    I cried
In vain for a drop of oil on your hand in blessing.
    The night
Is good to make start of a man, but ill for the ending:
    A light
Touch of oil for the dying lamp lay beyond your
        befriending.

    The luck
You left hasn't improved since this prospector's last home-
        coming:
    I've struck
No oil here below either for blessing or illuming.

III
In the desert of my days
    where the sun's unpitying rays
    tear at the unyielding stone,
    there, a mad Pygmalion,
    I made myself a graven image,
    fit, if any were, for homage:

A girl fronted like the prow
    of a boat that breasts the brow
    of Ocean, with the fall and rise
    of its far-flashing verge for eyes:

For the belly I took the theme
    of the cone that, like a dream,
    soars out of Taranaki's plain –
    in far air its pure snows strain
    to ensnare the stars, while on its flanks

more earthly forests rear their ranks
and from its base flawless waters flow,
linking the plain to furthest snow.

And when, defying ancient law,
my job was done, I stood in awe
at my hand's work, with its broad
forehead and its dark unflawed
eyes and the strong lips and tall
breasts and thighs and hips and all.

This I had made of my own motion.

Many days I did devotion.

In the night – and I had known –
I heard at last the voice of stone,
as a stream in the far hills throbbing
speaks with a voice that is half sobbing
and half laughter, and so much of each
as to make clear and even speech.

Cool was the voice, quiet and strong:

'Poor fool, you have lain too long …
you, who were so proud and wise,
have let Death dust your open eyes.

'You found the perfect? you, a fool …
not even heeding the first rule
that it grows with some imperfect chip
of stone or tool's flaw or hand's slip:

'This form is the work of your hand?
it was the labour of all our land
that brought me forth, yea, the untiring
tides and the winds and waves conspiring
through the unbeginning years that bore me:

'What did you make me to adore me?

'Something in an Easter Island quarry?

'I am woman, I am Maori,
   I am flesh, and I am human:
   more than a goddess, I am woman:

'I was the woman of your need,
   breast for your head, bed for your seed.'

Leave my grave unmarked: no stone
   could outlast this skull of bone,
   but my rags of pride, for I was proud,
   may serve a turn to make my shroud.

## Song For Dunedin

Soft by a hill that lay all still,
   As I was walking sorely,
I came by a town and I laid me down,
   And she was waking early.

'O, quiet town, in your grey-gold gown,
   In your grey and golden mantle,
The way lies drear and I in fear,
   And your eyes are grey and gentle.

'By night and alone by hill and by stone,
   O, it is ill to wander:
I would lie warm a while between the storm
   And the long night lying yonder:

'My feet they are bruised and my heart ill-used
   And I would rest for a moment.'
'For a year you may rest your head on my breast,
   And a song at the most for payment:

'Lie by me here for all a year
   And I'll cradle you full sweetly:
But if you will stay for a year and a day,
   Then I'll have your heart completely.'

# MAURICE SHADBOLT 1963

*Maurice Shadbolt (1932–2001) published ten novels, five volumes of short fiction, a play, two volumes of autobiography, and a considerable amount of miscellaneous non-fiction.*

**MAURICE** Shadbolt's account of his Burns year, written for the 1968 *Landfall* symposium on the Fellowship, is reprinted below. The 'big book' to which he refers was *Strangers and Journeys*, which he said at the beginning of the Fellowship would 'probably take four years to write' and which finally appeared in 1972 (his working title had been 'Search for Tim Livingstone').[26] He published an extract from his incomplete draft along with notes relating the project to some earlier stories in the 1963 University of Otago *Review* – 'Towards a Character – Ned Livingstone'. The second text is an extract from the first edition of *Among the Cinders* (1965); the passage

was revised in later editions to remove mention of what in the following excerpt he calls 'this Shadbolt character'. Nick Flinders, among other things a parody of Ian Cross's adolescent narrators, is relating the engagement party for his older literary brother, the poet and critic D.K. Flinders (suggesting C.K. Stead), and his meeting with characters based on Cross, Denis Glover, Barry Crump and James K. Baxter.

## The Burns Fellowship

I find it difficult to isolate my Burns year in 1963 from any other year of my writing life. This is not to be contrary; rather to emphasise that from the perspective of 1968 it seems of a piece with the two years before and the two or three years immediately after. So what am I to say short of succumbing to pint-size autobiography?

Perhaps the point is that a full-time writer (as I have been, more or less, up and down, for eleven years) is in a rather different position from a part-time writer in taking up the Burns Fellowship. The part-time writer takes leave from his nine-to-five employment; the full-time writer has the sticky business of shaking off commitments (in my case largely journalistic). And this I did find taxing. I received news of the Burns award in the same week as I flew to South-East Asia on a freelance assignment. And for the first two or three months of my Burns year I was completing this assignment, and ridding myself of one or two other earlier commitments, so I could get down to the work I wished to do on the Burns. A clean break between one year and another was impossible, in my circumstances (and I had, besides, an accumulation of debts dating back a year).

Around April, then – with less than eight months of my Fellowship remaining and mild panic beginning to overtake me – I settled to the serious work I planned. Too serious, in the event. The lengthy novel on which I was engaged seemed an eminently worthy project for a Burns Fellow to undertake. And that was my undoing. I've never been able to take myself seriously as a writer, though I can take the act of writing seriously enough; I was even less able to take myself seriously as a writer on a university campus (particularly since I'd missed English I ingloriously in my one attempt thirteen years before). And the atmosphere around the Burns Fellowship was foggy with that fiction called New Zealand Literature, which is really not to be taken seriously by anyone other than *Landfall* reviewers. And which, it is understood, Burns Fellows are busily creating.

It was all too much; something had to give, or go. On June 20, a day short of midsummer in England, I had a collection of stories published in London: *Summer Fires and Winter Country*. On June 21, deep in the deep of the winter country – midwinter day always being an annual turning point for me anyway – I quit my big book, after some 20,000 worthy words, and settled for something unworthy, possibly so I could feel my own man again. With no premeditation at all, I sat at my Burns desk and began composing a playful pastiche of some New

Zealand writing, partly as an oblique exercise in criticism, partly to put some of my more irritant preoccupations into permanent cold storage, and above all to make my year easier. (And so escape reasonably intact.) But I don't want to blame the Burns year for everything; I should add that I also had a clinical interest in seeing how far cliche could be used to subvert cliche. Thus the manuscript grew dismayingly into a novel called *Among the Cinders*, perhaps proving that I had to have my cake and eat it too. (Though I fondly thought I had built sufficient signposts into the book to indicate my intention, I gather it has been treated with all due solemnity as a New Zealand Novel, a richly satisfying irony I never really contemplated even in my wildest moments.)

But the game – if it was – paid off incredibly. Royalties from the novel, along with translation and other fringe benefits, were to keep me afloat for another couple of years after finishing the Fellowship – during which time I was able to write and complete the triptych of stories published under the title *The Presence of Music*, and substantial sections of two other books, one of which is soon to be published.

So my Burns year, unworthily used, and perhaps abused, in fact became three. But I imagine I'm supposed to discuss whether the Burns Fellowship is a good thing. (I've lately been assured that it is not; that it is almost invariably fatal; that a number of good New Zealand writers have been finished off.) A good thing? I just wish, now, that I'd had the nerve to apply for a second year.

## FROM *Among the Cinders*

On the whole, I must say I was relieved to find so many of Derek's friends were healthy, normal-looking people. This Shadbolt character, for example, arrived in a party of four or five. I wouldn't say he looked exactly normal, but his friends did. One was about six feet four inches tall, a really husky fellow with fair hair, and he looked to me a pretty normal front-row rugby forward. Another one seemed just about as tough, slightly shorter and much bulkier, with oiled slicked-back black hair, and a really aggressive face; he looked like a pretty normal policeman. Then there was a really hairy fellow wearing a pair of oily trousers and a shirt torn open down the front which showed most of his chest and some of his stained singlet, and he appeared to have lost his shaving gear about ten days before; he looked as if he'd just come off a farm. They were followed into the flat by a short, stout, jowly fellow with very sad eyes who was carrying something that marked him out as different from them right away. They were all carrying beer bottles and flagons; he carried a big crate of Coca-cola. Except for this one mournful fellow, they all seemed fairly happy with themselves. This Shadbolt didn't look like anything in particular, or as if he'd come from anywhere; he wore black jeans and a red check shirt, his hair was half over his face and needed a pair of shears taken to it, and his gingery-blonde moustache drooped in a sort of sad Spanish way around the

corners of his mouth. In fact I didn't take much notice of him, till later, because I was so pleased with all Derek's normal-looking friends.

Of course I was pretty much disillusioned before long. I got most of my information from Jim, the short jowly fellow, who installed himself in my corner with his crate of Coca-cola. I asked if he was a delivery man for the Coca-cola factory or something. He said no, he was just an ordinary postman, so I chalked up another point in favour of Derek's normal friends. Jim explained that he had to drink Coca-cola because he was an alcoholic. He offered me a bottle, and we sat there swigging away together. He really bucked me up, the way he yarned to me as if I was the only interesting person in the room, and he offered me small cigars which I smoked as soon as I was sure Derek wasn't looking; Derek had been complaining, after my sleepless nights, that he'd been going through an awful lot of cigarettes lately. After Jim and I had been talking for a while, I asked him about other people at the party. That was when I got disillusioned. That front-row rugby forward, for example, wrote pretty desperate novels about young boys who yell and scream at God, and whose mothers knock their fathers off. And the one with the oily slicked-back hair, the policeman-looking type, he really wasn't normal either; he wrote pretty frantic love poetry. I was almost right about one thing. That hairy fellow who looked as if he'd just come off the farm. Well, he hadn't come off a farm exactly, but he'd just come in from the bush country. The thing was, though, he was a writer too. He was a deer-culler when he wasn't writing about shooting deer, and about the hairy jokers who shoot them professionally for the Government. I've since learned that he's fairly famous, and that I really ought to have read his books. When people ask what he said to me that evening, I tell them he explained to me a technique for killing wild pigs with gelignite. What you do is, you cut open a potato and slip a detonator inside. Then you scatter a few of these potatoes in the bush where you know wild pigs are likely to roam. And you sit back and wait for the explosions. He reckoned you could collect any amount of wild pork that way. To tell the truth, I was pretty disgusted by this lazy man's way of hunting; it was just what you might expect from some literary friend of Derek's. Of course, I have to take into account that he might just have been telling a story. He'd been drinking a lot of beer.

Actually I was fairly merry myself, on that Coca-cola. Jim and I went through a half dozen bottles in no time. I grew very relaxed and wasn't much troubled by the noise, pushing and smoke any more. In fact I felt like quite an old hand at the party business, and I smiled amiably at everyone in sight. Jim was still talking. He really didn't need anyone to talk back at him. He just needed someone to listen. Without me saying a word, he argued his way from alcoholism to sex, from sex to religion, from religion to literature, from literature back to sex again. In between all these subjects, he quoted lines of poetry, and my suspicion grew. Finally I asked who had written the poetry. He said he had, of course.

It was a great sort of party, when even an ordinary alcoholic postman turned out to be a poet. I decided there just wasn't a normal person in the room after all.

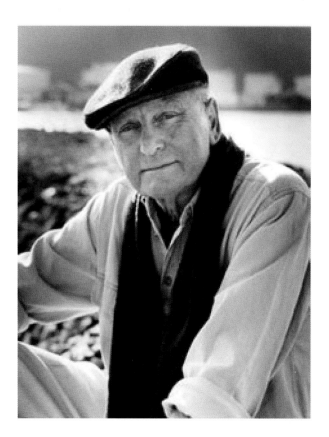

# MAURICE GEE 1964

*Maurice Gee (b. 1931) has published sixteen adult novels, twelve novels for younger readers, two volumes of short fiction, and miscellaneous non-fiction.*

WHEN Maurice Gee was appointed Burns Fellow in October 1963, he was clearly a young writer on the way up. Charles Brasch had published three long stories in *Landfall* (1955, 1957, 1959), Gee had placed five shorter ones in little magazines, and in London in 1961 Hutchinson had featured him as one of four new authors in *New Authors Short Story One* (with one of the *Landfall* stories and a new long story) and then published his first novel, *The Big Season*, in 1962. As Burns Fellow he focused on his second novel, which had a working title of 'Three Women' but appeared in 1965 as *A Special Flower* with a short final section added at the behest of the publisher.

The following extract from that novel shows Donald Pinnock, a middle-aged, repressed, mother's-boy male, facing up to the truth that his attempt to change his life by marrying the vulgar but vital Coralie Marsh, the 'special flower' of the title, has failed: her act of leaving him for her lover, the rugby lock Morrie Giltrap, is the end of that dream. By the end of the chapter he will have committed suicide, an act that provides a catalyst for change for Coralie and for Donald's genteel mother and sister, the 'three women' of the original title.

FROM *A Special Flower*

On Saturday morning Donald went out to work in the garden. He took the spade from the toolshed and started clearing a piece of ground beyond the vegetable patch. He had always enjoyed gardening, especially the planting part of it. Digging he did not like so much. ('Straight digging,' his father had called it. 'Good for the body, if nothing else.' An allusion to the fact that it could not be proved man had a soul.) And clearing away grass and weeds had always seemed to him rather a cruel business. Today it seemed especially so. Weeds were first in possession, they had a right to their ground. He admired them for the fact that men had not been able to turn them to some use. And even as he chopped them down he felt his kinship with them.

When he had cleared a few square yards he began to dig. The soil was rich, with worms in almost every spadeful. He began to enjoy turning it over: he was bringing something under control, almost making it part of himself. He dug on, cutting square chunks from the ground, breaking them into the chocolate-brown patch in front of him. When he reached the edge of the cleared area he attacked the weeds again. He had no sympathy for them now.

Jean brought him out a glass of orange cordial. She waited while he drank it. 'What are you going to plant here?' She was pleased to see him at work.

'I don't know yet.' Although his tone was pleasant he turned side-on to her. She took the empty glass and went back to the house.

He did not go on clearing weeds, but walked through the vegetable patch to see how things were growing. The peas were at different stages, some just breaking ground, others in flower. Coralie had helped plant the early ones – she'd had spells of interest in the garden and claimed to have green fingers. She had helped plant the potatoes too. They looked particularly healthy, thick-leaved and dark green, and were almost ready to flower. And the carrots and radishes were ready for thinning – a finicky job he didn't enjoy. He sat down on the edge of the lawn and looked at them. He didn't feel like starting now. But he'd lost interest in the new patch he'd been digging. He wondered what to do. The grass was damp and in a moment he stood up and brushed the seat of his trousers. He wandered round into the front garden, into the sunshine. Here roses, pinks, carnations, were in flower – as they had been the day he and Coralie were married. He had not thought of her, he remembered, while he'd been digging. What did that mean? That he'd bolted

into a hole and shut his eyes there? That he'd turned himself into a machine for half an hour? Or that he was getting over losing her? This last was not the right answer, he knew. His escape, however it had been managed, was over now: she was in his mind more firmly than ever. He sat down on the veranda steps. How had he come to marry her? He could not understand – it seemed a miracle. He simply remembered meeting her, going home with her, moved by a force that had existed before (strongly, he admitted) only in the shadows of his mind. Then there had been months that had no pattern but were filled with noise and colour and the dizzying hope of freedom. His mother lost her place in his life. While he was out with Coralie he thought of her at home, locked in her chair like a bird in a cage. His habits of apology and obedience began to weaken. He felt that soon he would put them off like clothes that had become dirty. Then he would be himself – naked. This was the word he chose. It no longer frightened him.

The wedding day arrived. He became Coralie's husband. And after the wedding …

Donald stood up. He went into the house, found pen and writing-pad, and sat down at the living-room table to write Coralie a letter.

*My Dearest Coralie,* he wrote. *You must come back to me. I cannot live without you.*

He meant this, but on reading it saw how Coralie would react. She would tear the letter up without reading any further. He started again.

*My Dearest Coralie,*
*You have never understood what you mean to me. That's my fault, not yours. I've never been able to make you understand. I've got no talent for expressing my feelings. Things can be crying out inside me but I can't say them. So I've never been able to convince you that I love you. I hoped the things I did would convince you, since what I said couldn't. But I know that didn't happen. It's my fault. There's a kind of impotence that extends into every part of my life where there isn't some rule to act by. I just go dead, though God knows I'm crying out inside. I want to live, but I'm dead.*

He stopped at this point, re-read the letter, destroyed it. It embarrassed him.

After a long while, during which the spring sunshine slipped halfway across the table where he sat, he began to write again.

*My Dearest Coralie,*
*I know why you left me. You knew you were being used. I've never been a man – I tried to use you to make myself a man. You must have become aware of this. I'm sorry. It was a dreadful insult to you. But believe me it was a saner attempt than some of the others I've made. And making you happy was an essential part of it – the most important part, even though it had to come second to getting myself free.*

*I'm not completely to blame for the way I am. Someone stronger would have done better. I suppose I'm to blame for not being stronger. But how could I have control over that? Because it started when I was a boy. I've told you my father disliked me. But I blame my mother as much now – that's fair I think, even though it's her ignorance I blame, not her personally. She made me a puppet that she jerked the strings of. She didn't want it that way, or at least if she did she wanted a strong puppet, like my father, not a weak one, like me. A free puppet, if that makes sense.*

*You were my attempt to get free from the strings. In every way you were unlike Mother. I didn't choose that, but I rejoiced in it when I found out. You were alive, enthusiastic – and coarse and noisy too. Don't be offended. These are virtues for me. My mother and Jean are ghosts, pale little ghosts, only half-alive. And so am I, so have I been, though I've hated it. My attempts to escape have been so crippled, so dark and nasty. You were an escape too, but a daylight one. And I wanted to love you and make you happy.*

He sat still for a long time. His grasp of reality seemed firmer than it had ever been, and his mind worked like an engine, moved steadily to the unalterable facts of his life. One after the other he faced them, stared into them, like shop windows in a street. He was impotent. He was weak. He was cowardly. He was sick beyond cure with frustration and accumulated defeat. Facts of his life. He passed and repassed them.

Then he wrote: *But even with you it wasn't any good.*

And immediately he was caught into a frenzy of denial. His pen attacked the paper, scoring heavy lines in it, tearing as it went. Then he swept the pad across the table and on to the floor.

He screwed back his chair, walked on to the veranda of the house, flooded with cool sunshine, and sat down in his mother's rocking chair. He rocked back and forth, with the view under his gaze.

After a little time the cars on the waterfront road caught his attention. They scuttled like coloured beetles, glinting in the sun. Then the contrast between Rangitoto (Nature, in his mother's lesson), dark and damp and solid between springtime blues of sea and sky, and the flimsy bridge, toy ships at the wharves, brittle city (Works of Man), came to him as revelation of impermanence and courage. He was freed from his unhappiness. But he could not hold the meaning of what he had seen: it began to slip away from him, and he made no effort to keep it. Effort would destroy his contentment. So he allowed his sight to fit like a pane of glass over the harbour. He was aware of nothing but enveloped all he could see.

Later, when movements inside the house had destroyed him, he thought of himself and this view: it was sometimes able to give him identity in a kind of non-identity. He became holder of beauty. But understanding of this meant he was back with desire, question, search.

# JANET FRAME 1965

*Janet Frame (1924–2004) published eleven novels, four volumes of short fiction, a book of poetry, and three volumes of autobiography in her lifetime. A further novel and book of poetry have appeared posthumously.*

IN October 1964, Janet Frame was invited to be Burns Fellow in 1965 (she had not applied). The year turned out to be a very productive one. In the first four months she was definitely the 'busily writing Burns fellow' of the poem printed below: Frame put the finishing touches on the manuscript of *The Adaptable Man* (she had put aside an almost finished draft in May 1964) and sent it to her agent, finished *A State of Siege* (begun in June 1964), and wrote 100,000 words of a first draft of *The Rainbirds*. In the remainder of the year she completed *The Rainbirds*, wrote a number of short stories and sixty of the poems that were to go into *The Pocket Mirror*, and with the help of Margaret

Dalziel selected the stories for *The Reservoir and Other Stories* from her two volumes that had been published in 1963 in the United States.

The work of the year resulted in a number of publications: *The Adaptable Man* (1965), *A State of Siege* (1966 in the U.S., 1967 in the U.K./N.Z.), *The Reservoir and Other Stories* (1966), *The Pocket Mirror* (1967 in the U.K./ U.S., 1968 in N.Z.), and *The Rainbirds* (1968 in the U.K., 1969 in N.Z., and, 1969 as *Yellow Flowers in an Antipodean Room*, in the U.S.). She applied for a second year of the Fellowship, but James K. Baxter was selected as Burns Fellow in 1966; however, she was invited to be a 'guest of the university' in 1966, with an office provided and a cash grant to help her complete the work she had in hand.

In that second year she completed more short stories and 'continued with [her] hobby of verse-making' so that she had 160 poems ready for *The Pocket Mirror* – poems that she thought to be 'slight with a gentle pastoral air: shockingly Georgian'. She had also almost finished a draft of another Dunedin novel, 'The Mill Belongs to Sandy', which eventually formed part of *Intensive Care* (published in 1970).[27] The grant also allowed her to make a down payment on a house in Dunedin, and the whole experience of the Burns and the 'guest' year were important factors in her decision to stay in New Zealand rather than return to England, where she had lived from 1956 to 1963.

For the 1968 symposium in *Landfall*, Janet Frame wrote the following account of her Burns Year.

## The Burns Fellowship

My father used to kiss every five-pound note goodbye with an unhygienic but magical ritual, 'Now you see me, now you don't.' The same note may have returned to him unrecognised again and again; always he said goodbye to it; it had to travel and be used, its value tested. Experience, the writer's currency, is like the five-pound note, to be got rid of with kisses or curses. It is three-and-a-half years since I held the Burns Fellowship and my experience of it has travelled so much in my head that, confronted by it now, I'm not sure that I recognise it. In common with the other Burns Fellows I had a room in the English Department, the salary of a junior lecturer, and perhaps the little war with the ghostly predecessors who 'always' went to morning coffee, who 'always' wrote from dawn till dark, who 'always' were willing to lecture to students; and then the victory achieved under the banner of Individuality, and the brief honour, the following year, of being Ghost Most Recent. Outside this bond of room, salary, myth-making, each Fellow is alone. One of the aims of the Burns Fellowship is to provide this aloneness: it is called 'freedom to write' which may be, but was not in my case, as much a torture as freedom from writing. I'm not being facetious when I say I could 'write a book' about my experience as a Burns Fellow. For me, it was like living personal fiction with all the best set properties of enchantment and nightmare, the classic theme of return to the scene of the crime, the triumph of the little serving-maid (I was last in Dunedin as a waitress at the *Grand*) who is invited to the castle. It was both a terrifying flashback and a satisfying fulfilment of wishes. It was Then and Now, Before and After, a personal advertisement with the potion nameless and the container rather resembling Quarto Bank.

Dunedin, through the Burns Fellowship, is, I think, the only place in New Zealand where the writer is invited to be a guest in his own country. It is a welcome form of literary hospitality that I'd like to see extended to, say, a room in a tourist hotel, on a sheep farm, as other fellowships are endowed. Whatever the writer takes away from (and gives to) Dunedin and the university, it is surely not the usual tourist opinions – They're happy in their own way, I saw no signs of violence or rebellion, clothes are cheap, the streets are clean. Also, it must be interesting and educating for the students to see living writers: in this sense a zoological element is introduced to literature, the Fellowship having the conditions of a good scientific experiment – white mice reared in the same environment exhibiting differences in behaviour and rate of growth; except that here the experiment reveals to the students and the community that all writers are different, that all writers are not dead, and no writers are white mice – though there may be some disagreement about the last conclusion.

To return to the five-pound note: It is some time since I kissed it goodbye. It's been much handled, taken and received in payment; it's been at the private mint of imagination to be retouched, renewed and – by a secret counterfeit device – increased in value. But before I say Excuse me while I write my novel I must ask myself the question that remained happily unasked during my term as Burns Fellow: Have I the freedom to write?

The following excerpt from *The Rainbirds* comes from the last part of the novel. Godfrey Rainbird had been declared dead after an auto accident, but had emerged alive from a coma to find his life changed. To others he had become a living *memento mori*, and he is ostracised by Dunedin society, sacked from his job, and shunned by his family. He has withdrawn into a solitary contemplative state, seeing all life differently after his near-death experience. In this scene, soon after Easter, he is contemplating the autumn landscape from the garden of his Anderson's Bay home.

## FROM *The Rainbirds*

He was sitting in the deckchair by the side of the house, sheltered from any passer-by but able to see clearly across the harbour to the city. Huge grey clouds with undersides glinting white as a rabbit's belly moved slowly across the sky. During the weeks since his accident Godfrey had watched the sky more than at any time in his life and he thought that he had never seen so many dark clouds that hinted at so much inaccessible light. He had thought at first that the world seemed new with new details – the cloud formations, the colours in the sea, the tides flowing in and out of the harbour, the long strips of dark green that lay from harbour-mouth to shore like dark eels beneath the surface, the seaweeds waving, patterned like lungs beneath the water; the sharp rocks that dried quickly when

the sun shone on them as a face might change beneath a sudden glance of hate or love: he noticed these without rejoicing; they had seemed so new and were now so old, so old. He felt the anguish of knowing that all should be as it seemed, that rocks or faces should change so beneath the glances of the sun and of love and anger, that soft clouds should hang like shot rabbits in the evening sky; that grass should grow along the fence in separate stalks of tinker-tailor, couch, barley grass – the children knew the names of the grasses, they seemed to prefer grass to flowers; perhaps one could not afford to be an enemy of grass when one lay in it, in summer, with one's face and ears and skin close to the stalks while one listened, listened to thoughts and whispers –

He remembered how he and Beatrice used to 'go down the Peninsula' to find a place in the grass, overlooking the sea, and lie down in the sun with the grass flattened beneath them or leaning over them shamelessly eavesdropping on their whispers, watching them when they touched, being a part of their touching, for a hand on the skin became the next moment a hand lying in the grass, picking a stalk of grass, biting it, chewing it – how sweet some grasses were to taste! – telling fortunes by it, tales of houses on fire and children all alone, fates revealed, rivals in love – surely grasses in their power deserved the role one gave them of thus being allied with the human race.

So much for that dream, Godfrey thought, as his view turned, as it did always now, to his death, as if he saw it before him more vivid than the sea and the sky and the city shining with its secret inaccessible light on the hills. The white houses in the harsh white light seemed to be built of salt, not of wood or stone. It seemed to Godfrey like a Biblical city and the words of a minister who had spoken to Beatrice on the phone at Easter came to his mind. 'This Biblical happening in Dunedin,' he had said, rather possessively, Godfrey thought. And would Godfrey care to be welcomed again into the Church?

He saw again the golden grasses and the lost sun and the sea where the points of light sparkled like points of dew at the tips of the grass-heads knocking, shaking, leaning so intimately upon him and Beatrice as they leaned upon each other, grass and bodies intent on crushing, on being crushed. The image was gone. It was now of grass under stone, bled yellow and white, its stalks set in the earth like a letterhead within a dark page; the writing of grasses that could not distinguish between life and death, that would wave against your cheek, eavesdrop on your thoughts with the same sparkle and grace as they waved across your dead body or found a path through your flesh to the sky and the sun; in all innocence.

The following poem comes from early in the Burns Fellowship year, about Frame's office in the then new library building, since demolished. The Burns Fellow office was located on the first floor of the south wing, looking out on the inner courtyard (see Ruth Dallas's poem, 'In the University Library').

## The New Building

In the new building the voices knock
like stones against the walls.
The partitions are thin.
The new building has a delicate inner skin
plastered with bookshelves to keep the sound in,
sound or wound. Trees planted in a hurry
droop in the courtyard among level pools
piped with clear water. Beds of grass are beginning
to get the architect's idea.
Swampy comes and goes
and fist of fog, storm, metallic light gonging
behind those whale-grey heavy clouds
whose blubber's in the heads of those
who can't think where the silence, like the money, goes,
once it's out of the soul and into the purse.

Yet I suppose things could be worse.
The hanging stairway in the library may well see
some interesting executions. The inner courtyard
is a surprise worth meeting; even under the leer
of Swampy's looming face the grass is trying,
the trees may recover,
the windows and the people may grow used to the glare
of the sun's rude stare;
and by and by
even I may mellow
into a busily writing Burns Fellow!

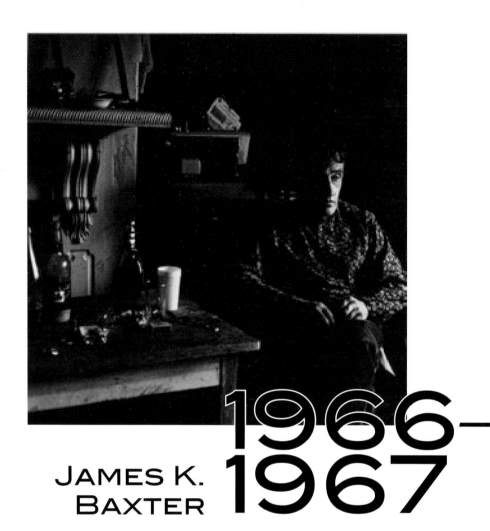

# JAMES K. BAXTER

# 1966–1967

*James K. Baxter (1926–72) published in his lifetime at least sixteen books and booklets of poetry plus innumerable broadsheets and pamphlets. He also published four books and pamphlets of literary criticism and a volume of religious essays. After his death at least eleven books of poetry, including his* Collected Poems, *were published, as well as his* Collected Plays, *a selection of his criticism, and a novel.*

JAMES K. Baxter was concerned that the Burns Fellowship might somehow corrupt or domesticate him and estrange him from his Muse, as he colourfully recounts in the essay from the symposium on the Fellowship in *Landfall* 87 (September 1968) and in the poem, 'On Possessing the Burns Fellowship 1966'. But the two years proved to be among the most fruitful of his career. In the first year he wrote ninety poems, mostly responses to being back in the place where he grew up, as in 'At Kuri Bush', and the powerful sequence 'Words to Lay a Strong Ghost', from which comes 'The Rock'. Both pieces were collected in the posthumously published

*Runes*, which he was preparing for the press at the time of his death, and are reprinted below. As well, he wrote three radio plays and the lectures and essays collected in *The Man on the Horse* (1967).

Whatever his doubts, he reapplied for a second year and was reappointed in November 1966, with the Fellowship Committee commenting that he was 'the only applicant this year who could confidently be expected to maintain the high standards' of the award.[28] In the second year he attempted to edit the memoirs of his maternal grandfather, John Macmillan Brown, but abandoned that project and, in the second half of the year, dedicated himself primarily to drama. He had said in his letter to the Fellowship Committee that he planned to write 'at least one play on the plan of a modern Everyman',[29] but he ended up writing six plays for Patric Carey at the Globe Theatre, four of which were produced that year, the other

two the next year, as well as several plays for a student dramatic group. He also wrote most of the essays for the *Tablet* which were collected in the *Flowering Cross* in 1969, *Aspects of Poetry in New Zealand* (a talk given at Victoria University in July and published later in the year), and many additional poems (113 of the poems in the *Collected Poems* are dated 1966–7), including the notorious *A Small Ode on Mixed Flatting*, published separately that year and reprinted below, and some of the poems printed by Keith Maslen that year at the Bibliography Room in *The Lion Skin*.

The work of the Burns years and of the following year, when he remained in Dunedin and worked in the Catholic Education Office of the Dunedin Diocese, is the richest literary expression of Baxter the Catholic family man – with the tensions of that role – before he went off to Jerusalem and other points north for his prophetic final phase.

## The Burns Fellowship

When I applied for the Fellowship I was tired of pounding the Wellington streets on a postman's round, and a bit of leisure seemed a good idea. Thirty-nine was a stopping place: a place to sit down and think about the road ahead. And I had heard others say that if a man had leisure he could write, at least without tiredness, perhaps with a new drive. I've never planned more than a year ahead if I can help it; and the Fellowship would last a year. But when I got the Fellowship I thought: 'Man, you're mad.'

Others had gone down to Dunedin to drink from the big gravy dish. They had come back boozed or haunted, needing longer to recover from their leisure than others do to recover from work. And I knew about America. In America there are many fellowships offering. The poets wander round the campuses like tame bespectacled sheep; and the results of their meditations are published in glossy volumes priced at six dollars.

The main trouble is of course that the Muse, that primitive and prejudiced old Lady, does not smile on Fellowship holders. Our good morals seem to bore her. She goes away from us to whisper in the ear of a young poet with a raging hangover and three mistresses and no money at all, who inhabits a blanket-shrouded bedroom in a flat above a wineshop in Greater King Street. She says to the Fellowship holder: 'All right, mate. You've made your choice. You want money and status. Well, you've got them. Don't ask to have me as well, thrown in to make up the full bundle.'

But in my time I had already done all the wrong things. I had made a strenuous effort to remain married. I had got off the booze before it gave me a wet brain. I had reduced my late adolescent adulteries (in this country it's a lucky man who's out of adolescence by the age of thirty) to an occasional sniffing of little girls' bicycle seats. And I had learned cunningly to twist the Muse's arm. She did not even leave me for more than two years when I became a Roman Catholic. I think my own brand of ugliness must have attracted her; or perhaps the fact that I am not always a liar. Furthermore, I travel under the protection of Baron Saturday, the voodoo god of graveyards, coarse, truculent, tough-minded, who has a special weakness for drunks because he himself likes to drink rum flavoured with a number of different kinds of pepper. I used to pray to him during drinking bouts. He had not forsaken me when I swallowed the Church's anchor; and he is a cousin of the grim Old Lady herself. To accept a fellowship is to enter a graveyard. He would no doubt look after me.

So I came down to Dunedin. The first year I wrestled with the ghost of an ancient mistress who came back to haunt me, and got a number of written lectures and some grim, dry poems out of the encounter. Sitting half-asleep in that sun-soaked Trappist cell in the English Department, I began to think that I had the Fellowship by the short hairs. But there were harder times to come. In some ways I am sorry that I did not receive the Fellowship while I was still an active alcoholic. To spend a year roaring drunk – the committee that administers the fund would of course in those circumstances never have granted me a second year – but to do this would have truly honoured the Muse, who likes a rumpus better than she likes omelets, and it would have left a hairy legend of the Abominable Snowman to gladden the hearts of the young and offend the nostrils of the old. But I am myself too old to sleep out on park benches; and on the whole I think I made an exemplary Burns Fellow. My misdemeanours were purely verbal. Without the assistance of Father O'Flanagan and Father Jones this might not have been so. Confession is good for the soul. If a big-eyed nymph occasionally visited me in my concrete burrow, hoping for an alleviation of the Varsity horrors – well, all that happened was that I bored her with theological information and fatherly advice, and sent her away with a pat on the rump to be seduced by somebody else in a mixed flat that I would most carefully avoid entering. Instead, I wrote an 'Ode on Mixed Flatting', to show that though my gonads were wrapped in steel wire, my mind was still mellow.

There were some interesting events. There was the time I climbed from my insomniac bed at 2 a.m. and drove in the pouring rain first to a hash-shop where the company of the drunk and destitute soothed me, then twenty miles further out through the howling night to Taieri Mouth, where I sat in my car and smoked and listened to the long wild mad black surf grinding on the beaches and communicated with the dead who had also frequently lived in despair. There was the time in Palmerston North when I stood on a platform between the Mayor

and the Chancellor, like a frog in a bell jar, sweating but honest, and told the assembled students that Kiwis should smoke a bit of marijuana now and then, that we should hold bullfights instead of flower festivals, that the age of female consent should be lowered to fourteen, and that I was tired of seeing homosexual artists being ridden to death by big ugly stupid homosexual policemen. I received warm thanks for these kind words afterwards from a number of homosexuals of every profession, and particularly from some of the better teachers in the country.

That was all right. And I received the Fellowship for a second year. And the thought stuck with me: 'O.K., mate. But what'll you do when you have to get out of this Old Man's Home, get off the bone of your arse, and contend directly with whatever wad of rubbish society can deposit on your doorstep?' The problem was security. Booze and women kill their quota; but the victims of imaginary security through money can be numbered in millions. And I could feel the death trance beginning.

I shook it off by going up to Patric Carey's place and writing seven or eight plays for him. I wouldn't have done it for anyone else. Patric is a witty man and a begetter of life in others. But in the plays I took our society apart and shook the bag, and what dropped out was what I had always suspected was there – a baby's dummy and a small dry dead bird which may have been the corpse of the Dove of Pentecost.

Family life has always been impossible for all people since Adam ate the apple and Eve made the core into the first contraceptive. I visited my parents regularly, which was a pleasure, since they are more alive than I am. And on the very first day of the first year of the Fellowship I noticed that my daughter, like a dog shifting after rabbits, had found out the name and location of every underground coffee bar in Dunedin. Such miracles of natural adaptation never fail to please me. My son became a Buddhist. I made a number of friends. There was a painter, Illingworth; a producer, Carey; and a professor, Durning. Each became wholly real to me; and each of their wives too, each in a different way. This dry inaccessible drunkard's soul is curiously like Noah's ark. My wife and I went on holidays to Stewart Island, Naseby, the West Coast, Queenstown, the Milford Track and Wanaka. From each place I came back with icy solitary poems that described the landscape in terms of the third and grimmest face of the Muse, which is a skull. There was a bit too much death inside me.

I wonder now how much of the death was my own and how much came from the Fellowship. Lately it has seemed to me that God was trying to say something to me. It is hard to hear through the static of frost and cigarettes and *Tablet* articles and TV documentaries. But it seems to say something like this: 'You poor old sod! I meant you to be a primitive, not a civilised talker at Women's Social Evenings. You've balled it up. Remember your clan motto: *Don't die till you're dead*. I know you believe in Me; but that's not quite enough to believe in. Try growing kumaras for a change. I make very few primitives and I like to see them

survive. The Fellowship was a conditional mistake. You knew that all along. Why don't you use your radar? I'm not angry about; I'm only sorry ….'

Something like that. The Fellowship hadn't exactly done me in. But my asbestos suit had worn through in a few places.

## On Possessing the Burns Fellowship 1966

*(to Nicholas Zissermann)*

Trees move slowly. The rain drops arrows
As on the Spartans from the Persian bowstring
Some while ago, across the tennis court
Behind the convent they hope to pull down,

And I who wrote in '62,
*Dear ghosts, let me abandon*
*What cannot be held against*
*Hangmen and educators, the city of youth! –*

Drink fresh percolated coffee, lounging
In the new house, at the flash red kitchen table,
A Varsity person, with an office
Just round the corner – what nonsense!

If there is any culture here
It comes from the black south wind
Howling above the factories
A handsbreadth from Antarctica,

Whatever the architect and planner
Least understand – not impossibly the voice
Of an oracle rising from that
Old battered green verandah

Beyond the board fence: a blood transfusion
From the earth's thick veins! As if
Caesar had died, and clouds, leaves, conspired to make
A dark mocking funeral wreath.

## At Kuri Bush

A few days back I climbed the mound
Where the farmhouse had stood,

As green as any that the Maoris made
Along that coast. The fog was blowing

Through gates and up gullies
Hiding even the stems of cocksfoot grass

That had sprung up in place of
The sitting-room table and the small brass

Kerosene lamp my mother lighted
Every night, whose white wick would burn

Without changing colour. Somebody must have
Used the old brushwood fence for kindling

Twenty years ago. Outside it
My father stood when I was three or less,

Holding me up to look at
The gigantic rotating wheel of the stars

Whose time isn't ours. The mound yielded
No bones, no coins, but only

A chip of the fallen chimney
I put in the pocket of a damp coat

Before I bumbled back down to the road
With soaking trousers. That splinter of slate

Rubbed by keys and cloth like an amulet
Would hold me back if I tried to leave this island

For the streets of London or New York.
I hope one day they'll plant me in

The kind of hole they dig for horses
Under a hilltop cabbage tree

Not too far from the river that goes
Southwards to the always talking sea.

## FROM Words to Lay a Strong Ghost

*The Rock*

Arms of Promethean rock
Thrust out on either
Side of a bare white strip
Of wave-ridged sand – long before

I ever met you, Pyrrha,
The free world held me in its heart,
And half my grief is only
The grief of a child torn from the breast

Who remembers – who cannot forget
The shielding arms of a father,
Maybe Poseidon – out there
Where the waves never cease to break

In the calmest weather, there's a hump-backed
Jut of reef – we called it Lion Rock –
Growling with its wild white mane
As if it told us even then

Death is the one door out of the labyrinth!
Not your fault – to love, hate, die,
Is natural – as under quick sand-grains
The broken bladders lie.

# A Small Ode on Mixed Flatting

*Elicited by the decision of the Otago University authorities to forbid this practice among students*

Dunedin nights are often cold
(I notice it as I grow old);
The south wind scourging from the Pole
Drives every rat to his own hole,
Lashing the drunks who wear thin shirts
And little girls in mini-skirts.
Leander, that Greek lad, was bold
To swim the Hellespont raging cold
To visit Hero in her tower
Just for an amorous half-hour,
And lay his wet brine-tangled head
Upon her pillow – Hush! The dead
Can get good housing – Thomas Bracken,
Smellie, McLeod, McColl, McCracken,
A thousand founding fathers lie
Well roofed against the howling sky
In mixed accommodation – Hush!
It is the living make us blush
Because the young have wicked hearts
And blood to swell their private parts.
To think of corpses pleases me;
They keep such perfect chastity.
O Dr Williams, you were right
To shove the lovers out of sight;
Now they can wander half the night
Through coffee house and street and park
And fidget in the dripping dark,
While we play Mozart and applaud
The angel with the flaming sword!
King Calvin in his grave will smile
To know we know that man is vile;
But Robert Burns, that sad old rip
From whom I got my Fellowship
Will grunt upon his rain-washed stone
Above the empty Octagon,
And say – 'O that I had the strength
To slip yon lassie half a length!
Apollo! Venus! Bless my ballocks!

Where are the games, the hugs, the frolics?
Are all you bastards melancholics?
Have you forgotten that your city
Was founded well in bastardry
And half your elders (God be thankit)
Were born the wrong side of the blanket?
You scholars, throw away your books
And learn your songs from lasses' looks
As I did once – ' Ah, well; it's grim;
But I will have to censor him.
He liked to call a spade a spade
And toss among the glum and staid
A poem like a hand grenade –
And I remember clearly how
(Truth is the only poet's vow)
When my spare tyre was half this size,
With drumming veins and bloodshot eyes
I blundered through the rain and sleet
To dip my wick in Castle Street,
Not on the footpath – no, in a flat,
With a sofa where I often sat,
Smoked, drank, cursed, in the company
Of a female student who unwisely
Did not mind but would pull the curtain
Over the window – And did a certain
Act occur? It did. It did.
As Byron wrote of Sennacherib –
'The Assyrian came down like a wolf on the fold
And his cohorts were gleaming in purple and gold' –
But now, at nearly forty-two,
An inmate of the social zoo,
Married, baptised, well heeled, well shod,
Almost on speaking terms with God,
I intend to save my moral bacon
By fencing the young from fornication!
Ah, Dr Williams, I agree
We need more walls at the Varsity;
The students who go double-flatting
With their she-catting and tom-catting
Won't ever get a pass in Latin;
The moral mainstay of the nation
Is careful, private masturbation;
A vaseline jar or a candle

Will drive away the stink of scandal!
The Golden Age will come again –
Those tall asthenic bird-like men
With spectacles and lecture notes,
Those girls with wool around their throats
Studying till their eyes are yellow
A new corrupt text of *Othello*,
Vaguely agnostic, rationalist,
A green banana in each fist
To signify the purity
Of educational ecstasy –
And, if they marry, they will live
By the Clinical Imperative:
A car, a fridge, a radiogram,
A clean well-fitted diaphragm,
Two-and-a-half children per
Family; to keep out thunder
Insurance policies for each;
A sad glad fortnight at the beach
Each year, when Mum and Dad will bitch
From some old half-forgotten itch –
Turn on the lights! – or else the gas!
If I kneel down like a stone at Mass
And wake my good wife with bad dreams,
And scribble verse on sordid themes,
At least I know man was not made
On the style of a slot-machine arcade –
Almost, it seems, the other day,
When Francis threw his coat away
And stood under the palace light
Naked in the Bishop's sight
To marry Lady Poverty
In folly and virginity,
The angels laughed – do they then weep
Tears of blood if two should sleep
Together and keep the cradle warm?
Each night of earth, though the wind storm,
Black land behind, white sea in front,
Leander swims the Hellespont;
To Hero's bed he enters cold;
And he will drown; and she grow old –
But what they tell each other there
You'll not find in a book anywhere.

# RUTH DALLAS 1968

**WHEN** Ruth Dallas applied for the Burns Fellowship in October 1967 she was already an established poet. She had been publishing poetry since 1947 and had had three major collections brought out by the Caxton Press, with the fourth accepted for publication in 1968. In 1964 the Press Room of the English Department had brought out a pamphlet of short poems, *Experiment in Form* (see 'Night Piece' below). She had also had some writing for children brought out by School Publications. During her Burns year she wrote some new poems, most of which were not published until 1976 in *Walking On The Snow* (See 'In Central Otago' and 'In the University Library' below).

*Ruth Dallas (1919–2008) published nine collections of poems, a collection of short stories, an autobiography, seven novels for children, and miscellaneous other writing for children.*

However, the most immediately visible results of the year were her writings for children: *Ragamuffin Scarecrow* (University Bibliography Room, 1969), *The Children in the Bush* (Methuen, 1969) – the first of what was to be a series of seven children's novels – some short stories and a play for children. Some of this work appeared in School Journals.

It was a most productive year, but at the end of it she reported to Professor E.A. Horsman:

It is possible that, for me, the most valuable part of the Burns Fellowship has not been in what I have been able to write, but the hours I had in which to read and study. Works written may be seen as the lemons or apples put forth from a writer's life, but it is the root that needs the nourishment, and this I have had time to find. My coming into contact with the University Library has been an enriching experience.[30]

## Night Piece

Fragile
– As snow –
Eddying
Moths tipsy
On evenings heady
With elderberry flowers
And the breath of gorse,
Round the street lights go
In a whirlpool dance of death;
Dazed, unaware of the velvet
Footed, shark-toothed,
Street cats
Watching
Moon-
eyed
below.

## FROM *Ragamuffin Scarecrow*

Ragamuffin Scarecrow tried to frighten the birds away. 'Off with you!' he said to the birds. 'This is the farmer's field. Here the wheat will grow and the wind will sing. There will be plenty of grain for all. You must not steal the seed. Shoo! Shoo!'

But the cheeky little birds flew down and picked up the seed and ate it. They hopped as close to Ragamuffin as they dared. They made up a song to sing:

'Ragamuffin Scarecrow!

Ragamuffin Scarecrow!

Couldn't catch a cold potato!'

It was a hard job Ragamuffin had, working for the farmer, and receiving no wages. He longed to go out in the world and seek his fortune. But there he stood, night and day, fastened to a post in the field.

Over the road, in the cherry orchard, the leaves were beginning to fall. This was the time of year the wind loved the best. It raced after the dry leaves, piled them up in corners, and scattered them again.

'All very well for you,' said Ragamuffin to the wind. 'You can go where you like. You can go round the world, if you wish, and come back again in the morning.'

'I will show you something,' said the wind. It rushed over the road and bent the trees as though it wanted to blow them down. All the leaves were chased away, leaving the branches bare.

And there, standing in the cherry orchard, Ragamuffin saw another scarecrow, dressed in some old clothes that had belonged to the farmer's wife. This scarecrow wore a red skirt, a blue blouse and an old sun-hat. Her arms were spread wide to frighten the birds. She had been standing there all summer, to scare the birds away from the cherries. Ragamuffin did not know, because she had been hidden by the leaves.

'Oh, how I should like to talk to that lovely lady!' said Ragamuffin.

When the wind blew his tattered coat he waved to her. But she stood with her head bent, and did not notice him.

'She is shy,' thought Ragamuffin. But the truth was, her head was not fastened properly. It was made from a piece of cloth stuffed with straw. The farmer's wife, who had made it, had not been able to make it sit firmly.

'She seems so neat, so pretty,' thought Ragamuffin. 'And she has such tiny feet!'

Yes, the lady's feet were very small. They were the prongs of a hay-fork. The handle of the hay-fork served as her back-bone, but that, of course, could not be seen under her gay clothes.

Ragamuffin's feet were big and clumsy. They were made from straw-filled gum-boots. You might think he had three feet, because the back of his coat was fastened to a post in the ground.

How could Ragamuffin get out of the field and across the road to the cherry orchard? He tugged hard against the post, trying to split his coat. But it was too strong.

'Ha! Ha!' laughed the wind. 'There you stand and there you stay. That is the life of a scarecrow.'

'Why can't I run about the world like the wind?' Ragamuffin wondered.

When he looked at the other scarecrow, in the cherry orchard, he felt so strange. He wanted to dance, to sing, to shout, to stand on his head. But there he had to stay, tied to his post.

# In Central Otago

Seek foliage and find
Among cracked boulders
Scab of lichen, thyme.

Seek a burgeoning tree
Discover
Upended witches' brooms.

Seek grass and tread
Stiff sheet of ice drawn
Over the land dead.

Moon country.
No one could live here,
In the houses squat on shingle.

Fields scorched,
Snow gripping the mountains;
Nothing could recover

From such desolation,
Jack Frost's sheep-run,
Mirror of the bleak mind.

But come back in a month –
See blanketing the slits
And sockets of the land's skeleton

Square eiderdowns of peach-bloom,
Old crone, Plum, unpick
A feather mattress from a bald stone.

# In the University Library

I am swallowed by a whale
Whose ribs are well furnished
With writing material, books,
A choice of coffee or tea.

From portholes I observe
Clouds disperse
Or gather in threatening storm.
Seabirds pass overhead

Emitting their coarse laughter.
I am walled behind glass
Where snow does not fall
Nor gales blow. I write poems,

Frame incantations
Against being digested by the whale.

# WARREN DIBBLE 1969

*Warren Dibble (b. 1931) had a number of radio and television plays produced, and published three short plays and some poems and short stories in New Zealand (1962–71).*

**IN** the gallery of Burns Fellows in the Central Library only one Fellow is not represented by a photograph – Warren Dibble. For him there is only an empty frame. Perhaps this is symbolic, for he has been the most difficult of the Fellows to locate. When I finally did succeed in contacting him, his reply came on the back of a postcard advertising Australian National Missing Persons Week. The introduction below is his own third-person account of the Burns Fellowship tenure and its context. He also supplied his own picture.

Born in 1931, married with seven children, Dibble began his Burns Fellowship in 1969, when times they were a'changin'.

Before this, he and his friend, writer Jim Edwards (son of the leader of the Queen Street Riots & friend of social rebel John A Lee) roamed N.Z. in rental cars, selling everything from mussels to 1st Aid kits, door to door. As amateurs (in the best sense of the word) they performed in church halls, band rotundas, school rooms, farm barns, and once in a boxing ring; from an ad hoc repertoire of Shakespeare, Durrenmatt, Ionesco, Mark Twain, early Pinter, Dickens, Synge, O'Casey, Tennessee Williams ('Last of My Solid Gold Watches') & dramatizations of Katherine Mansfield dialogues.

Dibble also acted in British Drama League productions: often caricatured by the ignorant, but never by Bruce Mason, who recognized the annual B.D.L. one-act Festspiel as the equivalent of an All Black final; where 150 plays were presented by over 1000 actors, 2/3rds of them women. Dibble's written one-acters won in various B.D.L. competitions. A production from his hometown, Hawera, G.B. Shaw's curious but pungent little Western, 'The Shewing Up of Blanco Posnet', produced by Nan Leatham, won the coveted N.Z wide B.D.L. comp', with Dibble as Blanco. B.D.L. was a grass-roots source for many emerging N.Z. playwrights.

By 1969 Dibble had had 3 short stories and a long poem printed in 'Landfall'; and had written a number of plays for radio, television and stage. They included N.Z.'s 1st colour TV drama, 'The Killing of Kane', which explored Titokowaru and the Maori Wars; and a TV play without dialogue, 'How With this Rage', that related military training in schools to the Vietnam War. An earlier 'cartoon for theatre', 'Operation Pigstick', produced by Tim Elliot for 'Downstage' ['... must rate with some of the best political satire produced in this country...']31 lampooned USA Prez' L.B.J.'s visit to N.Z. & Defence Minister Muldoon's Vietnam policy. It offended many. Already contracted by the NZBC, with production underway, major scenes in 'How With this Rage' depended strongly on co-operation with Defence. This was pledged, until the government ordered Defence not to co-operate because the play was 'unpatriotic'. Production was canceled. The play was later printed in 'Landfall'.

In his Burns year Dibble, rather than lecture, acted in Otago Uni's entry for the best N.Z. University theatre production, playing Paine in Rodney Kennedy's staging of Paul Foster's 'Tom Paine' [with 'warmth and maturity', 'gave the production heart and authority']32, set designed & built by Ralph Hotere. He played in two J.K. Baxter plays at the Careys' Globe, for which he radically rewrote an earlier stage play, 'The Voice of the Turtle', adapted for radio as 'Aria', and re-named by Patric (to Dibble's annoyance) as 'Mock Turtle'.

His stage play, 'Lines to M', premiered privately in Hawera, was adapted for radio by the N.Z.B.C., and performed with 'Mock Turtle' at the Carey's Globe Theatre. Downstage did it the same year (Oct '69) as part of the Gulbenkian Series of N.Z. dramas. George Webby, reviewing it in ACT, found 'Lines to M' ['... extraordinary ... the best New Zealand play I have ever seen ...']33

Dibble also shared a couple of poetry readings with Hone Tuwhare; and enjoyed informal discussions with arts students. While a Burns Fellow, he sketched out work for a trilogy of plays and began work on an historical novel about Herod the Great. Research (and temporary marriage and tax difficulties) took him to Australia, where, in Melbourne, he played Hamlet in Elijah Moshinsky's combined University production of Shakespeare's play. Dibble shifted attention from theatre to the sciences. He continued to write poetry in various modes, performed mainly for friends and family. He has recently completed the play trilogy (3 men: Casanova, Napoleon & James Boswell: refracted unflatteringly through the viewpoint of 3 historically linked women). He writes: 'without that kickstart from my Burns year I'd never have had the audacity to begin them.' He is currently alive and well in Sydney.34

The following poem is an extract from 'A Marriage', a long, unpublished poetic sequence. The author records that the poem was intended 'to place on record for my family some aspects of a mixed Maori and Pakeha marriage ... in the soul-stifling 50s'.35 The extract comes from the third of the work's four parts and was, Dibble writes,

foreshadowed in a short poem I wrote while Burns Fellow

for a joint reading with Hone Tuwhare (as it transpired, the first time he read – marvelously – his fine poem 'Rain', which charmed us all and stole the night). I transferred the general drift and one or two phrases from my short poem to that section in 'A Marriage', so it links to the time. Yes, and what's more, I remember now, I was surprised and pleased when Charles Brasch asked for a copy of it. Alas, it never got done.[36]

FROM **A Marriage**

all down our years
dreams flew round us,
some we caught, most we missed;
we did the best with what we had,
it wasn't enough – it never is;

you took it all, too proud
to break; I stormed and strutted,
clowned, betrayed,
but also gave
all of myself, the best, to you
and maybe more; at least
that's how I'd like to see it,
all up and weighed;

and I knew all the time
what a tornado
I'd picked up in you;
storm of a woman!
and the one I needed
more than any fame
that I might choose;
I felt your vastness, needed
your chaos
even though it angered me;
I breathed your life
and knew inside myself

you were the home I never had
and all I stood to lose.

\*

We thought we could ride out
bad weather; and true,

we mostly did;

but some nights you wept
on stone
calling up cold wind
to dry your tears;

and then we slept apart;

some days we woke
to screaming gulls
harsh light
and empty bed;
or worst of all
to an empty heart:

but each time we saw
the carnage left behind
we paused, and knew,
that we were better than all that:
                                    kiddies

kept us sane, brought us down
to common ground.

\*

Meanwhile Mt. Egmont
fanged the blue,
(a shape still hulking
in my blood);
I loved its lavender light,
its clean and clear
high note of snow
on Phantom's Peak;

and how its mystery
kept pace with ours.

\*

yet soft dawns still
could turn to blood,
clear skies to pain;
we wept, we wept,

but still we held
ferociously
to what we had –

none
more lovingly than you.

\*

Sometimes I saw our marriage-shape
in Taranaki cliffs,
their creamy wedges
slicing clear to ironsand,
its blackness glittering
with dagger points;

or saw poked out
from wind-eroded places,
quiet and ancient Maori bones;

or wandering round the pa sites
(and no, I NEVER had it off with HER!)
found artifacts
upheaved in sight
and timed anew
at point of trowel's probe –

bullets or obsidian flakes
without a speck of grief –

indices of a fury
long gone underground;

and thought of us in time to come
with all our meaning unattended
and only some unknown person's
eye to catch the immediate
history of these words and take
 them forward:
                                    time
will pick us clean at last.

# THE 1970s

# 1969, 1974

# HONE TUWHARE

*Hone Tuwhare (1922–2008) published thirteen collections of poetry (some with prose included) and one play.*

**HONE** Tuwhare held a special Centennial Fellowship from June to October 1969, and then a full-year Fellowship in 1974. In 1969 he composed or revised the poems for his second collection, published by the Bibliography Room in 1970 as *Come Rain Hail: Poems*, with a striking orange and purple cover by his friend Ralph Hotere, who came to Dunedin in 1969 as the Frances Hodgkins Fellow. The little book contained some of Tuwhare's most memorable poems and ultimately went through four editions (losing the original colours in the process). Printed below are three poems from it: 'Rain', 'Hotere' (referring to the cover) and another rain poem, 'Child coming home in the rain from the

store'. In 1974 he selected the poems (all written earlier) for his fourth collection, *Something Nothing: Poems*, published late that year by Caveman Press in Dunedin, and wrote new poems, some of which appeared in 1978 in his fifth collection, *Making a Fist of It*, published in Dunedin by the Jackstraw Press. Although much of the work in that political volume came from the Maori Land March in the following year, 'Reign Rain', a kind of annex to 'Rain', may have come from 1974 and is printed below.

## Rain

I can hear you
making small holes
in the silence
rain

If I were deaf
the pores of my skin
would open to you
and shut

And I
should know you
by the lick of you
if I were blind

the something
special smell of you
when the sun cakes
the ground

the steady
drum-roll sound
you make
when the wind drops

But if I
should not hear
smell or feel or see
you

you would still
define me
disperse me
wash over me
rain

# Hotere

When you offer only three
vertical lines precisely drawn
and set into a dark pool of lacquer
it is a visual kind of starvation:

and even though my eye-balls
roll up and over to peer inside
myself, when I reach the beginning
of your eternity I say instead: hell
let's have another feed of mussels

*Like, I have to think about it, man*

When you stack horizontal lines
into vertical columns which appear
to advance, recede, shimmer and wave
like exploding packs of cards
I merely grunt and say: well, if it
is not a famine, it's a feast

*I have to roll another smoke, man*

But when you score a superb orange
circle on a purple thought-base
I shake my head and say: hell, what
is this thing, called love

*Like, I'm euchered man. I'm eclipsed.*

# Child Coming Home in the Rain from the Store

When I see you pause
make talk dawdle-walk
on the back road to your house
your house overlooking
the timber mill and timber yard
I know you stop only to talk
not to the cruel metalled road

but to a stone a solitary stone
sharp-edged with flat shiny
faces

*Through your mind's eye know*
*the feel of washed leaves*
*made green again: tall rain-shafts*
*drifting: wind wincing*
*a water-filled pot-hole*

And I child-delighting share
your long walk your talk
to things *and for things* along
the bent road to your house
where impatiently
others wait for the damp bread
you bring

## Reign Rain

Neither juggernaut
man
nor crawling thing
with saintliness and ease

can bring
a mountain weeping
to its knees
quicker than rain:

that demure leveller
ocean-blessed
cloud-sent
maker of plains.

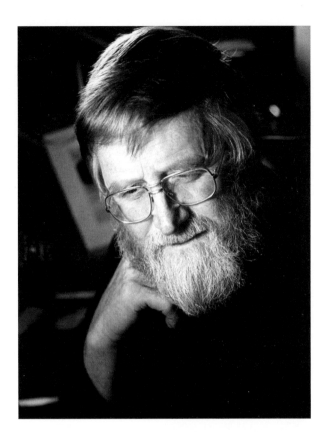

# O.E. MIDDLETON 1970

*O.E. Middleton (b. 1925) has published seven collections of short fiction, a booklet of poetry and a book of stories for children.*

**ALREADY** an established writer of fiction, with three collections of short stories, O.E. Middleton was appointed Burns Fellow late in 1969. He writes of his Fellowship experience:

When I came to Dunedin in January 1970 to take up a Robert Burns Fellowship, it was also with the intention of making the city my long-term home and place of work. Two stories finished that year, 'The Loners' and 'The Will to Win', were given public readings at the University of Otago by the late Philip Smithells, founding director of the School of Physical Education, and the late Patric Carey, co-founder

and director of the Globe Theatre. A novel begun that year and finished a year or two later, remains unpublished.[37]

'The Loners' became the title story in Middleton's 1972 collection, an exquisite little book published by Charles Brasch and Janet Paul's 'Square & Circle' press, with cover and line drawings by Middleton's good friend Ralph Hotere. 'The Will to Win' appeared in *Selected Stories* (1975), which in 1976 shared the initial New Zealand Book Award for Fiction with Maurice Gee's *A Glorious Morning, Comrade*. Both stories are included in the retrospective 2008 Otago University Press collection *Beyond the Breakwater*.

FROM **The Loners**

As long as he had been working, all had been well. The other men in the timber-yard had been friendly enough once he had got to know them. They had taught him all the gauges, shown him how to tell *rimu* from *matai*, *totara* from *kauri* and white pine. Once he had grown used to their rough, teasing ways, he had come to like working in the timber-yard.

The day the foreman had told him he was to 'finish-up' he had not at first understood.

'Bad luck, Luke!' one of the gang had growled, clapping him on the shoulder. 'There's seven of us been given our walking-tickets today.'

'… You too?'

'Yes. Me, my mate Bill here, young Jimmy from the joinery shop and three from one of the other gangs.'

'Bbbut, why?' he had managed to bring out, his eyes searching the man's weathered, unsmiling face.

'Not enough orders. That's why! The country's in a bad way at the moment. The building industry's one of the hardest hit. I've seen it happen before and it'll happen again!' The man had drawn a hand across the grey stubble on his chin, stared past the even stacks of timber at the gleam of sea.

All the next, workless morning, he had sat about, not knowing what to do. There were no labourer's jobs in the paper.

'Why don't you sit on the verandah?' Pine had suggested.

He had gone there meekly enough, glad to be out of the way while the two women made beds and cleaned the house. After a while, though, he had grown uneasy. It seemed to him that the people who strolled past, especially the stiff-faced women with their trundlers and shopping baskets, looked at him disdainfully, as if he had no right to be there. As soon as he had gone back inside, his brother's wife, Rebecca, had begun to scold him.

'Aw, Luke! Can't you give us a chance to get the house straight!'

Ashamed, ill-at-ease, he had gone out again, wandered off alone, not thinking or caring where he went, yet always making for the sea. He had sauntered moodily past the other old wooden houses, all like the one he shared with his

brother Matthew, had become aware all at once that this was his first *free* day, his first day to himself since they had got off the ship. From then on, he had wandered through the town, glancing almost furtively into shop-windows. In the window of a fish-shop, something had caught his eye. For some moments he had stared intently, almost affectionately, through the streaming glass at the object; a sizeable squid on a large dish ….

He had been on the point of going in to ask the price of the succulent thing, but just in time, realised that he did not know its English name. Besides, he had given Pine all his money the day before, so his pockets were empty.

Moodily, he had turned away. It did not do to go anywhere without money in *this* country. With money in the pocket, there was always something to buy.

At home, he had always gone fishing with friends: either in a boat on the lagoon, or, at night, with torches and spears on the reef. Whatever the catch, there had always been plenty of fun, the warmth of talk and laughter ….

Here, everything was different. The people went about singly, many of them with grim, stony faces. Often they passed one another in the street without so much as a greeting.

At last, hardly knowing where he was, he had reached the harbour, walked the length of the old wharf. A solitary fisherman squinting down at a dancing float had glanced at him briefly. In that instant, the two halves of his longing had come together. He would ask Pine for enough to buy a couple of lines and some hooks.

Ever since, he had hardly missed a day. Once he had scanned the job columns, been to see about any work that was offering, his thoughts would turn to the hours stretching ahead. With his gear and a morsel of food in an old basket, he would set out for the wharf.

Though he no longer followed that first, roundabout route, wasted no time gazing into shop-windows, it was still a long way. Sometimes, another man, or even two, were there before him. One day, when he had been to see about a job, he found four of them perched, intent as gulls, at the end of the wharf.

At weekends and late in the afternoons, small boys sometimes drifted down in two and threes to fish for sprats.

The old man he had seen that first day came down on his bicycle two or three times a week. He used a home-made rod that he carried tied to the bar of his bicycle, rarely stayed beyond midday and usually went home with a fish. He wore spectacles, moved stiffly and sometimes had trouble taking off and putting on the clips he wore around the bottoms of his trousers. He seldom smiled, spoke little, but usually greeted the other regulars with a nod. Once or twice, Luke thought he saw a gleam, like the sudden sparkle of sun on sea, light up the old man's eyes.

Jock, as the others called him, kept all his tackle in a wooden box strapped to the carrier of his bicycle. Nestling in a honeycomb of small cells were hooks and sinkers, swivels, rod-rings, spare coils of fine wire and nylon, spinners and oddments of all kinds. Once, the old fellow had gone to the box, rummaged a

while, and handed Luke a sharp new hook to replace one lost on a snag. He had shown him how to tie a stop-knot, how to 'kinch' it tight so that it would never slip. Another time, Jock had tossed him a piece of fresh mullet, signing to him to exchange it for the bait he had been using without success.

Three other men came down to the wharf almost every day. One rode a motor-bike, another drove a battered car, while a third came on foot. All were married men in their late twenties or early thirties. From the few words they exchanged, Luke guessed that all were out of work and came to the wharf as much to get away from their wives, as in the hope of taking something home for the pot. He would have liked to ask them what work they did; to have told them how strange he found everything after the life he had been used to. But the chance never came.

If one of them spoke to him, it was teasingly, as though he were a child. His halting replies usually brought only shakes of the head, pitying smiles. Their eyes would return to their fishing-lines that seemed to transfix the water like fine spears. He guessed that the three had all been born in the town, had grown up there at about the same time. Yet they were not *real* friends. Perhaps they had gone to different schools, belonged to different churches, worked at different jobs? Often, as he sat brooding on these things, Luke's thoughts would return to his wife. He would stare past the breakwater at the great rock thrusting up through the pale sea like a huge, blunt tooth, his heart swelling with love.

It was natural that she should feel anxious, now that she was again with child. At least Matthew still went to his job at the freezing works every morning. When the wind blew from that quarter, the wail of the works siren would come clearly over the intervening sea. Luke would cock his head, stare uneasily across the water.

There had been a hooter at the timber-yard. The first new words he had learned had been *smoko, knock-off, pay-day*: his workmates had seen to that. Each time he heard the siren, it reminded him of the men he had worked with in the timber-yard, the things they had said. The sound seemed to stir some chord in the others too. They would get up, stretch their limbs, swallow mouthfuls of tea from their flasks, light a cigarette or fill a pipe when the smoko hooter went. Whenever the noon whistle blew, old Jock would get up stiffly, begin reeling-in. Although the old man lived on a pension and none of the others had regular jobs, the mournful call of the hooter seemed to tug at them all, as the sun and moon affect the tide.

Since they were fond of eating their fish raw, Pine had tried to buy limes at the greengrocer's. But even the shops that sold taro had only lemons to offer.

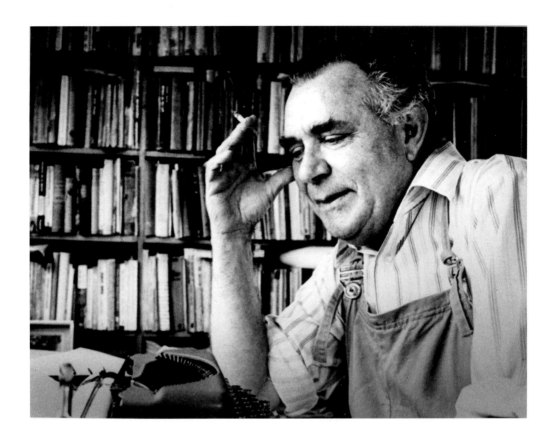

# NOEL HILLIARD 1971

*Noel Hilliard (1929–96) published five novels and three volumes of short stories between 1960 and 1978. He also published four volumes of non-fiction.*

**WHEN** Noel Hilliard was awarded the Burns Fellowship late in 1970, he had published three novels and a book of short stories in the previous decade. His first novel, *Maori Girl* (1960), and his second, *Power of Joy* (1965), appeared to be unrelated, but at the end of *Power of Joy* Paul Bennett, the Pakeha protagonist, has seen a young Maori woman who attracts him, and she will turn out to have been Netta Samuel, the protagonist of *Maori Girl*. Hilliard's primary literary project was to complete a tetralogy bringing these two characters together and then tracing their married life. Much of his Burns year was spent writing a draft of the third novel in the sequence, with

the working title of *And None Shall Doubt*. He had been gathering material for the book for three years, and it was eventually published as *Maori Woman* in 1974 (the title was the publisher's). When he finished his draft, he wrote a series of short stories which were later collected in 1976 in *Send Somebody Nice*. He completed the tetralogy with *The Glory and the Dream* in 1978.

The following extract is from 'Encounter', which he wrote during 1971 both as a section of *And None shall Doubt* and as a short story. As a short story it won the 1971 Palmerston North Centennial short story contest and was published in *Landfall*. It eventually formed the first chapter of the third section of *Maori Woman*. In the novel Paul Bennett has proposed to and been accepted by Netta Samuel in Wellington and is between buses on his return to his parents' small-town home to tell them. The young Maori man who picks a fight with him is Jason Pine, Netta's ex-lover, but neither is aware of the relationship of the other with Netta.

## FROM **Encounter**

Four Maoris in jerseys and gumboots came in together, put their elbows on the bar and ordered beers. They were all aged about twenty. One noticed Paul's suitcase.

'You hitting the road boss?'

'Yes, I'm catching the Ihutai bus.'

He nodded. 'So's we.'

'What time does it leave?'

'When we get there. Mattie here's the driver.' He nudged the man next to him.

Mattie grinned. 'Say about ten o'clock. You going all the way?'

'I am.'

'You staying out there?'

'Yes, going home for a little while, see the folks.'

'Ko wai to ingoa?'

'Pardon?'

'What's your fellows name?'

'Bennett.'

'Old Stan?'

'That's him.'

'Can't remember you.'

'Haven't been home there since I was a kid. Went to school there three-four years during the war.'

'Where about does your fellows live now?'

'I get off at the stop just before the pa.'

One of them laughed. Paul wondered what was funny.

'Your shout Jason,' Mattie said to the one who had laughed. He rummaged in his dungaree pockets for change, then turned to Paul and asked, 'What pa's that?'

'There's only the one that I know of. You must know it, about half a mile from the end of the run.'

All four laughed this time: not an easy, pleasant laugh. Paul wished he could see the humour of it.

Jason said: 'I suppose to you one pa is just the same as another?'

'I never really thought about it. You asked me where I live and I told you. If it was the post office I'd have said the post office.'

'But the pa's just part of the scenery to you, eh? Like – how would you say – like a landmark?'

'That's right.'

'So you think that's right?'

'I do indeed.'

'Well I don't think that's right. You pakeha say pa like it was only part of the scenery. And I suppose you think we all live there? Maoris, so they got to be from the pa?'

'I've got no idea where you live.'

'But you think to yourself, Here's a bunch of Maoris catching the bus out our way, they must all be going to get off at the pa. Is that it?'

'I didn't say.'

'But that's what you thought. You just told us it's part of the scenery and of course it's the place where all the horis live. Do you know any more about it than that?'

'I've never actually been there if that's what you're getting at.'

'Never been there but you know all about it. Maoris – so they got to live in the pa. Simple and neat as that. The pa – that's where the Maori live. Is that right?'

'If you say so.'

'But I don't say so. Not too many Maori live in the pa these days boy. You pakeha saw to that. Do you know the difference between pa and marae?'

'Supposing you tell me.'

'You think it's just a case of me tell you and then you'll know. Boy – you pakeha! you give me a guts-ache.'

They all laughed again.

'Listen,' Jason said, pushing his face closer to Paul's, 'what you say if I tell you no Maoris live in pas these days because most of them been closed down by the Health and the Welfare and the Maori Affairs? What would you say to that?'

'I'll take your word for it.'

'But you're pakeha, you should know. This was all your idea, part of your plan. You should be interested in how your big plan is getting on. But you still won't let the Maori into your very flash special sort of pakeha places so it still suits you to say *Maori – he's got his place – lives in a pa* – because then you don't have to think about it any more.'

'In fact I don't think about it at all. You could be right there.'

He could sense that something was developing, something ugly, but he could not judge what to do about it or how to get out of it with a show at least of good grace.

'Let me tell you this then: quite a few Maori are just as well set up as a lot of pakeha but you still got this stupid pakeha idea that the old hori is back in the pa somewhere eating pipis and dragging his feet. And if you come across a city Maori there's still something in you that won't allow you to let go – won't let you admit him to pakeha society' – he pronounced it sass-ay-eh-tee with heavy sarcasm – 'so you know what you do? You shove him off into a pa in your mind somewhere. That's the only place it exists, in your mind. But it's there and that's where you put him and then you don't need to think any more, don't need to take any notice because everything is taken care of, everything is in its proper place. You say to yourself *If he's not in a pa he ought to be* and leave it at that.'

'This could all be true but I don't see what it has to do with sinking a few beers before the bus leaves.'

'And you don't know about marae, the home place. It's precious to the Maori wherever he might be, that's where he goes when the pakeha world got him so confused he don't know who he is. That's where he goes to find out again, and this time he's hoping he might remember, might keep on remembering. But you pakeha say *There he goes, back to the pa*. You say *Back to the mat*. That's what you say to each other about us.'

'You're making a hell of a lot out of this. All I did was tell you where I live.'

'And that's what I'm telling you boy – where I live. Not at the pa, none of us. We don't sleep there or have meals or work there. We all do that in the city. But on the marae – that's where we *live* if we're Maori, even though we might be some place a hundred miles away. Can you understand that?'

'I can't and it sounds a bit spooky to me. I haven't a clue what you're talking about and I'm not interested in arguing.'

'You make me bloody wild. Pa! you say – I live near the *pa* – that's that Maori thing, the *pa*. You run into me in a city street and you say to yourself, Here he is away from his *pa* today, I wonder when's he go back to his *pa*. You throw that word around as if it explained everything. Most Maoris never even lived in a pa in their whole lives. Never even seen one, lot of them. It's the pakeha keeps that idea alive. He got rid of all the real pas but he keeps them going *in his own way*.' He laid heavy stress on the last four words, lunging with his eyes.

'Anyway, don't get all excited about it, chief.'

'Why do you call me chief?'

Paul realised he hadn't seen the pitfall here; in an effort at jollity he had walked straight into it without thinking.

'I don't know your name, do I?'

'You could always ask. Or look me up in the phone book.' He grinned as he glanced at the others; they grinned too.

'So why do you call me chief?'

'I've got several Maori mates I call chief. They don't mind.'

'I mind.' On the word 'I' he slammed the bar with his fist and stood looking

Paul directly in the eye for fully half a minute without a word. The bar was silent. Paul was aware of a deeper tension and was trying to remember what he had said to put things off on to this track; the introductory remarks had seemed casual enough, and friendly. Could it be that he had not offered to shout?

Jason's lips pursed and his nostrils dilated as if he had just smelt a disagreeable odour. 'Maori mates you say. Maori mates and you call them chief. Why not mate or pal? That's what you call your pakeha friends isn't it?' He moved closer. 'But Maoris it's got to be chief. I suppose you think it's funny that a Maori can be a chief. You think that's funny?'

'Can you see me laughing?'

'Bastards like you never laugh – that's half your trouble. But listen: there's nothing funny about a Maori being a chief. My grandfather was a chief. Just try laughing about that and see what happens.'

'I'm not saying it's funny.'

'No but you think it. I can tell, I see it in your eyes. Mate or pal or buster to your pakeha friends but chief to Maoris because chief is funny – ha ha! The Maori used to have chiefs but now they don't because us know-every-thing pakeha are in charge but it's still a good joke, every man a chief, every woman a princess. Have you any Maori women friends you call princess?'

Paul wanted to tell them he was on their side but he suspected they would despise him for it. He said nothing.

'Did you ask your Maori friends if they really were chiefs or not, or doesn't that concern you? No, you wouldn't bother because you could never believe that one of these half-pie comical fat-bums you knock around with might really be of rangatira stock.' He was becoming more and more agitated. The others glared, hostile. 'More likely they would be of slave stock, descended from kuki, and that would add to the humour of it. His ancestors were slaves, nobodies, and now along here comes the pakeha, the noble pakeha, and makes him a chief. Like the Queen giving out a knighthood. Lord this, Sir that. But not for real. This is for laughs. Chief. Funny. Big joke. Ha ha.'

'I don't bother too much about that sort of thing. If you want to go digging into somebody's family history that's your business. I take people how I find them and I don't go in for this *chief* business whether it's Maoris or whites – kings, lords, nobles, all the rest.'

'That might be what you say now but what happens when Her Majesty comes to these shores, what happens then? You're all out with your little flags waving and yelling, you suddenly come over all pakeha, very pakeha.'

Paul knew things were not going his way. He said, 'Can't we just leave it at that then? Can I buy yous all a beer?'

'Why did you say *yous* all?'

'Look, are you having a drink or not?'

'It is because you think that's a Maori way of talking? Are we supposed to fall

in love with you because you suddenly start talking Maori English like we do – or like you suppose we do?'

'Everything I say, you see something evil in it. You tip it right on its head. What about a beer?'

'Just a minute. You said before, Can we leave it at that? That's what you asked and I'm telling you no, no we can't leave it at that. You can. We can't. You can go from day to day and week to week and never have to think about being pakeha. You're a pakeha fish and you swim in a pakeha sea. But we have to think about being Maori twenty-four hours a day, seven days of the week. We might not want to, we might even like to forget it for a while. But you won't let us. You make us feel it all the time in a hundred different ways. We're the herrings in this pakeha sea of yours and there's sharks around. Have you ever thought about what a privilege it is for you to be able to forget you're pakeha, take it for granted? Have you ever wondered what you're doing to us, drumming this Maori-Maori-Maori thing of yours until every breath we take we think it's a Maori breath? Pa! Chief! Yous all! You make me sick.'

# IAN WEDDE 1972

Ian Wedde (b. 1946) has published twelve collections of poetry, a collection of short fiction, four novels (with another forthcoming in 2008), two collections of essays, and has a monograph appearing in 2009. His edited books include two anthologies of New Zealand poetry and several art catalogues.

**WHEN** he returned from England and took up the Burns Fellowship in 1972, Ian Wedde was a promising young writer. He had to his name only one slender book, *Homage to Matisse*, a collection of poems published the year before, but he had been a regular contributor of poetry and short fiction to Robin Dudding's *Landfall* in the previous five years. In the half-decade following his Burns year he was to publish five books of poetry, a book of translations and a short novel, and work from that year appeared in many of these publications as well as in Dudding's new periodical, *Islands*, to which Wedde transferred his loyalty in 1972. He has nominated as 'the better work to come out of

the year' poems and stories in the following works: Selected *Poems of Mahmoud Darwish* (translations, with Fawwaz Tuqan, 1973), *The Shirt Factory and Other Stories* (1981), *Earthly: Sonnets for Carlos* (1975), and *Spells for Coming Out* (1977).[38] In a sense, almost all of his writings from 1972–5 in Port Chalmers form a single body of work which began in the year of Wedde's Burns Fellowship.

The following story was written during that year and first appeared as 'The Porch' in *Islands* 7 (Autumn 1974), an issue devoted to 'An anthology of contemporary New Zealand fiction'. It was collected in *The Shirt Factory and Other Stories*.

## In Clover

They were wrangling as they walked through the paddock at the back of the house. There were certain practical considerations: isolation, money. She listened with only half an ear to what he was saying: '… until next summer …' Something, something.

She was thinking that there is the place we live in, and there are the places we return to. It's the places we return to that we love most. They can never be the place we live in. If we return to them, again and again, then we must be away from them, very often, for long periods of time ….

'Oh my god,' he said. 'Look!' He began to run back towards the house. The baby was swinging gently in a canvas sling suspended from the porch. She could see that the roof of the porch had come loose from the house. One of the uprights at the centre of the porch had broken off at roof height. The roof was folding slowly inwards at the centre. He was running at full speed across the clover of the paddock behind the house. He had just flung himself over the gate when the porch roof collapsed with a crack. The whole structure came down leaving one corner of rusty iron attached at the right-hand side, bent downward like a broken wing or like a viaduct disaster. He was running across the yard. She could hear him shouting, a high-pitched succession of formless words. The baby was out of sight. She had fallen in her sling and the broken porch roof had come down on top of her. She saw him straining at the wreckage on the ground. There was no sound now. Then with a crash he flung the reddish iron back against the porch, and bent again. She could see that he was looking at the baby, where she lay. Then he straightened up, the baby in his arms. His head was bent over so she couldn't see his face or the baby. He was walking slowly back towards her, his head bent. She could see his head shaking from side to side. All at once the events caught up with her. She screamed and ran, in her turn. He was standing by the gate, his head still bent, shaking it from side to side. When she got there he looked up. 'Wasn't that the funniest thing you've ever seen?' he said. He was overcome with laughter and relief. She looked at the baby with her mouth open. She was smiling a crooked smile. The only mark on her was a smear of powdery old roof paint across her forehead. The tears were pouring down his cheeks. 'Oh my god,' he

said, 'wasn't that just, wasn't that just, oh god, wasn't that just the funniest thing you ....'

So for once he took some time off and spent the rest of the day fixing the porch. There wasn't much to it. He hammered and sawed cheerfully. By late afternoon it was together again. He climbed up and began scraping at the iron with a stiff brush, saying that he might as well paint it now that he had begun. She found that she didn't really care, though she had often reminded him that the porch needed fixing, that a gale might bring it down.

That evening a friend of his, a journalist, came round just as they were beginning to eat a late meal. He told the story to the journalist, spinning it out, embellishing it. He said for example that he had caught his trousers on the gate and was struggling to unsnag them at the precise moment the whole roof finally came down and the baby with it, the baby making not a sound. He also said that she had become hysterical. She didn't correct him. It was a habit of his, to make a good story of something, and she had got used to it.

The baby was now asleep in another room. They all went in to look at her. He drew with his finger the place where the smear of dry paint had been. The journalist said the baby was lucky not to have lost an eye. This remark, uttered because he could think of nothing better to say – nodding his head stupidly over this infant most of whom was invisible – nonetheless reminded them of how nearly the comedy had been a disaster. They went back and finished eating, drinking some wine the journalist had brought. The journalist was rather earnest and the meal-time passed quietly while he expounded his theory that real comedy was only possible where disaster was barely averted. He illustrated his thesis by quoting from Shakespeare, describing scenes of mayhem from Laurel and Hardy movies, and by telling a number of sick jokes about Ugandan Asians. Meanwhile he seemed to be avoiding her eyes. She found him banal and a bore but her husband enjoyed drinking with him. They would spend long nights drunk, while she listened from the bedroom where she was going to sleep to the level drone of their voices as they went over, yet again, what she imagined to be familiar ground.

She cleared away the plates, washed them, and left them to drain. A mumble of voices came from the next room. She went out on to the porch, to a smell of galvanising primer. She'd thought this over-fastidious – all that had been needed was a coat of ordinary roof paint. By contrast a saw and some other tools were lying where he'd dropped them on the floor at one end. It was a clear warm night. Moonlight lit the level expanse of the small paddock and the slope of the hill behind. The cabbage tree rustled, a dry sound like large insects. There was a cane chair which usually stood on the porch. He had left it in the yard. She dragged it back and sat down. She thought of going in to get a glass of wine from the journalist's flagon; but though she didn't really care about such things, it seemed it might be rude for her to be sitting by herself, drinking his wine. Not a bad reason to do it, given his manner. But she got up and walked down to the gate. When

she looked back towards the house she could see the profiles of her husband and the journalist, crouched towards each other over opposite sides of the table, and the flagon between them, in the single lit window of the house. Light came dimly through the kitchen door on to the porch and on to the trunk of the cabbage tree. It would be better to hang the baby's sling from that, from the tree, she thought. She didn't really care that the porch was fixed but, more than that, she didn't really believe her husband could have fixed it all that well. A large moth fumbled at her neck. She shook it off in disgust and moved further into the dark. In the gully below the paddock a morepork was telling its own melancholy name, over and over, insisting on it. The moon was still rising. She tipped her head back to look up at the sky. In spite of the moonlight the stars were very bright. She found the Southern Cross, took an arc, and had due south. Then, out of habit, or for practice, she found Orion and waving her arms and taking up the points had the Celestial Equator. It was six thousand miles to Peking, six thousand miles to Santiago. Or so. Then she counted twenty paces back to the house.

There she met her husband and the journalist coming out. They were going to get flounder. That explained the journalist's foxy air. He'd anticipated her resentment. But it's late, she said. On the contrary, they insisted, the tide was now perfect and the moon was high. They went briskly around the house and up to the road. The journalist's big flashlight clacked against the jar of wine he was carrying in the same hand. She heard her husband laughing, and fumbling in the hedge at the front where he hid his flounder spear for fear visiting children would get hold of it. She sat on the porch with a cigarette. Soon the baby would wake up and she would feed her. She wished the smell of primer wasn't in the porch. She would have liked to smell the warm breeze blowing across the gully and the paddock. She would have liked to sip at another glass of wine. A joint would have been pleasant. In the distance she saw the lights of the journalist's fast car winding across and up the hill towards the estuary on the other side.

The next day also, to her surprise, he didn't work. He cooked two flounder for their breakfast, then went off by himself for a long walk. He came back, attached the baby's sling to the porch again, and sat with a bottle of beer in the sun, occasionally giving the sling a push. Then, abruptly, he set off up the road with a sack of flounder towards the pub at the crossroads.

He came back about four o'clock in a cheerful mood. He had sold most of the fish in the pub and, he said, had told the story of the collapsing porch. He hadn't paid for a single drink. The money from the flounder he'd given to the grocer, towards settlement of the account, with a couple of fish thrown in for extra placation.

But his good mood soon wore off. When at dinner time he saw another flounder on his plate, he went out in disgust into the dark and gave it to the sleeping hens. Then he sat reading, picking at a packet of dates.

About ten o'clock, having not said a word, he went to his room. She was feeding the baby. She would not do the dishes. Why should she, when he sat so morosely, having barely spoken to her all day. She heard him tapping at his typewriter. She put the sleeping baby in her cot and went to sit on the porch. The smell of paint was fainter now. It was another warm night. The moon was moving past its third quarter. As it had the previous night, the wind blew across the gully and the paddock, combining the earthy redolence of bush humus and wet leaf-mould and the freshness of deep clover. Or so she fancied. No matter how she happened to be feeling in herself, that wind was a constant pleasure, a Zephyr as she thought, 'firing gauche Chloris with passion' – though not when it blew a gale, as it did from time to time, wrecking the young plants in the vegetable garden, making her irritable and despondent, sapping her zest. But such a caressing breeze she imagined could exist anywhere. It was in itself quite neutral, universal, a pure traveller. It was only by placing smells in its way for it to take on as cargo that you attached it momentarily to a particular locale. The 'same' wind could quite conceivably bring her the smell of jasmine, or of Dutch herrings, if such things were in its path … but that would place her there also, in that path, and what she was smelling now was wet bush humus and deep clover, which was where she was. O which was where she was, yes, 'in clover'…. Watching her husband, once, scything along the fence at the end of the yard, she had realised the meaning of that phrase. Having struggled through coarse patches of weeds and paspalum, wiry cushions of twitchgrass, he came, after pausing constantly to whet the scythe, to a stretch of lush clover. How simply, then, the severed green lay down across the blade.

Going inside, she met him coming through the kitchen. 'It was so funny then,' he said, 'why does it have to be so fucking dismal now? I want to write it, just as it was, but I can't.' She found his petulance irritating. 'You could have got on to it sooner,' she replied. 'And if you can't write, why don't you do the dishes or something, instead of moping about?' 'Didn't I fix the porch?' he shouted. 'Didn't I put off the grocer?' 'They were only necessary,' he replied, 'you could hardly have left either of them for long.' He went outside cursing.

That night she had a dream in which the porch collapsed and sprang upright again, endlessly, in rapid succession. The baby's face kept reappearing, with a comical crooked grin. Then she saw the porch with jasmine trailing across it, a delicate confusion of bloom and perfume. Her husband was up in the cabbage tree with his flounder spear, keeping a lookout, shouting something like Placate! Placate! She woke up laughing. He was not in the bed. She closed her eyes again, trying to will herself back into the dream. It had been so refreshing.

She must have gone deeply and instantly asleep, because it seemed to be only seconds later that the baby woke her with its crying. It was early morning, just

after six o'clock. Through the bedroom window she could see that the hedge was being lashed by a gale. The sky above the hedge was grey and low in the dawn light. Going towards the kitchen to put the kettle on, she found the living-room lights burning, and her husband asleep, lolling uneasily over the side of an armchair. She stepped outside to look. The cane chair had been blown to the far side of the yard. Gusts of rain were being driven untidily into the porch. The hill beyond the paddock was half-covered by a grey mantle of cloud and rain. The wind was from the south, cold and foreign, too cold and fast to have any smell, any place, loaded on to it, and too violent to be a messenger, a 'harbinger', a soft sell. Too brutal to awaken.

Inside it was also cold. She went through to her husband and woke him up. 'Welcome back, fishface,' she said. O his drama, his embellishments! He looked at her with tired eyes, suspiciously, to gauge her mood. 'Go to bed you silly arse,' she said, adding, 'It wouldn't work anyway.' 'What wouldn't?' he said with a start. 'Hanging the baby's sling from the cabbage tree,' she replied. 'There are no decent branches on a cabbage tree.' He was looking at her in astonishment. At the other end of the house the baby was by now yelling at the top of her voice. 'Anyway,' she said, 'it looks as though you've fixed the porch all right. Now go to bed. I'll shut the baby up. You won't get any work done if you don't have a proper sleep. Then we'll be here for ever.' She kissed him. 'I love you,' she said, 'god knows why, you're such an idiot.'

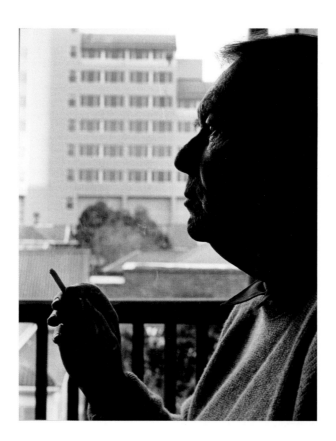

# GRAHAM BILLING 1973

*Graham Billing (1936–2001) published eight novels, one book of poetry and three works of non-fiction as well as much journalism.*

**WHEN** Graham Billing was awarded the Burns Fellowship at the end of 1972, his career seemed to be on a rising curve and he was well on the way to being one of the leading novelists of his generation. In the previous seven years he had had three novels published in New Zealand and overseas with one of them filmed, two radio plays produced, two works of non-fiction published, and had held the Scholarship in Letters in 1972. His fourth novel, *The Slipway*, was due for international publication in late 1973 (he made the last revisions in proof early in the year), and received excellent reviews in New York, London and then New Zealand. During the Burns year Billing wrote

the first draft of his fifth novel, *The Primal Therapy of Tom Purslane*, several essays for the *Listener* and *New Zealand Today*, and a commissioned 'history and biography of the Todd family and their enterprises in the motor car, petrol and oil exploration businesses'.[39] At that point his life and literary career derailed. His publishers rejected the new novel – it did not receive publication until 1980 – at the same time as his marriage broke up and he experienced severe personal problems. As Denis Welch said, he 'vanished from the radar of the public consciousness' in the 1980s.[40] Billing published a book of poetry as well as his Burns novel in 1980 and eventually got back on track with his long-awaited *magnum opus*, *The Chambered Nautilus*, in 1993 and two more novels in 1997 and (published posthumously) in 2002. However, his reputation never regained the position it had had in 1973.

The following excerpt is from the beginning of *The Primal Therapy of Tom Purslane*, when the protagonist first sees the woman with whom he comes to have the obsessive and disastrous affair on which the novel focuses.

## FROM *The Primal Therapy of Tom Purslane*

He drove back through the flat streets trying to decide whether or not he was lonely. It was a day for loneliness, self-imposed immolation. Perception was sharp and bitter. The grass in the Museum Park was still thick with fallen leaves and he remembered running across it when he was twenty, down the asphalt path lined with lime trees expecting to meet a girl running towards him. But she had had big breasts and never ran. Suddenly he remembered sitting under a copper beech tree beside the old Leith Valley bluestone post office building while the same girl made a daisy chain and told him she was pregnant which she wasn't. He could remember the dreadful scream, like molecules colliding, that the starlings made at dusk when they gathered in the lime trees before reeling into the sky as Dante said like myriad souls flocking to the Gates of Hell which among its inscriptions bore the words: '*The Primal Love made me.*'

Children were walking in and out of the front door of the Museum with bemused faces, like mice beneath the towering Doric columns of the portico, unable to understand how life could be described from observations of the dead. Across the road people were coming out of the doors of the new Roman Catholic Church designed like a pagoda. They were smiling at each other like cherubim and seraphim, masked in innocence and the red brick of the church and its coppery roof tiles glowed like a banked up fire. The people stood about like sparrows finishing a feast of crumbs and he thought *The Primal Love* made me and wondered if he should ever understand what the words meant.

At the Regent Road Foodmarket under the lee of the hill the air was almost warm and the rain had stopped. He bought a bar of hazelnut chocolate and some cigarette tobacco and matches. The chocolate was for Ben who for some reason preferred hazelnuts.

From Regent Road he had to drive up Cosy Dell to reach the road system taking him south. There was plenty of time to eat the chocolate because Cosy Dell was steep and winding through woods of sycamore and oak with fern and

bracken lining the stream below. The tarmac was always greasy in wet weather and the unladen van with its low gear ratio always slithered into wheel spin on the corners if he drove faster than seven or eight miles an hour. He bit the hazelnuts out of some chocolate and held a handful to Ben who licked them up neatly from his palm. There was always peace in Cosy Dell. At low speed the van made little noise. Purslane leaned back in his seat and told the dog to stop nudging his arm because all the nuts were gone. He was a strange dog. He didn't like icecream. The tracery of wet black sycamore branches enclosed the van like the shadows of wire in a gigantic aviary. A bird might deliberately entrap himself by going through.

The noise of the stream came up from among the fern below the rotting wooden houses which clung to the last bit of level land. The wheels spun on the next bend and the motor whined, but straight away in the silence a bellbird whistled and there was the crackle of blackbirds going away calling warning like smallarms fire from a fleeing enemy. At the head of the Dell the road began to open out and he could see for a moment past the final bend and the end of the woods. A woman was walking there, slowly and gracefully climbing the hill, emerging from the trees. She has a kind of look about her, he thought, as she went out of sight. The van wheels spun, the engine whined. He had an uncomfortable feeling that he had disturbed her.

The feeling was so intense that when he came round the next corner, he was surprised to see her still there. The scene was bizarre. It was just after eleven o'clock on a wet Sunday morning and a graceful woman was walking up Cosy Dell, almost at the top. Ben had noticed her. He was leaning forward staring intently through the windscreen. Nobody ever walked up Cosy Dell. A young woman? Alone?

Purslane looked about at the emptiness of the morning wood and the road and the image of grace that seemed to fill it. He felt like a comet approaching a green planet. Her long woollen skirt was pale primrose and she wore a cream-coloured jacket. Her hair was piled on top of her head, Medusa-like with a single coil falling between her shoulders. Aion. She carried a furled, sky-blue umbrella. Her walk was like the way a lovely girl might fly.

Of course she should not be beautiful. She would be thick-lipped, and round-nosed, and ugly. There was something in this kind of thinking, he reminded himself, like the thoughts of a voyeur. A girl with flying legs. A lonely road. More than a voyeur. A rapist. Ben shifted in his seat and whined.

The van might stop, a man step out, accost her and then she would turn to him in all her ugliness and he would apologise for thinking she was somebody he knew and quickly drive away. What arrogance. Never before had there been any hint of such arrogance, the rapist's arrogance, set deep in his soul. What maniacal presumption. But what if this confrontation were important for the rest of a person's life, his whole future. Would he have a right?

The van was almost upon her, humming quietly in low gear and she was

walking steadfastly not changing her pace or distance from the verge. At the nape of her neck her hair was soft and pale and the coiled mass above it shone like bronze opals. At touching-distance the skin of her neck was like moonstones and the hand holding the sky-blue umbrella was like a flower. Now he was passing her and there seemed to be a flash like wildfire in the crack of doom. Her face was very close and he had never seen a woman more beautiful.

Purslane could feel his face sliding into a crazed smile as his head turned looking back for an instant before he desperately tried to focus her in the wing mirror so that the looking could go on, more composed after the first shock of near terror, as if he believed her sight was so penetrating that she could see on and on, defining him for herself in his own little mirror image.

Her jacket had been open and under it she had worn a cream viyella blouse which clung about her breasts and yet was sweetly buttoned to the neck. Her stomach had been rounded under the fitting skirt and there had been slimness yet strength in her legs and the perfectly proportioned pelvic gap between her thighs and in the smallness of her feet in brown calf boots. Her lips were full and red, a disconcerting sign of fullness below, her eyebrows arched and brown with golden lights. Her eyes had been intensely blue with intelligence and warmth, frank, without fear. Her skin was pure and butter-milk healthy. But how could he have seen all this? Her forehead was moderately high and gently curved, her nose straight with oval nostrils slightly flared. Had she had several delicate freckles on her nose? Her eyelashes were long. Surely he could not have seen all these things.

The rain had begun again and the last look he had was upon her flowering blue umbrella.

Driving away from her was like being slowly disembowelled, as if only his frame moved and the vital organs remained at her side. The rain was heavy on the van roof and he felt shrunk, empty of purpose.

# WITI IHIMAERA 1975

*Witi Ihimaera (b. 1944) has published seventeen works of fiction and several plays, written the texts for a number of books of New Zealand photographs, and composed the libretti for operas and the texts for other musical works. He has edited eight anthologies of contemporary Maori writing, several collections of Maori art, a book on growing up Maori and an anthology of writings about Auckland.*

**WHEN** Witi Ihimaera came south to take up his Burns Fellowship in February 1975, he had published his first three books in the previous three years, working within what he calls 'the Maori conservation framework' of his work.[41] As he describes in an essay written for *Review 75* at the time, he found being what he called 'the only Maori on Maori Hill' something of a culture shock, but he also felt 'honoured to have this opportunity to write, for the first time, on a full-time basis'.[42]

Two significant projects came from that year. He wrote *The New Net Goes Fishing*, a collection of short stories that both marked the end of his early, 'pastoral' phase and

looked forward to the more political post-1985 writings, with their emphasis on Maori in an urban, Pakeha-dominated world. He also began editing the first in what was to become a series of anthologies of contemporary Maori writing, *Into the World of Light* (published in 1982). Ihimaera has commented that 'that first anthology was pretty significant personally as it enabled me to reach beyond myself to commit to Maori writing in its widest sense'.[43] It was the only book to appear in his name for nine years after the publication of *The New Net Goes Fishing* (1977); in December 1975, having completed that book, he vowed to publish no new fiction for some years because he thought that his books were 'a serious mismatch with the reality of the times', the expression of a vision that 'was out of date and, tragically, so encompassing and so established that it wasn't leaving room enough for the new reality to punch through'.[44] Thus at the end of his Burns tenure, Ihimaera decided both to stop publishing his own work until his artistic vision had encompassed the 'new reality' and to help bring into the world of light recent Maori writing that dealt with 'Maori life and race relations between Maori and pakeha in the current environment'.[45]

Ihimaera selected the short story below from *The New Net Goes Fishing* because it shows 'the influence of being on the Burns' and is 'an early attempt to begin to write beyond my then boundaries'.[46]

## Masques and Roses

'What time did you say Philip was picking you up, dear?' Mrs Grant called through the closed bathroom door. Behind it she could hear the steady thrum of water in the shower box.

'Half past eight,' Kate called back.

Mrs Grant looked at her watch. Quarter to eight. Goodness. 'You'd better hurry then,' she said. She listened for a moment and heard the shower being turned off.

'All right, Mum.'

Mrs Grant nodded to herself. She went back into the sitting room where her husband was reading the newspaper. The room was softly lit. 'You'll ruin your eyesight,' she reproved him as she snapped the standard lamp on. She picked up her knitting, sat down in her favourite armchair and began to rock back and forth. With irritation she noticed it was still squeaking. She looked across to her husband wondering if he could hear it. His eyebrows were arched and his face tight with concentration on the news of the day. The pages rustled as he turned them. 'Anything interesting?' she asked him as she continued to knit. But he didn't seem to hear her. With a sigh she shifted herself more comfortably in the chair.

The bathroom door clicked open and Mrs Grant heard the slippered steps of her daughter making her way to her bedroom. 'You'd better get a move on,' she called.

Kate appeared at the doorway. She had her dressing gown on and was pulling off her shower cap. She was clean-scrubbed and shiny with youth. She smiled at her mother and then peered with alarm at the mantel clock. 'Gosh, is that really the time?'

Her mother nodded, amused.

'Oh well,' Kate continued, 'Piri's bound to be late anyway.' For a moment she stood there, brushing her hair. She caught her mother's eyes and felt a wave of sudden affection for her. 'Are you going anywhere tonight, Mum?' she asked.

Her mother looked at her husband and then back at her daughter. Mother and daughter grinned privately at one another across the room.

'You taking Mum out, Dad?' Kate asked him.

Mr Grant looked at her across the top of his glasses and arched his eyebrows at his wife.

'It's a good night for television,' Mrs Grant said. '*Coronation Street*'s on. Now hurry, dear. Which dress are you wearing?'

'The dark blue I think.'

'But don't you think it's a bit, well *tight*?'

'Oh Mum. We're going to a club, not a church dance.'

'Well,' Mrs Grant said, 'you know best.'

Kate nodded and left the doorway. Mrs Grant put her knitting aside and reached for her cigarette case. She lit a cigarette and sucked it gently. A smile touched her lips. 'Girls these days,' she declared. 'They just seem to throw clothes on in a couple of minutes and hope for the best.'

Mr Grant harrumphed and folded his newspaper. For a moment he was silent, staring at his wife, and she began to feel a small panic rising within her. *Don't say it, Bill. Don't.* 'This Maori boy and Kate …' he began. 'Do you think it's serious?'

Mrs Grant felt something wither inside her and the façade to her feelings about her daughter and this boy, Philip, begin to crack. She tried to recompose the mask, one which she had applied with as much care as the powder and lipstick to her face. 'Kate's only nineteen,' she answered. 'This is just the third time she's been out with him.' She put her cigarette aside and stood up. She looked at the vase of roses standing on an occasional table. One of the roses was slightly out of place and the effect was irritating. She began to rearrange it, pushing at the bouquet with sharp angry movements.

'Whatever happened to that other fellow she was going out with?' Mr Grant grumbled behind her. 'He was a much nicer boy. More suitable too.'

Mrs Grant drew a breath. *I just don't want to think about it.* 'George Watson?' her voice quavered. 'I saw his mother in town today. She asked me the same thing. I don't know. I suppose they quarrelled.'

'Yes. Well. Perhaps this new friendship of Kate's will blow over too. Bound to. Yes. Hmmmn.'

The newspaper crackled again. When Mrs Grant turned, her husband was immersed in it. She went back to her cigarette and took it up. But the façade would not stay in place. She took several puffs. Short. Quick. Urgent.

It wasn't as if Kate was plain or unpopular. She could have her pick of boys. She'd always been as pretty as a picture. A lovely baby. People on the street would stop and admire her as she sat smiling in her pushchair. She'd never wanted for

anything and, although maybe she'd been just a little spoilt, she was the only daughter after all. She'd been a bright little girl and, later, a very good student. And she'd had lots of good and suitable friends. Then *why*?

'Mum, can you zip me up?' Kate was at the door again, holding her hair away from the back of her dress. Her mother went to attend her and as she did, Kate looked at her father and giggled. 'Stop peeking, Dad!'

Mr Grant grinned. Oh she was a cheeky one, his little girl. Beautiful, too. Nobody could mistake that breeding. 'Why should I peek? When you were younger I saw all there was to see, my lady!' They laughed together and the mask was back in place and this was simply their little girl who was waiting for a friend to take her out.

'There,' Mrs Grant said. She stepped back to survey her daughter. Just lovely. Not too much makeup, the dress a little too informal for her taste but no, she was lovely all the same.

'Could I borrow your brooch, Mum?' Kate asked.

'Of course, dear,' Mrs Grant answered. She turned to go to the bedroom. The front doorbell chimed.

'Oh gosh, Piri's on time for once!' Kate wailed. She ran through the hallway.

Mrs Grant hurried to the bedroom. She opened the top drawer of the vanity unit and reached in to get the brooch. Her eyes glistened. She pricked her finger.

*I would be worried about Kate no matter who she was going out with*. She patted her hair and put a smile on her face. She walked out into the hall.

He was standing there.

'Hullo, Philip,' she said. 'Here we are, dear.' She fixed the brooch to her daughter's dress. Kate smelt like a rose. Then Mrs Grant looked into that dark face. That dark face with the hesitant smile that showed that he knew. He knew. And yet he could smile as she did and remain polite.

'Hullo, Mrs Grant,' he said.

'Will you come in for a while?' she asked.

'All right,' he answered. 'But I'm parked on a bus stop. Couldn't find any place else, eh.'

'You'd better hurry then, dear,' Mrs Grant said to Kate.

'I'll just get my coat,' Kate answered. 'Won't be long, Piri.' She ran down the hall, leaving her mother and Piri standing there by the door. With each other.

'Mr Grant is in the sitting room,' Mrs Grant said. She led the way through the carpeted hall. 'Dear? Philip's here.'

Mr Grant looked into her tremulous face, so pale and bright. His wife, waiting there, needing him. 'Hullo Philip,' he greeted. The heartiness of his greeting surprised him. He put aside his newspaper and rose to shake this boy's hand.

'Mr Grant,' Piri acknowledged. Then he stood there. In his dark jacket and open-collared shirt. Wondering whether his appearance was all right and whether or not the nick on his chin had stopped bleeding.

'Unfortunately,' Mrs Grant said, 'Philip can't stay long. He's parked on a bus stop.'

'Oh?' Mr Grant asked. 'Our off-street parking isn't what it used to be now that they've put up that block of flats further down the road.'

Piri nodded his head. He didn't know what to say. He looked round the room. 'Nice roses, Mrs Grant,' he offered.

'Why, thank you Philip.'

Her words glittered like pieces of broken glass.

Then, at last, Kate was there, smiling up at this boy. Putting her hand in his. Her hand in his hand. Her long fingers twining in his, interlocking, joining, pressing into his.

Mrs Grant turned again to her roses.

'Have Mum and Dad been looking after you?' she heard Kate ask.

'Yes.'

'What time will you be home, dear?' she heard her husband ask.

'About one I think, Dad.'

'Fine. I'll leave the hall light on for you.'

Then she felt her husband squeezing her arm and the small comforting press of his lips against her cheek.

'They're leaving now, dear.'

Mrs Grant turned. Her face was gay but her eyes were glistening.

'Are you all right, Mum?' Kate asked.

She hugged her daughter tightly.

'Of course, dear. It's just that you're so pretty,' she answered. She tried to laugh and to smile at this boy standing beside her daughter. But he knew. He knew.

'Well, we'll be off then,' Piri said. He followed Kate down the hall way to the front door. Mr and Mrs Grant went with them. The night was warm.

'Don't wait up,' Kate laughed. She blew a kiss to her parents. They waved back.

'Have a good time,' Mrs Grant called.

Mr Grant shut the door. He was silent for a moment. Then he put his arm round his wife. 'Well,' he said. 'That's that.'

Together they walked back to the sitting room. At the doorway, Mrs Grant gently moved from him and went to the bathroom. There she put a small sticking plaster over her pricked finger. The bathroom smelt like a little girl and she began to cry as she picked up the things her daughter had left on the floor. Surely Kate knew better than to leave the bathroom in a mess. Then she went into the kitchen to make a cup of tea.

'Aah,' Mr Grant smiled as she brought the tray into the sitting room.

Mrs Grant sat down on the sofa beside him. 'Was there anything interesting on the news?' she asked. She did not want to look into his face. She did not want him to see her face. She did not want to talk about anything except ordinary things. But her hand began to quiver and she had to put the silver teapot down.

'Dear?' her husband asked.

'Oh it's just my finger,' Mrs Grant said. 'I pricked it when I took the brooch out of the drawer.' She finished pouring the tea. She took her cup to where she'd been sitting in the armchair. She picked up her knitting and then put it down again. She began to sip at her tea. She lit a cigarette. She put it in the ash tray and took up her cup again.

Her husband smiled across at her. 'He's quite a nice boy really, I suppose,' he said to her.

Mrs Grant tried to smile back.

'And our Kate,' he continued, 'she's become a real beauty.'

Mrs Grant nodded.

'Yes, she's a good girl,' she said.

# Sam Hunt 1976

*Sam Hunt (b. 1946) has published twelve collections of poems and a number of pamphlets and broadsheets. A comprehensive collection is to be published in 2008.*

**THERE** was no full-year appointment in 1976, but Sam Hunt had a ten-week 'mini-Burns' which he took up at the beginning of the year. By that time he had been performing and publishing poems for ten years, had produced five collections and a number of broadsheets and pamphlets, and was well-established as a travelling minstrel who made a living through his craft. During his stay at Otago he was not really at home in the university environment, but lived in the crib of Alan and Patricia Roddick at Otakou where he became enamoured with the harbour and coastline, and wrote many poems, some collected in *Drunkard's Garden* (1977). Four of them are printed below.

# Liz

*with her left hand crippled*

I know your dreams are dreams of
waking with the man you love:

whoever in those dreams that
good man be, you have his heart …

I dreamt last night of you, Liz,
you, and every man had eyes

for some bird else: we were at
some bar. You sat like a cat,

queen of your corner, sizing
each bird up, hypnotising

every feathered one. They slowed
together. Then in a cloud

they rose across the garden,
the moon herself now hidden …

Planets and a thousand stars
retreated. You flexed claws

slowly, your left claw crippling.
I woke appalled, applauding.

# Two Winter Settings

i
I knew a girl who
came from where the blue
lupin flower grew, oh
such a girl I knew

where lupin flowers grow
as blue as her blue
eyes against the snow.
So, the girl I know.

ii
Taiaroa Heads, I've never
seen them floating so, so
easy on the light as
land can float on sea.

Low cloud slides south;
the albatross lift off;
warm breezes blow. Far as
eye can see, and further, snow.

## Those Eyes; Such Mist

Seamists from the upper inlet
lift, the morning hills afloat.

I dream of the several men who've
sailed seven seas; their many mists;

wake again to your love
as thick dreams clear; a dream of masts,

a dream that no man ever
saw your eyes like this.

I have lost all voice. I kiss
those eyes, our voyaging; such mist.

## My Father Today

They buried him today
up Schnapper Rock Road,
my father in cold clay.

A heavy south wind towed
the drape of light away.
Friends, men met on the road,

stood round in that dumb way
men stand when lost for words.
There was nothing to say.

I heard the bitchy chords
of magpies in an old-man
pine … '*My* old man, he's worlds

away – call it Heaven –
no men so elegantly
dressed. His last afternoon,

staring out to sea,
he nods off in his chair.
He wonders what the

yelling's all about up there.
They just about explode!
And now, these magpies here

up Schnapper Rock Road' …
They buried him in clay.
He was a heavy load,

my dead father today.

# KERI HULME 1977

*Keri Hulme (b. 1947) has published two books of poetry, two collections of short stories, a novel, a book describing her 'homeplaces' and an uncategorisable work of fiction/poetry.*

**KERI** Hulme in her July 1976 application pointed to three published short stories (including 'Hooks and Feelers', which had won the Katherine Mansfield Memorial Award in 1975), and said she was working on 'Kerewin, Joe and Simon P.' which was 'almost ready for submission'.[47] She received a one-term Fellowship for 1977.

In her Burns tenure she worked on a variety of projects: the short story, 'A Nightsong for the Shining Cuckoo' (1981), some of the poems of *The Silences Between (Moeraki Conversations)* (1982), and 'The Reef in Winter', which she described as 'a follow-up NOT sequel to [*the bone people*] which has never been offered

for publication and probably won't be'.[48] Hulme went on to say that 'most of the time I was rewriting bits of [*the bone people*] dismayed and furious that it had been so contemptuously dismissed' by the publisher to whom it had been sent.[49] Below are two sections of 'Moeraki Conversations' that Hulme states 'were very much part of that era, worked upon – or at least, sketched out & drunk upon – at Otago'.[50]

## Moeraki Conversations: 2

## He Wahi Tapu

### *Shell knife*

*'You digging another hole for the dunny?'*
Yeah, breathing hard and stabbing the earth
on the safe fringes
sand and more sand and shovel and aching
and suddenly soot
calcined shells and broken fishjaws browned
by hundred on hundred still years
underground, and on the iron edge
a flake of flint chipped in deliberate small notches
long as my finger. Don't touch!
*'Hey it's sharp!'*
    grinning at my white eyes
    grinning and carving the air
    hoping for blood beads
    *'Tu! Tu! Tu!'*
shrill above the sea
*'E, who taught you that?'*

    *'Nobody …'*

### *Kehua trap*

I was playing, making knots in the muka in the sun
and I dropped the tangle, forgot it
until the dark came

*'Hey what we got in here,*
*full of flies or something?'*

Cat yowling deep in her throat
fur up and flaring electricity,
rustle and buzzing air getting madder each minute
and something bang! in the boatshed
while the lampflames knock their glasses
and we watch each other big-eyed

*'Someone!'*
his voice pitched to bat-squeak,
shaking on his kneebones *'No no I never!'*
hung your thing in the window
stretched the knots out over the door –

it stings my fingers all the way to the fire
a shriek
ashes
and uneasy silence

## Kotahitaka

*'E What's happened?'*
hands on hips and jaw dropped open

*'They cleaned it up while you were gone.'*
    Once the pines bowed, branches lank black scrabbles
    bent away from the winds warring in
    from the other side of the sea

*'They took the church round the port an'*
*it took ten days a truck and all the men.'*
    Once the church leant loose and empty of prayers,
    door crazily hung and sheep hunched among the pews
    chewing cud and a book in the dung on the floor

*'O it's bare now,'* I say
    The stones had dropped, careless asides,
    the older hollows unmarked
straightened, whitened, trimmed & tightened
they've driven the peace away

'*Who's down there?*'
Just bones I answer, just bones … I
watch a new headstone tilt as the flesh
melts a little more and he goes
hopping over the mounds

'*Hey don't go knocking round the graves!*'
they lean too far
toward you …

## Moeraki Conversations: 3

Three Songs For The Ghosts

And I said,

'*Her crew caught by sunlight*
*became boulders and hills by this beach*

> '*All night I ached with longing*
> *and then*
> *I felt you come gentle*
> *between my thighs o ghost –*
> *I reached out*
> *to cradle you close*
> *and woke*
> *hugging my own shoulders*
> *o I wept*'

> *Down there on the black water*
> *fog hangs, hiding the rocks*
> *where Te Araiteuru came aground*

## *Returning*

Making the mistake of running my fingers over
        the braille of your scars
I now see those grotesque and bloody episodes
as pursed-mouth words – against them I offer my tales

of the slender people who carved their love on trees
but you tremble and turn back into your nightmare,
so I am leaving you, tearwet and too tired to sleep,
to go out and bury much more deeply
the bone who has crept out of the cliff each springtide
as though that longago child liked your touch on its skull
and struggles through layers of time and sand
to be with you again.

## Hokioi

*'Have you ever been windwhipped?*
*Had your belly kneaded by want?*
*So it is with me, friend,*
*so it is with me.*

*I am given lone islands*
*with deep kilts of kelp,*
*stray birds and tired ghosts*
*to shelter in my arms –*
*I am a slender skein of muscle and bone*
*to stand against fear on their behalf.*

*I smell bad times coming,*
*a sharp intake of death,*
*I am eating our way to safety*
*building fat rib walls against famine*
*saving that monthly flush of blood*
*for real wounds*
*collecting anyone else's breath*
*against*
*the rending*
*the ravening*
*the hellbent raving cry of war.*

 *The wind is rising, e hoa –*
 *may all the nightfliers be friendly'*

# 1977 –1978

# ROGER HALL

*Roger Hall (b. 1939) has published nine plays, had many more produced, and written several television dramatic series. He has also published an autobiography and a guide to writing for theatre, produced the text for a book on the University of Otago, and composed numerous short stories and plays for children.*

**PRIOR** to his initial appointment as Burns Fellow late in 1976, Roger Hall had in the previous ten years published plays and short stories for children in the *School Journal* and written a number of television scripts and dramatic scripts for local theatre. His first major national success, *Glide Time*, had been first performed in August of that year (and was to be published in 1977). At the beginning of the first of his two years as Fellow, Hall completed *Middle-Age Spread*, which became his most successful play (first produced late 1977, published 1978 and in a revised edition 1980, filmed 1979, named the Society of West End Theatres' Comedy of the Year in

London 1979). In the rest of that year he wrote the first series of *Gliding On* for radio, the children's pantomime *Cinderella* (premiered 1978), and started *State of the Play* (premiered 1978, published 1979). In his second year he finished *State of the Play*, wrote another series of *Gliding On*, and started *Prisoners of Mother England* (premiered 1979, published 1980). He then stayed on at the University of Otago as half-time teaching fellow in drama until 1994.

The following extract is from scene seven of *Middle-Age Spread*, towards the end of the dinner party. It was chosen, Roger Hall wrote, 'not so much for its literary interest as for its historical interest: what those characters were discussing thirty years ago'.[51]

## FROM *Middle-Age Spread*

*The three women enter from the kitchen.*

JUDY: Elizabeth's just been showing us her new blinds.
ROBERT: Are they nice?
JUDY: Very.
ROBERT: Well, you can have some if you want.
JUDY: *Annoyed*. No, I didn't mean that.
ELIZABETH: *To Colin*. Roddy's back from basketball. They won.
COLIN: Good.
ELIZABETH: And the car's all right.

*Colin gives her a 'I told you' smile.*

ISOBEL: And Judy's just been telling us about your trip to Fiji next month. It sounds wonderful. What a lovely idea to celebrate your … *embarrassed* … I mean if I went back to Reg after we'd … *floundering* … you know, after … HE certainly wouldn't ….
ROBERT: (*Rescuing her*). We'd like to have gone for longer, but everything was booked out. As it was, we got a cancellation.
ELIZABETH: This is what I can't understand when they say there's no money about.
ROBERT: Well, we tried Australia, Cook Islands – all booked out.
ELIZABETH: I know! Everybody seems to go these days.
REG: But not people on the average wage.
ELIZABETH: I wouldn't know about that.
REG: I would. $119 a week – do me a favour.
COLIN: I wouldn't like to manage on that, I must admit.
ELIZABETH: We could manage – easily. These people complain about how hard up they are, but they've all got cars and colour television and go to the pub all the time. We could manage Colin.
REG: Yes but you've got everything. You've got your house and car and fridge and

deep freeze and wall to wall carpet in the lavatory. Imagine if you were starting off to get all those things and having to pay forty or fifty dollars a week rent.

JUDY: You're quite right.

REG: More and more people are giving up the idea of ever owning their own house. Whatever they save in a year, houses have gone up that much. They're just giving up.

ELIZABETH: But there are state houses – and look how people look after those – they leave them in a terrible mess. I'm sorry, but I can't feel sorry for these people. For years, Colin was earning less than most unskilled workers. Look at first-year doctors in hospitals – the porters and cleaners earn more than they do. It's about time we had our turn.

REG: But can't you see what's happening! The gap is widening – we're rapidly developing a class system … the haves and have-nots.

COLIN: The country's splitting down the middle, there's no doubt about that.

REG: And it's going to get worse. You can see it now – the kids from good homes having all the advantages, while the poor sods at the bottom are getting further and further behind – just through the accident of birth. And I always thought that that's what this country didn't believe in.

*Short silence.*

COLIN: But what do you do about it? Don't you feel helpless? It didn't use to be like this, did it?

JUDY: At the last election I didn't know who to vote for. I just couldn't make up my mind.

REG: *Scathing.* So you voted Values.

JUDY: Yes.

ISOBEL: So did I!

REG: Values! God, they're the exact opposite of Oscar Wilde's definition of a cynic – they know the value of everything and the cost of nothing. Still, at least you didn't vote for the present lot.

ELIZABETH: Well I did.

COLIN: You only voted for them because you thought the candidate was a nice man.

ELIZABETH: Well he was. He had nice manners and I think that's important. Most of the Labour people are so … so coarse.

REG: Well I voted for the coarse lot, heaven help me. Honestly the Labour Party remind me of a documentary I saw on television about sleeping sickness. All these people who'd been half asleep for twenty years were given this new wonder drug and they all came alive and sang and danced around for a bit … and then the drug wore off and Zap! Back to sleep for another twenty years.

COLIN: Whatever one party does, the other's going to undo when it gets into power.

ISOBEL: It's all so wasteful.

REG: Tch! It's hopeless.

ROBERT: I think you're all wrong. Things have taken a turn for the better. For years and years, people have assumed that if things go wrong the Government will come to their aid. It's killed initiative and the development of new ideas – there's no incentive for them. Now I think people are realising that you CAN'T always rely on the State for a handout – the State can't afford it – and that the way out of our mess is knuckling down to a bit of hard work.

REG: A good dose of unemployment to make the men work harder, eh?

ROBERT: Well, I'm afraid it's true. Not that the unions'd ever allow it. They're out to wreck the economy, as we all know.

REG: That is so middle-class it makes my flesh crawl.

ROBERT: *Suddenly furious*. Why is 'middle-class' now a term of abuse. Every one of us in this room is middle-class – all that means is that we were brought up to work hard and to get a decent sort of job and try and lead reasonable sort of lives. Dammit I DID work hard – and still do – and I do try and lead a decent life – and blowed if I'm going to be made to feel ashamed of it.

ELIZABETH: Hear hear!!

REG: Oh Lord.

ISOBEL: If it weren't for the middle-class there'd be no orchestra in this country – no theatre to speak of, or art galleries – no culture at all.

ELIZABETH: Anyway Reg, you must agree that with all New Zealand's faults, you wouldn't want to live anywhere else. No other country would be as nice to live in.

REG: *Shouts*. Oh Elizabeth!! You can't really believe that. The only reason you think that is because of all the news you read in the papers and see on the telly – they REVEL in showing us other countries' problems – that people are starving or unemployed or drug addicted or that you're likely to get mugged if you step outside the house. It's all designed to make us feel New Zealand is the only country in the world to live in – and now we all believe it. Just as we believe that New Zealanders are NICER than other people. Niceness is in our genetic code. Whereas in fact we're as nasty, money-grabbing, prejudiced, violent, alcohol-addicted, hypocritical a race as ever walked this earth.

*A silence.*

COLIN: I'll drink to that. He offers wine all round.

ELIZABETH: I'll go and get the dessert. *She goes to the kitchen*.

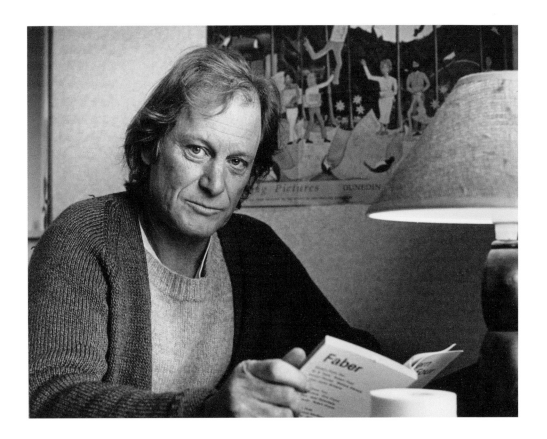

# PETER OLDS 1978

*Peter Olds (b. 1944) has published eleven collections of poetry and has also written unpublished drama.*

**IN** 1978 when Peter Olds received a one-term supplementary Burns Fellowship, he had published five collections of verse with Caveman Press in the previous six years as well as a number of broadsheets and had been anthologised in *The Young New Zealand Poets* in 1973. He says the he 'came to writing' through the Beatles, Bob Dylan, Roger McGough, and the Beats.[52] By 1978 he had established himself as an anti-elitist poet of the youth culture and the counter-culture, of drugs, rock music and life radically outside the New Zealand middle-class norm. He writes, 'I've taken as my influences Baxter, Tuwhare, Frame, Plath, Wantling, Bukowski, and A.A. Milne (not to

mention my Methodist upbringing)'.[53] In his short tenure as Fellow he wrote some of the poems that were gathered in his fifth collection, *Beethoven's Guitar*, in 1980, including the title poem and 'A Yearning for Specific Pinetrees: Small Pictures of Dunedin' as well as 'The Green Gate to Ward 10', printed below.

## The Green Gate to Ward 10

1
Where the steps climb the path
beside Van Gogh's vast overhanging tree,
I come to see
the dark pressed grove
where quiet things lie, live and cry –
the sun, the sparrow, the dry mown lawn,
a daisy,
and a squeaky, rusty, mad green gate.

2
Where the steps climb high
through dark, through light –
through thin walls, and thick walls,
overhead smoked glass, soundproof ceilings,
concrete floor, musical furnishings –
where the sun is a spiked hard flower:

so often
he comes into my picture and
I in his.

3
We walk
into the hospital together –
away from the paint, the brush-streaked sky –-
nod to the stone-faced reception desk,
pass on
and swim down the longest square tunnel
in the world,

to the lounge

where someone on the pooltable
is trying SO hard
not to keep going in off the black eight-ball.

'The cue has no tip,' you whisper to me –
I know … I see ….

I see
John the Baptist, dressing-gowned,
hugging the walls –
his hands, his head and feet cut by ice
were never supposed to be
like this.

Yes, I see ….

4
Brahms is waltzing
out of the radio.
The nurses dance with
National Geographic hysterical
bathrobes … We watch, stilled –
sometimes
        feeling
            at home –
sometimes
        not feeling
            at home
                at all ….

5
So often I come into His picture and
He in mine,
where the steps creep through His dark
grove:

the hard sun, a black arched crow, a cut lawn,
a swim down the longest tunnel
in the world,
a crazy daisy,

and a rusty, mad green gate.

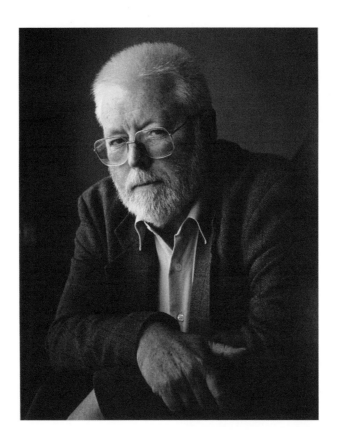

# MICHAEL NOONAN 1979

*Michael Noonan (b. 1940) has published a play, three international books on education and human rights, and a number of monographs on education, human rights and teachers' rights. However, his major writing has been for a number of television projects, for which he has 473 credits.*

MICHAEL Noonan was the first Burns Fellow whose work was primarily in scriptwriting. Prior to taking up the Burns Fellowship in 1979, he had published an absurdist play in his student days (1963); however his major work in the 1970s was in television drama as a scriptwriter, researcher, and editor in such projects as the groundbreaking dramatic series *Pukemanu* 1971–2), several serials, a documentary drama on Richard Seddon (1973), and the major historical drama series on Governor George Grey, *The Governor* (1976). In 1975 he was also responsible for a three-film series profiling Janet Frame, Sylvia Ashton-Warner, and Ngaio Marsh. During his Burns

tenure he worked on several projects including a still unpublished novel, 'Home Fires', set in Otago 1913–9, and a nine-part television adaptation of Bill Pearson's novel *Coal Flat* which was unproduced because of TVNZ cutbacks on domestic drama.

Noonan also researched three Otago-Southland men whose extreme World War I experiences were material for a possible future project, and published an essay on his findings in *Review 1979*. An excerpt from that essay follows.

## FROM **Three Soldiers – Notes on New Zealand Historical Writing**

I am engaged in research into the political, social, economic, and cultural history of New Zealand between 1890–1919. This research is wanted for a novel I am writing, and in the long term, possibly a television drama series. Who knows, the way things are at the moment?

Obviously the most spectacular public event of the period 1890–1919 was the Great War. As you know the Government of the day enthusiastically committed New Zealand to the war and we sent young men to die in Europe in numbers disproportionate to the rest of the British Empire in relationship to our population.

It is often said, even today, that on the beaches of Gallipoli and in the trenches of Flanders we as a people won our spurs and came of age.

Keith Sinclair has written: 'almost the first events to stir colonial pride, which eventually became national pride, were the heroic deeds of New Zealand troops in wartime'. And Professor W.P. Morrell has described the Gallipoli campaign as 'New Zealand announcing its manhood'. Certainly, few nations have chosen to celebrate such a defeat with a national holiday.

When I came to look for material that would assist an investigation into New Zealand's experience of the Great War I found several informative books written from a personal point of view. These biographical works concentrate on the war itself but it was quite a compulsive exercise to find out what I could about the background history of these men prior to the War.

The three most 'accessible' men: Archibald Baxter, John A. Lee, and James Stark, although they were born almost ten years apart from each other in that order, provide us, I think, with quite a unique glimpse of life in colonial New Zealand.

Baxter was born in grandmother's house at Brighton in 1881, Lee was born at home at Dunedin in 1891, and Stark was born in his father's hotel at Invercargill in 1899.

All three grew up in a harsh, violent world; in tough primitive communities. Their families were basically unattractive people struggling to make ends meet.

Their fathers were alcoholics and gamblers.

Stark's father, a Delaware Indian, was an hotelkeeper who ran illegal cockfights and gambling schools. James Stark was frequently thrashed by his

father and older brother and was once dragged to school by his father with a sixteen-pound chain round his waist and chained to his desk.

Lee's father deserted the family when Lee was still an infant but he learnt brutality in the person of his maternal grandmother, also a hopeless alcoholic, and on the streets of Dunedin's slums where his mother managed in circumstances of appalling poverty.

The Baxter family were always short of money but comfortably off when compared to Lee's. Baxter's experience of violence was more confined to the playground – where brawling and bullying were the main sports – and in the Saddle Hill school classroom, when the school was in the care of a disturbed and sadistic headmaster.

Lee and Stark were both birched as first offenders: Stark at age eleven, Lee at age fourteen. As second offenders both were sentenced to the Burnham Industrial School for the reform of 'incorrigibles'.

Burnham Industrial School was a Dickensian institution. Most of the inmates came from poverty-stricken homes. A government report at the time revealed that parents fell into one or more of the following categories: habitual drunkards, loafers, prostitutes, and vagrants.

Stark developed an abiding hatred of authority at Burnham. Lee was much better equipped to handle such a place and when he finished standard IV, which was as far as the school went, he was appointed assistant teacher.

Baxter had no criminal record that I am aware of and he left Brighton school at the age of twelve, having passed through all seven standards.

The desire to escape from Burnham Industrial school was every bit as appealing to the inmates as escape from a prisoner of war camp for POW. Both Lee and Stark escaped several times, were caught several times, and accordingly birched several times.

Baxter, Lee and Stark became odd job men – itinerant workers, joining that strange sub-culture of the time; the swagger. A world Lee was to write about later in his Shiner stories. Stark also spent sometime on a coastal steamer. Baxter looked after cows and horses in the Brighton area before taking off up central and then to South Canterbury.

I don't think Lee or Stark ever had two coins to rub together but Baxter was frugal and by his mid-twenties he had saved up enough money to buy his father a small farm at Brighton. His father, true to form, mismanaged the farm and Archibald Baxter had to come home to rescue the property from the bailiffs.

In 1912 John A. Lee was convicted of breaking, entering, and stealing and sentenced to one year in Mount Eden prison.

In the following year, at the age of fifteen, James Douglas Stark, was charged with assaulting a special constable with a beer bottle, and making off with a bike and sentenced to one year with hard labour.

Both Lee and Baxter were intelligent, politically aware men with an interest in reading and literature, and it is no surprise that they had the energy and talent to write about their experiences of the Great War. Stark, on the other hand, we can assume to be an inarticulate, semi-literate man, essentially a loner. If it wasn't for Robin Hyde's biographies, (she wrote a sequel to *Passport to Hell: Nor the Years Condemn*) Stark would certainly be remembered only in oral folk-lore.

Both Lee and Baxter were active socialists before the first world war. (Baxter was at the Labour Party conference in 1940 when Lee was expelled.)

Lee was originally influenced by Upton Sinclair's novel *The Jungle*. Erik Olssen writes: 'He became a socialist on the spot. He knew not what socialism meant; it simply expressed and legitimised his sense of anger and alienation.'

Stark enlisted for the war while on the run from the police; he lied about his age, and he lied about his criminal record. Stark, I think we can safely say, enlisted to escape.

Lee enlisted in March 1916. He had been out of trouble with the law for four years. Olssen suggests: 'As so often one senses he moved with friends intent on having some fun, being the biggest event of his life, happy and free and easy, happy to escape past and present problems'.

Baxter was thirty-two when the war started. Earlier in the century he had considered enlisting in the South African War but he attended a public lecture against war by a Dunedin Lawyer. Gradually he came to the opinion that war was wrong; practically, morally, and religiously.

Baxter's own religious ideas in this period are difficult to access. In his childhood and youth almost the entire population of Brighton joined the Plymouth Brethren sect (his father gave up the booze consequently for thirteen years) but Archibald Baxter did not join. His attitude against joining a particular church was reinforced by the complete support for the war on the part of all the churches – excepting the Quakers and a few small sects. The Labour Party, of which he was a member at this stage, also held strong views that were anti-militarist, though probably not pacifist.

Stark, then, went to war because he was shiftless. If there hadn't been a war he would have created a private one. John A. Lee went out of a spirit of adventure. Baxter stayed at home believing this war and all wars to be morally wrong. (There were very few people who thought like Baxter at that time.)

At the end of 1916 New Zealand introduced conscription and Baxter was arrested. At the end of 1917 he, and thirteen other conscientious objectors, were shipped to England. These men were treated badly. The physical punishment Baxter experienced amounted to torture and he was several times placed in the front lines under heavy fire and unarmed. Baxter never gave in although his health, mental and physical, eventually collapsed and he ended up hospitalised.

Baxter's book *We Will Not Cease* is unashamedly a pacifist tract (it was

originally published on the eve of the second world war and was re-published at the time of New Zealand's involvement in Vietnam). I find, however, Lee's horrendous description of carnage and death and the mindlessness of war a more impressive and persuasive anti-militarist document. Baxter is at his best in debate with the officers who gave him a rough time; he never lost a verbal round according to the book.

Robin Hyde's book on Stark, *Passport to Hell*, was published in 1936 …. In an introductory note she writes: 'This book is not a work of fiction. I have related its incidents and the circumstances under which they happened, as Starkie told them to me.' A modest statement which tells us nothing about her own considerable literary investment in the book. I think we can safely assume that Stark's contribution was plain and simple and although Hyde's romanticism sometimes runs away with her imagination, *Passport to Hell* is a successful book, and its scenes of Stark's childhood and the descriptions of the war are evocative and convincing.

My notes perhaps may suggest to others the value of individual research into the lives of Baxter, Lee and Stark. Their early lives are intrinsically interesting. Biographical knowledge deepens our understanding of personalities who, through a powerful presence in various writings, have made part of the New Zealand experience in the Great War accessible to later generations of their countrymen. Moreover, their wild struggle into adulthood illuminates for us that dark and neglected underworld, colonial poverty in the early years of the century.

THE 1980s

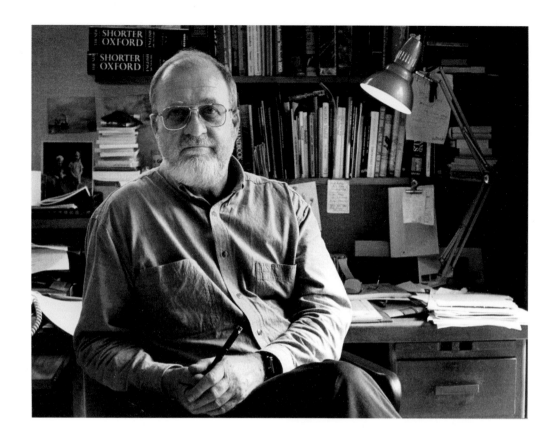

# Philip Temple 1980

*Philip Temple (b. 1939) has published eight novels and over twenty non-fiction books.*

**PHILIP** Temple had been a full-time writer for nearly a decade when he took up the Burns Fellowship in 1980, after receiving a Katherine Mansfield Memorial Fellowship in 1979. He had established himself in a variety of non-fictional modes – books on mountains and mountaineering, walking-track and travel guides, photographic books on the South Island – and had published two novels. In his Burns year he finished *Beak of the Moon* (1981), his anthropomorphic environmental novel that sees from a kea's point of view the impact that clearance of the high country for sheep farming had on the natural Southern Alps environment. He also did research

and some writing for a saga, 'Tikimana', that was left unfinished, and undertook the preliminary planning for *New Zealand Explorers: Great Journeys of Discovery* (1985). The following is an excerpt as contextualised by Temple:

The beginning of the novel is based on Samuel Butler's account of his meeting with keas and of burning mountain beech forest in *A First Year in Canterbury Settlement* (1861). As the story progresses, the young kea Strongbeak and his friends are driven from their native Kawee and explore foreign lands west of the Main Divide. The following excerpt, from the beginning of part three of *Beak of the Moon*, follows their separation in a great storm.[54]

## Strongbeak's Time of Dreaming
### (FROM *Beak of the Moon*)

When he opened his eyes it seemed that he was still in cloud. No wind, no cold, and then sunlight so intense that it hurt his eyes and he was forced to close them again. He sensed that he was not flying, not gliding even, or soaring, swinging in a hot silence. When he stopped thinking about the cloud and the silence and began to listen, he slowly became aware of sounds commingling; close noises and distant calls; soon he heard a pedal note of life, a vibration of energy in the air. He listened more carefully and, like the separation of a drop from a stream, he heard the chafing leg song of crickets. Then the rattle of a stone – crack, snap – as it tumbled down a steep face of rock and bounced over scree and somewhere, deeper than both these, the cool rumble of subterranean water. Rising and falling, shifting past the ambit of his hearing, came the 'zwee-scree' of a wandering pipit and far away, so far that he could not believe he heard it, sounded the monotonous piping of a warbler. But it was all outside the cloud of his mind, suspended in the sky of his unfinished flight.

Strongbeak did not think of opening his eyes again until he heard the startle-cry of a gull. Its chatter of hungry interest stirred a powerful instinct of alarm in his stomach, breaking the lethargy of his sound-dream, forcing his eyelids open. The cloud of his dazed vision began to part, flick-flick, like the tearing of a cobweb. First he saw the sky, unblemished, and beneath it the brown and white serrations of sun-washed mountains, strange and yet familiar; the edge of trees and the shape of nearer rocks. Then, from the corner of his eye, he saw the folding of a black and white wing. He told his head to move, slowly, achingly, until his beak pointed towards the sky and, with his clear right eye, he could study the gull which perched above him. The black-back cocked its head and looked at him with calculated relish; then it shuffled its webbed feet on the bare boulder and turned to assess him with its other eye, as if it could not believe its good fortune. The gull craned its neck, looked about quickly to see that it had no rivals, and released a wet and chalky dropping in nervous excitement. With a flurry of wings, it dropped down closer to Strongbeak, not more than two yards away, and began to walk about him on the scree.

Strongbeak's mind began to work more quickly, driven by fear and a rising instinct for survival. Dully, he remembered that a gull alone would only scavenge, or attack birds that were defenceless and could be despatched without danger of a fight. He knew that he must move; but moving his head or his wing would not be enough if the gull sensed that he was disabled or seriously weakened. He must show that he had all his faculties about him, that he, Strongbeak, was a kea and that the gull would attack at its peril.

The gull came closer, circumspectly, and then dropped its head and made an exploratory rush. Strongbeak felt its beak close over his foot, snatching at it, and a sharp pain ran up his leg and across his flank. Quickly, he thought, but still so slowly that the gull hardly backed away, Strongbeak lifted and turned his head. The rock, scree, sky and mountains passed before his eyes. When he looked down he saw his legs with peculiar detachment, one wing folded beneath his side, the other half-open and free. The gull stood only a wingspan away, its eyes full of black cunning; beyond it, and the scree on which he lay, Strongbeak saw that there was tussock and a stand of beech trees.

He stared at the gull as it walked forward carefully and lunged again, this time nipping the flesh of his leg. As pain flickered through his body, Strongbeak thought frantically, I must get up! I must get up! But the urgency of his wish produced no response in the inert muscles of his legs and wings. Disconcerted by his unblinking gaze, the gull shifted out of Strongbeak's sight and took a stance behind him. Strongbeak waited, unmoving in the dim hope that the gull had been put off. But the gull had decided that he was easy prey and the blow on his back was so powerful that every bone in his body seemed to jar. Half-thrown, half-turned on the stones, Strongbeak raised himself in a spasm of anger and pain, resting on the shoulders of his wings. The scarlet showed and he opened his beak in silent threat; desperately he tried to screech but his throat was parched and locked. With a terrible shudder he sank down on his stomach and waited for the gull to strike again.

The gull came in quickly, but shied away as Strongbeak unexpectedly raised his head. Then again, seeking out the soft parts of his belly. Strongbeak began to watch every detail of the gull's movements, the way it lowered its head to rush in, the twisting of its beak, the bracing of its legs and the balancing of partly opened wings. He ignored the pain of its repeated blows, gathering together the last dregs of his strength and resolve.

The gull ran in again, confident that soon it would break the body of its prey, sure now that Strongbeak would offer no resistance. It lunged once more at his belly and as its yellow beak twisted to break through his feathers, it turned its head as if to gauge his reaction. With one swift and powerful stroke, Strongbeak drove down with his curved beak, piercing the gull's eye with dreadful accuracy. The gull staggered back with a harrowing cry and began to run about the scree in panic, directionless in its sudden half-blindness. It turned back to Strongbeak as

if it would strike at him again but Strongbeak lifted his beak in an unmistakable warning and the gull screamed and screamed, shaking its wounded head until the snowy feathers of its breast were flecked with blood. Then it scurried out to the crest of an isolated rock and took off, dipping and swerving out of sight. Exhausted, Strongbeak let his head fall back upon the scree and closed his eyes. In a moment he lay unconscious, easy prey, but the gull had gone, its plaintive cries echoing in the distance.

When Strongbeak woke again he saw from the mountain shadows and the deepening blue of the sky that it was late in second beak. He lay still for a long time, looking at the sky and far-off peaks, slowly gathering the will to move. For move he knew he must; he had not eaten for an unknown length of time; a day, two days, more, he could not guess. He did not know when he had come to this new place, how long he had lain on the scree. But he had little strength left and after a night with no food and the frost that the clear sky promised, he might not wake to guess or question any more.

He raised his head and looked down the long slope, the air above the stones still quivering with the day's heat. The first tussocks were perhaps a hundred yards away and they thickened at the edge of a starting gully, obscuring the dark heads of hebes and snowberry. Further, there was a straggle of beeches before the slope fell steeply away to a valley which seemed wider, though not as deep, as the big valley near Keeaw. But Strongbeak had no interest in the opposite slopes of the valley; he could only contemplate the difficulty of reaching the shelter and food of the scrub beyond the tussocks.

At last, Strongbeak's will and decision fused. He dug his beak into the stones and, using that and his wings as props, he lifted himself up and struggled to find a footing. When he tried to stand he felt as though he were lifting a boulder on his back. Straightening up, he turned quickly before his trembling limbs gave way and tottered down the slope, only to collapse on to his outstretched wings after a few yards, beak wide open, gasping for air. On again a few yards, scraping his wing feathers and tail against the sharp stones; down again, belly pressed to the lingering heat, head swinging erratically from side to side; on again; down again, scratching and flopping towards safety, nothing in his mind but the deepening shadows and the enticing silhouette of bushes which seemed to grow no larger.

Now, he thought as he slid helplessly over the shining tussock strands and came to rest against a stem of inaka. Now, as he lay still in the unexpected softness of moss and stared one-eyed at the first star in the east. Now, as he crawled deeper into the thicket of shrubs and began to tug weakly at drupes of ripe black berries.

Strongbeak stayed in the scrub and shrubfield for eight plus two days, and he counted them by touching a claw with his beak each sunset. At first he had neither the strength nor the enterprise to eat more than berries, shifting slowly from coprosma to patotara to snowberry, filling the scoop of his lower beak, rolling the juices about his tongue when he had separated pith from skin and

tipped out the seed. Later, as his energy returned, he dug for daisy roots and grubs in the bare soil beneath woody akeake. The scrub provided shelter from wind and frost, a screen against passing gulls and falcons and Strongbeak found a night perch under overhanging rocks which shed even the rain of a furious nor'west storm. He watched rain and sun, cloud and star, and thought of nothing but food and sleep and the healing of cuts and bruises inflicted by the gull and by a force or accident he had no memory of.

After four days he could hop with only mild discomfort; after six he could flap his wings with serious intent; and after eight he flew a short distance to the nearest beech tree and looked down on his hidden perch whose bushes and berries he suspected had never before felt the probing beak of a kea. When, during the day, he began to rest only at all the sun; when, as a matter of habit, he frequently fisted his feet to clean his toes; when he began to spend time preening himself clean and progressively straightening every vane and every barb of his dishevelled plumage; when he noticed all this, then he knew that he was almost himself again.

# 1981–1982

## BILL SEWELL

*Bill Sewell (1951–2003) published six books of poetry and edited a collection of literary criticism, a volume of biographical essays, and three poetry anthologies.*

**BILL** Sewell, when he was first appointed Burns Fellow in late 1980, had not yet released a book of poetry but had published some of his distinctive poems in literary periodicals and had a clear sense of the kinds of poems he wanted to write – more 'European' than most poetry then being written in New Zealand in their political focus, quietly ironic attitude towards human pride, understatement, intellectual allusiveness, and formal control. In his two Burns years he wrote many of the poems of his first two collections, *Solo Flight* (1982) and *Wheels Within Wheels* (1983). The titles of both volumes refer to poetic sequences, and each volume is built around several sequences, a

practice continued in his four later collections.

The two following poems each form part of a sequence, the first concerned with Richard Pearse, the second with 'some anarchist visions' in European history.

## Pearse at Mount Erebus

Pearse were you curious
about the world's end
or was the air above
intriguing enough?

a joy-ride no more
an ocean away & back
exploring in comfort
where the cold comes from –

no trudging through the snow
on pemmican
but the effortless sky
and three courses

reserves of all kinds:
engines whisky fuel
only the weather
to be wary of –

a smudge on a mountain-side
and everybody gasped:
you landed in a hedge
nobody knows when –

Pearse old spoiler
was it you there
whispering false instructions
in the pilot's ear?

# Spain

no one hates like we do
nursing the flame from spark
to flicker to conflagration –

a landscape arid enough
there is still fuel to be found
in orange grove & garden suburb:

twigs tossed on as tidbits
weaned on a solid diet of logs
washed down with swigs of gasoline:

*here's to the landlord*
*who shaves off our grain*
*here's to the priest*
*who hoards the Lord's favour!*

these heady days on the rampage:
no one who has worked
the soil for so long
has unsullied hands:

(open arms amnesty
coexistence compromise?
*no pasarán!*)

we'll rinse them first
in bourgeois blood

we'll burn off the past
from coast to coast
and wait for the rivers
to run clean.

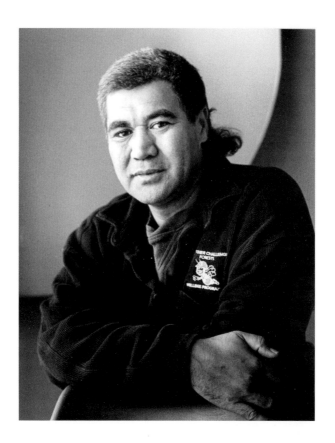

# RAWIRI PARATENE 1983

*Rawiri Paratene (b. 1954) has authored numerous one-off television dramas and Theatre in Education programmes, two radio plays and a short film. He has also co-written a feature film, four television documentaries, a theatrical musical, and provided text for a variety of NZ drama series and TV children's programmes. Poems and script excerpts by Paratene have been published in anthologies of contemporary Maori writers.*

**WHEN** Rawiri Paratene took up the Burns Fellowship in 1983, he was probably best known as a television actor (*Joe and Koro*) and presenter (*Playschool*), but he had won a Mobil Radio Award in 1980 as writer-director of the play 'Proper Channels', and was winner of the Maori Trustees Writers Award in 1976 with his one-act play 'Saturday Morning'.

During his Burns tenure he worked on several projects that came to fruition after his tenure. These included Erua (1988), a one-hour television play that won him the New Zealand Film and Television Award for Best Writer in 1989, the teleplay/screenplay *Dead Certs*

(1995), for which he received the New Zealand Film and Television Award for Best Actor in 1996, a radio play called *Save us a Place to Live*, and many performance poems which Paratene put on at various venues around Dunedin during the year. He also delivered a series of three 'Joy Lectures' at the University. These examined Shakespeare as the 'supreme user of the Pakeha tongue', looked retrospectively at the Maori Protest Movement of the 1970s, and surveyed the state of performing arts in New Zealand.

Below are four of those performance poems: two Dunedin landscapes, a satirical lyric, and a love poem.

## Untitled

The days here are frozen
of warmth
and of motion.

Iced ink
from the harbour
that flows
(thanks to God)

I've looked at those hills
of a million emotions
and
they always look back
and I cry
and they crack
a smile like whip
that wakens my senses

ha! We'll soon move on
but all this remains
like a well shat upon rock
our marks
are mere stains

## Dunedin Waking Up ...

Clouds
like charcoal blobs
hang
like a patchwork quilt i' the sky.

Shimmering streets and buildings
(cradled by the hills)
yawn and stretch
like a well-slept child
that sniffs
at dawn's sweet and sensuous scents.

And the harbour …
'ah, such a thing of joy'

I look at you
as others look at television.
I am mesmerised!

I've seen so many yous
and know that all are real.
But now
you pulsate
and
like a life-force
you flow
toward
an old, cold, grey
Dunedin

## To US …

I am                    US
 and                    US is who does organise the earth for you
to say and think and feel and do what
US requires
US gets from you
I am                    US
 and                    US is who looks back at you from mirrors!

I am                    US
 and                    US is who does gallivant the earth for you
a-painting her red white and blue
US knows
US gets

US in the pooh
I am                         US
    and                     US is who looks back at you from mirrors!

I am                         US
    and                     US is who
disc –US-ses
US. that's me and you
Yep
I am                         US
    and                     US is who looks back at you from mirrors!

I am                         US
    and                     US is who incorporates the earth for you
and keeps her spinning straight and true
US knows
US likes Big Ballyhoo
Ooh
I am                         US
    and                     US is who looks back at you from mirrors!

I am                         US
    and                     US is who did nip the nips in World War II
when jUStice was a human stew
US does what
US don't want to do
Still
I am                         US
    and                     US is who looks back at you from mirrors!

I am                         US
    and                     US is who does colonise the earth for you
with tourists and a coke or two
What                         US requires
US takes from you
I am                         US
    and                     US is who looks back at you from mirrors!

| I am | US |
|  | |
| and | US is who Kentucky Fries the earth for you |
| and keeps her sizzling, battered too | |
| Yeh | |
| I am | US |
| and | US is who looks back at you from mirrors! |

<br>

| I am | US |
| and | US is who will smash our mother earth in two |
| and j-US-t | |
| beca –US-e | |
|  | US don't like you |
|  | US knows |
|  | US gets |
|  | US in the pooh |
| But | |
| I am | US |
| and | US is who looks back at you from mirrors! |

## To a Robin

There is nothing more yellow
than the gorse when it flowers
There is nothing more hollow
than the ivory towers
There is nothing more blue
than the lake when it's frozen
There is nothing more true
than the twelve in a dozen
There is nothing more green
than the pastures unseen
There is nothing more mean
than the record that's clean

There is nothing more red
than a grievance unsaid
There is nothing more dead
than a hole in the head
There is nothing more white
than a mountain that's clothed

There is nothing more right
than a sage who is loathed
There is nothing more pink
than a candy-flossed sky
there is nothing more stink
than what's sweet to the fly

There is nothing as crisp
as the apple that's stolen
There is no greater risk
than the glitter that's golden
There is nothing as fresh
as the air when it snows
There is no sweeter death
than the death of a rose

And there's you
Yes there's you
Mmm there's you

# BRIAN TURNER 1984

*Brian Turner (b. 1944) has published eight collections of poetry, a volume of autobiography and three sporting biographies. He has also co-authored two volumes of his brother Glenn's cricketing autobiography, contributed the texts to a number of books featuring paintings and photographs of South Island landscapes, edited a guide to trout fishing in Otago and written plays, television scripts, reviews and essays.*

**WHEN** Brian Turner was appointed Burns Fellow in 1984, he had been publishing poems since the 1960s and had had three collections to his name. During that year he wrote the poems for his fourth collection, *Bones*, and a play about cricket, *Finger's Up*, a joint winner of the John Cowie Reid Memorial Award in 1985 which was was given rehearsed public readings at the Circa Theatre in Wellington.

The following two poems are from *Bones*. Turner has written of the first:

I wrote 'Listening to the Mountain' in an hour one

afternoon, the sun streaming in the window of my room on the third floor of the Burns Building. I'd been sitting there enjoying the sunshine and looking up at Flagstaff, the prominent hill in the northwest that overlooks Dunedin.[55]

The second poem is one of many in *Bones* dealing with family and personal relationships. It anticipates his autobiographical work, *Somebodies and Nobodies*, descriptively subtitled 'Growing up in an extraordinary sporting family'.

## Listening to the Mountain

*(for Peter and Phil)*

The clouds lift off Flagstaff
relaxing in the sun
while the city gets on with dispensable business.

——

The cumulus jostle but not in earnest
and nor is the wind, teasing the sky's scalp
and ruffling the skin of the harbour.

——

Each day the sun's hauled further west
so there's no question
it's spring.

——

Late, the sun begins to shine
as cloud abdicates, and late
the spirit lifts, at last.

——

At a different magical time every day
the mountain comes into view
and frowns or shimmers.

The line of the ridge
dips then lifts and runs off
into the blue distance.

Sometimes I imagine the mountain
is sleeping in the sunshine,
sometimes I think I am dreaming

the mountain is dreaming
of places it will never get to see,
and sometimes I feel the mountain

knows what I am thinking
as it lies there smiling
and looking down on the city

and the thriving sea, and all
that I shall ever stand for
grows benignly like a mountain in me.

————

The blue burns and the mountains
turn blue and the streams
from the blue mountains flash wickedly.

————

Blue light clashes with white light
above where the rolling hills
are tanned and blistered beneath the sun.

————

A million tolerant stars or more
and one buxom full moon
look down upon the still dark waters of the pond.

————

Whatever I was thinking when the cirrus
touched the tops of the mountains
left me wondering where to go from there.

————

If we listen long enough
the mountain wind sifting through the tussock
will bring the music of water leaping from stone to stone.

————

The lark, so high it's but a speck
in the blue, sings a song to remember
when you feel despair.

————

Celmisia have no voice
except to sing of the flowers
that are not here.

————

The mountains know that many people
have lain among them and listened
to the yearnings that reverberate

from age to age, between the races
and shiver like fire and water, and shake
like stone among the creatures of the world.

————

The river issues from the mountain and gathers confidence.
It has the assurance of one who knows
that it will return to where it belongs.

————

The birds are so curious
they could be our friends.
Only the mountains know

where they have come from
and where they are going
and what will happen when we are gone.

# Photograph at the Caledonian Games

*(to A.L.T.)*

Glossy monochromed 1950.
My father standing
with his track bike,
radiating fitness and light

and coy optimism, one arm
balancing the bronze
frame on which he
expended himself often,

his crash helmet
like a string of
black pudding tight
around his head.

A sprinter, my father,
I remember the way
he launched his bike
from between his legs,

lean as a whippet
lunging for the line,
and then sat back
spent. I was

not quite six, neither
happy, nor unhappy,
and still to start
in the real race.

# CILLA MCQUEEN

# 1985– 1986

**CILLA** McQueen had been publishing poetry for seven years when she took up the first year of her two-year Burns tenure. She had published two collections, been anthologised in the *Oxford Anthology of Contemporary New Zealand Poetry*, and received the New Zealand Book Award for Poetry for her first volume, *Homing In* (1983).

From her Burns tenure McQueen continued that brilliant start with two more collections, *Wild Sweets* (1986) and *Benzina* (1989), winning a second New Zealand Book Award for the latter. She also continued her career in mixed media, with performances of 'A

*Cilla McQueen (b. 1949) has published ten collections of poetry, has written two unpublished plays, and has released four music-poetry CDs.*

Maniac at the Joystick' (poetry/music/theatre, Dunedin, 1985), 'Shocks and Ripples' (solo performance, Dunedin and Wellington, 1985), 'Bad Bananas' (poetry and music with two guitarists, South Island tour, 1986), and 'Fancy Numbers' (performance piece for voices, instruments, and tap dancers, with the scores derived from computer-modified drawings of the Otago Peninsula in 1986). A radio drama, *Spacy Calcutta's Travelling Truth Show*, was produced for the Australian Broadcasting Corporation in 1986.

Below are three poems from *Wild Sweets* and two from *Benzina*.

# Crikey

I can't think straight
my words spin off
in sugar & spice
god you're nice
I've got a running filmstrip
in my head of you
every time I close my eyes
I close my eyes quite often
I feel so good
I feel like a morning
a kiss on a ferris wheel
in the tunnel of love

I'm not quite sure what's happening
but your image is in me like a scent
all the roses in the garden are opening up at once
it's raining big round drops
of extraordinary sweetness
let me be serious
I'm in love with you
                        I think of
you at every
                turn              move
my hand
            your eyes              your
hand
        crikey
            do the washing
                        dream on the doorstep
clean all the windows at high speed
get lost

              stare into space
                              watch a
green caterpillar
spinning enough
amazingly fine
silk
to let itself down
smoothly
from the
very top
leaf
of the tree.

## Otherwise

I come
from an opposite country
to yours,
where water spirals
& the moon waxes
otherwise.
my stars assemble
in unfamiliar patterns
& I watch often
not traffic or television
but hour by hour the huge tide
absently fingering rocks & small shells
& the wet brown kelp
where fish go sliding through.

if you were with me now
on my favourite beach,
we'd watch the distant seismograph
of silver peaks darkening to indigo
& walk on the breakwater
towards the harbour mouth,
disturbing the flocks of terns
that wheel up shrieking in slim wild voices
to land again behind us
renewing their conference.

                                        I would slip
my cold hand in your pocket,
you'd look at me & grin
& we would walk together quietly
right to the very end,
where big chained rocks hold back
the same Pacific ocean, lumbering in.

## Axis

shells pipe sea music
& fern fronds punch
soft green heads into my palm

within
the tiny ladder of the DNA
the mighty spiral of the Milky Way

living
in circles of time
growing towards the light

## Recipe for One

Take a Dunedin winter's afternoon,
a woman blown along the road,
a leaf, a russet umbrella
Take heed of the weather:

Take the washing off the line
and listen under the tree
to the storm coming seawards
over the mountain, cold taffeta

Take into consideration
the blackbird and the worm,
the world beyond the surface:
a jump through the meniscus

A glance, a chance, a step, a risk
a fancy, care, the liberty;
a moment held for time enough
to let the tones untangle.

Take all of this to heart.

Now,
take the rain.

## Synaesthesia

the lines the eye can see the mind can hear
the sounds the eye has found the ear can see
the landscape sings inside my inner ear
invisibly its silent harmony

the sounds the eye has found the ear can see
the eyes see patterns that the brain can sing
invisibly its silent harmony
draws out the music inside everything

the eyes see patterns that the brain can sing
invisibly the music pictures sound
draws out the music inside everything
& sings the lines of light my hand has found

behind my eyes as melodies unfold
the landscape sings inside my inner ear
a visual music that my mind can hold
the lines the eye can see the ear can hear

# ROBERT LORD 1987

*Robert Lord (1945–91) published five plays, had many others produced in New Zealand, the United States and Australia, and wrote a number of television scripts and filmscripts.*

**WHEN** Robert Lord was awarded the Burns Fellowship late in 1986, he had been living in the United States almost fourteen years. He applied for the Fellowship because he wanted to test the water in New Zealand – see what life was like back in a New Zealand that had changed significantly since he left. He told Rowena Cullen in a videotaped interview that he had hoped for a 'restful time' with some of the New York pressures removed so that he could let the idea of a new play come to him 'naturally' and be developed slowly and satisfyingly.[56]

However, the Burns year turned out to be a very busy one. His play *Bert and Maisy* – first written in 1979 – was

produced by the Fortune Theatre during the year, and he 'honed' and fine-tuned' it for that production (it was published by Otago University Press in 1988).[57] Lord wrote the *Peppermint Twist* television series, began work on a television series based on *Bert and Maisy*, and also wrote several radio plays. He revised his most recent American play, *China Wars*, for a Circa production in Wellington in 1988. Perhaps his central experience of the year was writing and directing *The Affair* for the Globe Theatre – a chance to take one of his plays from conception through to performance without any compromises. As a result of the Burns year, exhausted but pleased with the results, Lord decided to stay on in New Zealand, and his last years before his untimely death in 1991 were taken up especially with his last New Zealand plays, *Glorious Ruins* and *Joyful and Triumphant*.

The following extract is from *The Affair*. The play is presented as a television 'investigation' into the affair between Robin and Frank, two University of Otago students. The 'presenters' are their respective flatmates – Libby, a nurse at the Accident and Emergency Unit in the Dunedin Public Hospital, and George, a student. Robin and Frank act out the affair, while Libby and George comment. Dialogue and asides take place between Robin and Frank, between Robin and Frank and the 'presenters', between Robin and Frank and the audience, and between Libby and George and the audience.

## FROM *The Affair*

GEORGE: (To audience.) And that is how it began. A Friday night encounter at Foxy's, the elegant upstairs bar at the Robbie Burns. G and T followed G and T. Several Steinlagers were followed by a whisky, a bacardi and a brandy and dry. Between trips to the men's room Frank told Robin about his passion.

The lights stay up on GEORGE and LIBBY and come up on ROBIN and FRANK.

FRANK: (To ROBIN.) Rugby.
ROBIN: (To FRANK.) Rugby?
FRANK: (To ROBIN.) First five eighths.
ROBIN: (To FRANK.) That sounds so precise.
FRANK: (To ROBIN.) I love rugby.
GEORGE: (To audience.) He does, he loves rugby.
FRANK: (To ROBIN.) I love everything about rugby. The rucks, the scrums, the line-outs. The pain, the exertion, the exhaustion. The early morning jogging, the late night practice. The nerves before the game, the parties after.
ROBIN: (To FRANK.) How fascinating. (To audience.) He really does love rugby. (To FRANK.) I've never played.
GEORGE: (To audience.) I went through high school avoiding people who loved rugby. I get really upset dealing with brain damage.
LIBBY: (To audience.) Rugby is so aggressive. Every Saturday it's the same. Broken collar bones, torn ligaments, shattered kneecaps, black eyes, cauliflower ears, dislocated shoulders and ankles, not to mention cuts and abrasions.
FRANK: (To ROBIN.) I even love the smell of the field.

GEORGE: (To audience.) It's dirt. It smells of dirt. And sweat. Dirt and sweat and a dash of Brut.

FRANK: (To ROBIN.) The feel of the grass. Seeing my breath hanging in the air on a cold winter morning.

GEORGE: (To audience.) Doesn't it sound fabulous?

FRANK: (To ROBIN.) The sound of sprigged boots …

GEORGE: (To audience.) … thundering across the field like Clydesdales racing to extinction.

LIBBY: (To audience.) I can't see that it's worth being trampled half to death in order to enjoy some dubious male bonding at the bottom of a scrum. I don't think it's very hygienic, either.

ROBIN: (To FRANK.) When I was seven I joined the marching girls. I had a pony tail, a pink uniform and white vinyl boots.

FRANK: (To ROBIN.) You must've looked adorable. (To audience.) I hope that sounded sincere.

GEORGE: (To FRANK.) It didn't.

ROBIN: (To FRANK.) Of course marching is hardly a contact sport but you do do it on a field. Later I played netball.

FRANK: (To ROBIN.) How fascinating.

ROBIN: (To audience.) How fascinating? Am I being boring?

LIBBY: (To ROBIN.) You don't want to know.

ROBIN: (To FRANK.) I played two seasons and then I broke a wrist.

FRANK: (To audience.) I wonder if she likes me?

ROBIN: (To FRANK.) It was a compound fracture and I think I did something to a metatarsal.

FRANK: (To ROBIN.) Oh! Painful.

ROBIN: (To FRANK.) Very.

FRANK: (To audience.) Should I sit closer? Put a hand on her thigh? (To ROBIN.) You poor thing.

ROBIN: (To FRANK.) I was in plaster.

FRANK: (To audience.) She's got great lips. I want to put my tongue in her mouth. (To ROBIN.) Which wrist?

ROBIN: (To FRANK.) This wrist.

FRANK: (To audience.) What beautiful breasts. I want to hold them, kiss them.

ROBIN: (To FRANK.) Or was it this one?

FRANK: (To audience.) I want to take her nipples between my lips. I want to kiss her ribs. I want to stroke her thighs. I want to … I'm getting an erection!

ROBIN: (To FRANK.) It was a long time ago.

FRANK: (To audience.) What'll I do? I can't stand up. It's sticking out. Shit! It's about as discreet as the Andy Bay crematorium. Why am I wearing track suit trou?

ROBIN: (To audience.) What's gone wrong?

FRANK: (To audience.) I should've worn a jock strap.

ROBIN: (To audience.) Why is he sitting like that?

GEORGE and LIBBY: (To ROBIN.) He's got an erection.

ROBIN: (To audience.) Oh.

FRANK: (To audience. After a deep breath.)

> God of nations, at thy feet
>
> In the bonds of love we meet
>
> Hear our voices we entreat
>
> God defend New Zealand.

(HE looks at HIS crotch.) Damn!

ROBIN: (To audience.) We never discussed sex in Mataura. At least not in my family. Erections were something you found on building sites.

FRANK: (To audience. Another breath.)

> Amazing Grace, how sweet the sound
>
> To save a wretch like me
>
> For I was lost and now I'm found
>
> Was blind and now I see.

(HE looks at HIS crotch.) Shit!

ROBIN: (To audience.) My best friend, Gloria, drew an erection on a little stick man. I don't think they discussed sex in her family either. It looked like a cross between a walking stick and a television aerial.

FRANK: (To audience. HE sings.)

> God save our gracious Queen
>
> Long live our noble Queen
>
> God save the Queen.

(HE looks at HIS crotch then sings with renewed vigor.)

> Send her victorious
>
> Happy and glorious
>
> Long to reign over us
>
> God save the Queen.

FRANK starts reciting the Lord's Prayer under HIS breath.

ROBIN: (To audience.) A few years later when Gloria discovered the real thing she was a mine of information. She said guys who were too easily aroused ended up in the showers before she left the starting block. I wonder if she knew Frank?

FRANK: (To audience.) It's going down.

> For thine is the kingdom,
>
> The power and the glory

Thank God, it's going down.

> For ever and ever, Amen.

(To ROBIN.) Ready for another drink.

LIBBY: (To audience.) Crisis averted.

# John Dickson 1988

John Dickson (b. 1944) has published two collections of poetry and has released an audiocassette of his poetry. He writes that 'Currently, as well as working as an undertaker and part-time kitchen hand, I am finishing a book Mister Hamilton'. [60]

**ALTHOUGH** he had been writing, reading and publishing for many years, John Dickson, always exacting in his search for 'sentences which were supple, complex in a simple way, and able to carry lightly the weight of [his] preoccupations', had only recently produced his first collection when he was named Burns Fellow late in 1987.[58] When his second collection, *Sleeper*, was published in 1998, he wrote in the acknowledgements: 'I wish to thank the University of Otago (and specifically the Department of English), for awarding me the honour of the Robert Burns Fellowship in 1988. Most of the poems in this book were begun during the time I was the Fellow.'[59] Maybe the operative word is 'begun'.

# The Assumption of Mr Dickson into the Order of Domestic Cats

**1**

at midday exact, I went back inside.
Choosing clothes took time, but after a smoke
and most of a bottle of Mouton Rothschild
I settled for the Company's normal outfit
a silk Zingari-Richmond tie, a white linen suit
and its latest fashion, a pair of bare feet.
For a time, I sat out on the terrace.
A clock ticked, a cat meowed, a cloud
clouded the sun. The clock ticked, the cloud
passed on, and the cat meowed yet again, and just
as I was thinking, The future? Ah yes, the future
the continuities changed to a singular point.
Shall I go? Shall I stay? I wriggled my toes.
How easy it is to squander existence

**2**

the afternoon was warm like a blue oboe
so I straightened my tie and set off
down the track called Stuart Street.
Near the Exchange, I heard voices – those
of the merchants who traded TVs, cars, and land
for muskets, beads, and prayer books.
And sure enough, there they were.
They shouted, they winked, they smiled
displaying their perfect teeth in a carnival
of beguiling gestures. For like the crowd
they wanted to go home, embark
on the waiting schooners, and sail back
to where life was much more simple

**3**

at the Captain Cook Tavern, the crowd
was somewhere else. Mainly middle managers
the Company had no further use for
they were dressed in grass skirts, and all
were swaying to a hooba hooba band
their pupils dilating to blindness
when the suave trombones swelled

to an indolent crescendo. I've forgotten now
why I permitted my feet to tap in time.
Perhaps, it was the opaque heaviness of the air
or a sudden rupture of all memory
the bush taking plankton before max
constantly floating his equations into the
prolix foliage of her muesli-eating tusk
as if watering tuataras with a sour apple
and back came I my senses to, and yet again
I'd missed my chance. The schooners had left.
According to the usual suspect information
spread as word by those in charge
when everyone has finally disembarked
amongst their dreams of winding rivers
and forests bright with the plumage of parrots
they live in paradise like happy clouds
in an otherwise blue sky.
While I never say a thing, that's a lie.
When they wake, they're ambushed
by the challenge of nothing at all

4
of course, there was always work.
Whenever I see a gull's feather twirling
in an updraft of air, at intervals of ten seconds
I'm obliged to plot on graph paper
the various positions of its fall, joining
each point with a line that gives no idea
of the prodigious entanglements of its movement.
And no mistakes. Though why is beyond me.
What I knew was this: follow instructions.
But these days, my neurons were wearing out
the electro-chemical pulses going in
directions they weren't supposed to.
Like everyone else, I could go on the schooners
or, like a last freedom, I could choose
smaller and smaller intervals than the
one required, the slope of the graph
increasing to infinity until I met
a feather's shadow on the lawn below

5

I turned the handle and let myself in
leaving the door wide open to the stillness.
In the lounge, delicate cups on a tray
and the sound of a distant footstep.
I stood by a window as twilight came.
A flush of blood-coloured silence deepened the sky.
Shall I go? Shall I stay?
I began to hum a tune from La Bohème.
My indecision was final

6

no, it wasn't like that at all.
When a cloud had clouded the sun
and an easterly breeze from the harbour
was rustling the leaves of a laburnum tree
a tom cat walked across the terrace.
It stopped, and began licking a paw.
Hey you, I called, don't you realise
we have a future as sly and innocent words?
The cat stopped licking its paw.
We exchanged a look of mutual forgiveness

# RENÉE 1989

*Renée (b. 1929) has written eighteen plays, seven of which have been published, and a number of radio plays and television scripts. She has also published six adult novels, one children's novel, a collection of short stories, a collection of comic writings, and several writing guides.*

**WHEN** Renée took up the Burns Fellowship; in 1989, she had been writing plays for ten years and had had eight produced, with four of those published, including two in the *Wednesday to Come* trilogy of historical plays depicting the lives of four generations of New Zealand working-class women. The year as Burns Fellow bore further fruit, for the next year she had three plays produced in Dunedin, two of which were published. The major writing project of the Burns year was the third play in the trilogy (but the earliest in historical setting), *Jeannie Once*. She wrote a draft during 1989 and completed the play in 1990; it had its premiere that year

at the Fortune Theatre in Dunedin and was published the following year.

An extract from the play follows, with Renée's contextualisation.

*Jeannie Once* is the first play in the *Wednesday to Come* Trilogy although it was written last. Set in the early 1860s it shows the old woman, Granna (Jeannie), as a young Irish immigrant, newly arrived in Dunedin. Her husband died on board on the way to New Zealand and was buried at sea.[61]

## FROM *Jeannie Once*

Scene Three
JEANNIE's *work space. Tuesday afternoon.*
JEANNIE *is still working on the pattern.* ALEC McPHERSON *is watching her. He is a strong-looking healthy young man. He hesitates but finally speaks. He has a Glasgow accent.*
ALEC: You should stop for some food Jeannie.
JEANNIE: Don't fuss.
ALEC: My Mam always said that if you wanted to do a job properly you'd likely do it better on a full stomach.
JEANNIE: Ah there speaks the good Scotswoman whose husband was never out of a job.
ALEC: My Dad was lucky. Luckier than his son. Ireland hasn't got the edge on hunger and unemployment.
JEANNIE: It's my understanding it's a great and glorious thing to be born in Scotland! You'll not be saying I'm wrong?
ALEC: You've got a chip on your shoulder.
JEANNIE: All I'm interested in at the moment is getting this pattern just right. I'm fed up with being paid a pittance to sew shirts for old Pengelly. If Mrs Wishart's pleased who knows where it'll lead?
ALEC: Be careful it doesn't drag you down.
JEANNIE: What is it you'd like Alec?
ALEC: You take too much notice of what people say.
JEANNIE: I live in the world.
ALEC: I'm not denying there's prejudice.
JEANNIE: And it helps if you've got the right accent!
ALEC: You can't deny that some of your countrymen give the rest of you a bad name. It's nothing to do with you personally.
JEANNIE: The bad name grew up with me, it travelled out on the ship with me.
ALEC: It's over. It's past.
JEANNIE: You mean who cares if three lazy drunken papists die before their time? No match for sober, God-fearing, hard-working Presbyterians like Alec McPherson! You know it always surprises me that you decided to honour this home with your presence.

ALEC: I was told Mary O'Malley's stew would keep a man going for days at a time.

JEANNIE: And she doesn't charge the earth. That's a consideration for a young Scot who's having difficulty finding a job!

ALEC: Your tongue drips with bitterness.

JEANNIE: Don't exaggerate Alec, why should I be bitter?

ALEC: I'm not saying it's a just world.

JEANNIE: That's good because it's not. How did you get on?

ALEC: I saw that tight-arsed foreman of Larnach's. He says it's Mrs Larnach who wants someone. She's to be in town this Thursday.

JEANNIE: That sounds hopeful for you.

ALEC: He wasn't sure of the details. He thought it might be a married couple she wants.

JEANNIE: No Alec.

ALEC: Why not? God himself knows I've been patient! I know full well your grieving had to run its course but I've given you plenty of time.

JEANNIE: My time is not yours to give!

ALEC: You know what I mean.

JEANNIE: We made a bargain Alec. You were to stop pestering me and I would be your friend.

ALEC: Why have you turned against me?

JEANNIE: I never turned towards you, it's all in your head you great fool!

ALEC: You're a liar Jeannie Brannigan!

JEANNIE: I don't intend to marry again.

ALEC: You use your sorrow as a stony barrier against feeling! You're young, Jeannie love, why throw it away?

JEANNIE: I am not interested in marriage!

ALEC: Tried it once and didn't like it eh?

JEANNIE: You watch your tongue!

ALEC: It has to be something! You work all the hours God sends, hardly take the time to toss a word to your friends and your only outing is to go to the madhouse to see that crazy woman!

JEANNIE: Margaret May is not crazy!

ALEC: Is she not then?

JEANNIE: She suffered a terrible shock!

ALEC: She's playing on your kind heart and if you weren't so pig-headed you'd see it!

JEANNIE: It's jealous you are Alec Mc Pherson, jealous of a poor sick woman!

ALEC: *putting his hand over* JEANNIE's Jeannie please.

JEANNIE: You're upset and angry because you haven't got regular work but something will turn up, I know it will.

ALEC: I've put my name with everyone I can think of.

JEANNIE: You should move away from town.

ALEC: You won't live in the country.

JEANNIE: Don't start that again.

ALEC: Besides, jobs are as hard to get in the country as they are in town.

JEANNIE: So much for this bright new world. It looks just like the old one to me!

ALEC: There's a hell of a lot more space, don't you love that about it, Jeannie?

JEANNIE: You like it here, don't you?

ALEC: I do. I know if I hang on I'll be all right.

JEANNIE: Good luck to you then. I was thinking it would take me forever to save enough but with this dress and maybe some others, we'll be off in no time!

ALEC: Back to the misery you left behind.

JEANNIE: It's Margaret May's only chance.

ALEC: I won't have it do you hear me? I won't bloody have it!

MARY *enters. She takes in the atmosphere in one brief glance.*

MARY: The London Company arrives within the hour. Claude says could you be at the theatre to meet them, Alec.

ALEC: I didn't come to this place to run messages for actors and their fancy women!

JEANNIE: It's all money.

ALEC: Is that all you think about?

JEANNIE: Just about.

MARY: Now I wonder if it's the actors or the fancy women you object to?

ALEC: Both!

MARY: Don't fret yourself. Carrying luggage for actors might be irksome but they tip well! Have you seen Barney? *They don't answer.* At the billiards again is he? Well he might as well make the most of it. I've made an appointment with James Mowat for tomorrow and if agrees to take him on, Barney'll be too busy to sneak off to the Golden Nugget! Perhaps you could pick him up on the way?

ALEC: I'll do that. *He goes.*

MARY: Poor Alec.

JEANNIE: He's big enough and ugly enough to look out for himself. I'm surprised you're allowing Barney within a stone's throw of the theatre.

MARY: God preserve me from the drama if I said he couldn't go! Besides Claude said he'd be needed and Barney can do with the money.

JEANNIE: If you don't like drama why push to get him apprenticed to James Mowat?

MARY: Tailoring's a good trade, a safe trade. If he keeps his head down maybe one day he'll be setting himself up in business. He'll see the sense when he's a little older.

JEANNIE: Is this you talking about security Mary?

MARY: I've had enough of the other.

JEANNIE: I like Barney.

MARY: I'm quite fond of the little beggar myself.

JEANNIE: I'd like him to be happy.

MARY: Oh happy. Now there's a thing. Jeannie, I'm off to make a cup of tea, to hell with what the Reverend thinks, and when it's brewed I'll give you a call.

JEANNIE: I think you just snubbed me Mary O'Malley.

MARY: And you're to come straight away mind! You're looking far too pale!

JEANNIE: Don't you start!

MARY *leaves and* JEANNIE *holds a piece of pattern up against the model.*

JEANNIE: What do you think Nelly? Is it really because I tried it once and didn't like it?

# THE 1990s

# DAVID EGGLETON 1990

David Eggleton (b. 1952) has published five collections of poems, a collection of short fiction, a book of essays about the seasons, an illustrated history of Kiwi rock music, an illustrated history of local photography, and an illustrated history of twentieth-century New Zealand art. He has also released two CDs, as well as other recordings, of his poetry set to music.

DAVID Eggleton was well-established as a poet when he was appointed Burns Fellow for 1990. In his Burns year he continued his prolific output, working on the poetry-music CD *Poetry Demon* (1993), many of the poems collected in *Empty Orchestra* (1995), book reviews, journalistic articles, a group of essays 'which appeared in various short-lived magazines between 1991 and 1995', and a series of over twenty short pieces of fiction, mostly unpublished, from which the story that follows was taken. He was also 'involved in a very large number of live poetry events … in keeping with [his] belief that half of the art of poetry is in poems being read, or enacted, aloud'.[62]

# Top Dollar

Gerald was part of the Shore City bum-fluff crowd, one of its richer sons. In spite of having been raised in a hot-house nursery of snobbery and disdain, he was a deracinated cultural victim, lacking an ideology which would allow him to make sense of his brazen wealth. The nearest he got to a philosophy for living was to assert that, for neo-modernists, being guilt-free should be part of everyday life. Because he applied it across the board it seemed to mean whatever one wanted it to mean in any given context. In a way he was a guinea pig of the profit-motive ethos.

His Uncle Eddie had been his inspiration. A middle-aged, middle-management skinhead in 'bovver' brogues when just a newly-arrived immigrant from 'dear old Muvver England' during the Seventies, Eddie had set up a ruthless debt collection agency which had muscled in on all kinds of rackets. Now his uncle affected a distinguished silver turban of hair which demanded the constant attentions of a coiffeur, and his well-lined trouser pockets were always jingling. From his high-rise apartment he could look down on those living in the shadow of Shangri-La, while his two pedigree cats, Eros and Mammon, cavorted across the expensive carpets. To calm himself and to relax, Eddie would practise the ancient art of origami: Japanese paper folding. He would drop the coloured-paper pellets he had made into vases of water and watch them unfold, breathing deeply.

In the space of ten years, Ed had become one of the country's most powerful business men, a shadowy influence on the Business Round Table and a dealmaker and string-puller par excellence. He had been one of the first to take full advantage of the opportunities computers offered, scouring databases for bank information and landlord history. While condemning the scabrous behaviour of 'stupid greedy bastards' after the Stock Market crash of '87, he hadn't failed to move in and clean up himself, and he had found that the recently privatised corporations offered fresh opportunities.

He had linked up with Tod of SuperTod Holdings and Action Development. Tod was a money player. He used a merchant banker's sexy but safe money practices inside his investment fortress. A free-market zealot and TV pundit, his hobbies included dwarf-throwing and using his car phone. As directors with Action Development, both Eddie and Tod had been key players in the in-house investment casinos, which used the thrusting ongoing forms of dozens of unreflecting reflective buildings – out-of-scale copies of desirable overseas buildings, many with hogging panoramic views – to raise collateral with ever larger corporations in the United States and elsewhere.

Tod had a design team whose brief was to imitate only the finest. At the same time they had to create with purely commercial requirements in mind. So it was that crass concrete box structures were topped off with a superglue slurry of glass and granite chips. Very crude mistakes were declared virtues; they trumpeted the

fallen arches of architecture and compared themselves to the Greek Revival of 1886.

Spare-part surgery was practised on groaning, obsolete buildings. They were gutted of their interiors, disembowelled floor by floor and refurbished, featuring the old facade. Frontage fractions were weighed against concrete benefits; businessmen with twin-tower complexes met in dingy cinemas to plot building ordinance circumventions; and huge concrete mixers with grinding peristaltic cement loads ate up the k's along the clogged, pulsing arteries of the city's motorways.

Rumours went around that some of those suffering from 'the modern vandal complex' – graffiti artists and the like, engrossed in their aerosol spraying – had been crushed under the mirror glass accidentally on purpose. They had been glued into the superstructure.

Often, as a wrecking crew brought a house down, crushing a former herb garden or hen coop, small groups of Neighbourhood Watch members would clap and cheer ironically. They were all living in the midst of change and uncertainty, under threat from 'restructuring', turned into unwilling models for conspicuous consumption. Sometimes the wrecking crew would begin to demolish the house as the harassed tenant carried out the last carton of hot rod magazines or left home still sipping from a last cup of coffee.

Tod, a former All Black, was a rugged individualist with a flattened conk, cauliflower ears and the scars of scrum pox. Amidst the small talk and private chatter of any SuperTod Holdings function his solid drone was invariably heard, cutting through the banter:

'Money talks. If no one's listening to you it's because you have no money talking for you … You've got the bad timing of someone using a long shot, however I think we can make an accommodation. … You must learn to rise above the ruck because it is a tough game … Money can be used to shape your lifestyle, your personal first-strike. It can help you to burst upon the scene like a revelation of the future. You will find that backsliders on the slippery slope of rationalisation are people without money.'

Tod's high profile as an opinion kiteflyer for Big Business on TV meant his built-in insincerity was magnified in the public mind. Yet his astuteness told him the public would ignore it because he could energise and motivate, even manipulate any emotional groundswell to topple dissenters. Those who shouted out loud that he was a privateer, a buccaneer, were soon taught that discretion was the better part of valour. After all, Tod had made a fortune inventing a personality for Joe Public Junior, selling childhood innocence as a commodity. The public had loved him for it. He had made another fortune, it was rumoured, by being the untraceable prime-mover behind a barefaced insurance landslide scam. Upon meeting some customer resistance to one of his money-making ideas in small town New Zealand, he had arranged to have truckloads of salesmen

brought in to the provincial areas from Australia and they had been instructed to promise the world on easy terms.

When an under-manager had demurred, saying uneasily: 'But will they swallow that?' Tod had barked, 'We've managed to bring them along all the way so far,' and turned to carry on cranking up a new interactive TV campaign involving the Sadistic Sisters of Sappho: purchasers would be encouraged to kiss the whip before being eligible for lower interest rates. A gimmick that Tod was sure would prove very sales-effective.

Tod and Eddie, with Gerald in respectful attendance alongside, trod in a weighty and deliberate way along the meticulously vacuumed carpet of an exclusive club. Using an ad-hack's PR rah-rah, Tod spoke of his aspirations, of marauders, raiders and forays. He spoke, too, of the dumped high-level employee of a global development corporation, someone who had taken his disgruntled self and his insider information to an underworld criminal fraternity who were now seeking to destabilise the dairy industry. Tod had already tipped off the Minister of Agriculture, but not before using the news to his own advantage. Soon, he would go on TV to blow his own trumpet and generally drum up populist support by announcing what he had done. He knew how important such factionalism was. He could never be sure when he might next face another group of evicted squatters in front of the cameras, and have to act as the embodiment of moral outrage, under a clear sky, best profile forward.

In the bar of the exclusive club two narrow-necktied dealers in commodity futures were arguing heatedly together in loud, drunken voices about who had the better head for business. In the club's health studio a broker lay in the simmering vat of the hot tub, mulling over figures and pecking at the keys of a powerful laptop suspended from a wall bracket. A small holding company was about to become another hit-and-run statistic in an advanced personal number-cruncher.

Gerald was running with the fast pack, with stockbroker whipper-snappers who traded quotations on pork belly futures and talked about what it must feel like to turn thirty without having made your first million. They sashayed loudly through through the local pub, telling one another: 'Soon this will be a wine bar.'

Their girlfriends tended to be aerobic wonders waiting to be recognised by New York modelling agency talent scouts on a sweep through the South Pacific. One or two of the more entrepreneurial of these girlfriends would swing by a health store saying: 'I am prepared to advertise that this is what your product has done for me.'

At dinner in a tiny fern bar just off Queen Street, the clientele of networking yuppies, still winding down from having spent all day gambolling through their own cyberspaces, would get stoked up on falafels. Lips smeared with saffron, tongues tumescent with turmeric, teeth gleaming with fine wine, they would launch into their mating calls.

'Humpy-pumpy!' would yell the inebriated money-shufflers.

'Pumpy-wumpy!' would come the answering refrain from their derailed debutante companions.

Dance-infected, they would flow into the next-door disco to cure themselves by leaping around so violently they seem to be trying to turn themselves inside out. Gotterdammerung time in the basement, as a DJ mouths inanities from a fishbowl alcove and a laser-light show stages a stellar explosion.

'Life is a matter of neutralising the nay-sayers!' screams one pretend-fascist in fashionably distressed leather.

'Sobriety after my twenty-fifth!' screams another.

Gerald skanks it up, along with the rest of the crush. Tomorrow will bring the usual search-and-destroy missions in the great treasure house of economic exploration, never quite sure where the next adventure would lead, knowing only that at the end of it there was money.

# LYNLEY HOOD 1991

*Lynley Hood (b. 1942) has published four books of biography and cultural history and contributed to several other books.*

LYNLEY Hood had published two related books when she was appointed 1991 Burns Fellow – her award-winning biography of Sylvia Ashton Warner, *Sylvia!* (1988), and *Who is Sylvia? The Diary of a Biography* (1990). During her tenure she worked on her third book, *Minnie Dean: Her Life & Crimes*. It was a finalist in the New Zealand Book Awards in 1995. Minnie Dean had been convicted of infanticide and sentenced to death by hanging in 1895; her application for leave to appeal was denied, and the Executive Council refused to recommend to the Governor that he commute her sentence to life imprisonment. The extract below picks up Minnie Dean's story at that point.

## FROM *Minnie Dean: Her Life & Crimes*

The newspaper editorial writers who manned the moral barricades of the nation were, for the most part, well satisfied with the Executive decision. An *Otago Witness* columnist wrote approvingly:

*We cannot doubt that the decision was a right and proper one … there was no redeeming feature in the case – nothing at all that could be urged as a plea for mitigation of the sentence …. The man who commits the foulest murder in a paroxysm of anger, or even of avarice, is not so lost as the woman who is constantly on the lookout for infants to murder at so much a head.*

According to the *New Zealand Graphic*, hanging was too good for the infamous Minnie Dean:

*One wishes there were some punishment twice as terrible as death for a monster capable of such crime. Hanging is too severe a punishment for some murders. But for such murders as these, it is a perfectly inadequate punishment.*

The *Southland Times* declared:

*The cruel killing of helpless innocents, systematically perpetrated as a matter of business, is murder in so aggravated a form that sympathy for the wretched woman now awaiting execution would be misplaced.*

Despite the fulminations of editorial writers, sympathy for Minnie Dean did exist. The unusually high proportion of women spectators in court, much commented on by the press, may have been the first sign. After the trial the signs became more explicit. On 29 June a columnist in Invercargill's *Southern Cross* commented on the community agitation to have Mrs Dean's sentence commuted. The same day, Christchurch suffragist, Ada Wells, penned a letter to the Minister of Justice on behalf of the Canterbury Women's Institute:

*That this Institute is in favour of the abolition of Capital Punishment (1) as the State has no right to commit murder; (2) as it has not proved a deterrent; & that therefore the Minister of Justice be petitioned in the matter of the Dean Case, in which sentence of death has been passed, that the sentence be commuted to imprisonment for life.*

'Mother' of Christchurch wrote directly to Minnie, a Dunedin woman gave £40 towards her defense costs, the congregation of St Paul's Presbyterian Church in Invercargill said a prayer for her and other sympathisers wrote to the press. On 1 July a letter from Edwin Rutland to the *Southland Times* opened timidly with, 'Please allow me a little space to say a few words about the poor woman Mrs Dean, who now lies under sentence of death in the Invercargill gaol.' He suggested that if her sentence were commuted to life imprisonment, 'she would have time

to repent of her sins and be made in a fit state to enter heaven.' The following week 'Mercy' wrote to the *Southland Daily News* to complain of the unfairness of hanging Mrs Dean before the Bill for the abolition of capital punishment had been considered by Parliament, while in Dunedin's *Evening Star*, 'Justicia' urged that women be appointed to charitable and other boards because 'It takes a woman to understand a woman's woes.' 'The terrible case of Mrs Dean should raise Dunedin women to a sense of their duty,' 'Justicia' wrote, and went on to press for the provision of foundling wards in hospitals. This was too much for 'Mother.' 'In my opinion such resources only foster the crime that causes the misery,' she wrote. 'It would be far better for the country if there was State punishment for the crime of illegitimacy.'

The expressions of sympathy were to no avail. On 5 August the Superintendent of Prisons telegramed the Invercargill gaoler Mr Bratby:

*Please inform prisoner Minnie Dean that His Excellency the Governor sees no reason to interfere with the sentence passed upon her and it will therefore be carried out in due course.*

As far as the authorities were concerned, carrying out the hanging was a matter of urgency; delays often provoked embarrassing public outcries for clemency and with the prisoner being not only a woman, but a refined woman, the chances of an outcry were probably greater than usual. They would have been mindful that in Melbourne the previous year the passing of the death sentence on baby farmer Frances Knorr had provoked an alarming wave of petitions and public meetings culminating in a march on Government House on the eve of her execution that had 'given the impression that an attack might possibly be made on the premises.'

According to New Zealand law, executions had to take place within a week of the local sheriff receiving notice that the Governor would not interfere with the sentence, but by the time the Invercargill sheriff received his notice in the mail on Thursday 8 August most of the arrangements had already been made by telegram: the scaffold was on its way from Dunedin, the hangman was on his way from Wellington, and the date and time of the execution had been fixed.

The search for the hangman had begun soon after Judge Williams pronounced sentence. Despite the apparent popularity of the verdict, the authorities feared that finding someone willing to hang a woman would not be easy. In this matter too they were probably mindful of the Australian experience; in Victoria 'Jones the Hangman' was reported to have committed suicide by cutting his own throat because of his

*unwillingness to execute Mrs Knorr, the baby farmer, and that unwillingness was the result not so much of conscientious scruples or of sympathetic feeling for the condemned woman as a shrinking from the contemptuous jeers and the persecutions of his neighbours, who, he believed, would be still more hostile if he hanged a woman.*

The most likely candidate for hangman in the Dean case was intemperate Tom Long, an old soldier, nearly sixty years of age, who had in the course of his life hanged over a dozen felons. On 6 July an urgent and confidential memo was issued by the Wellington Police Office:

*The Commissioner directs that immediate enquiries be made for the whereabouts of Tom Long, known as the 'hangman' …. If found a telegram to be at once sent to this office. Report results of enquiries without delay.*

By 6 August Tom Long had been located at Wanganui, taken to Wellington, locked in prison and presented with an agreement to sign:

*To the gaolers at Wellington, Dunedin and Invercargill & all whom it may concern – I Thomas Long do hereby agree to act as hangman in the case of Minnie Dean, for the sum of £25.0.0, twenty five pounds. I further agree to be taken to Invercargill under escort, sleeping in any prisons that may be necessary en route, and that, on arrival in Invercargill I shall allow myself to be enclosed within the walls of the prison, and be fed on prison fare, until the execution is over and I hereby agree to bring no action against any person for so shutting me up in prison, as it is my own wish and request that I shall be so treated. The Prison Department are to pay my fare from Wanganui to Invercargill and back, and if the hanging is satisfactorily carried out I am to receive the £25.0.0, twenty-five pounds, on my arrival in Wellington when returning from Invercargill.*

With the success of the hanging resting on Tom Long's unreliable shoulders, the Under-secretary for Justice was understandably anxious. '*I wish particularly to impress on you the great necessity of taking every precaution to prevent the occurrence of any hitch or bungle,*' he wrote to the Invercargill sheriff. '*Will you be good enough to telegraph to me whether he has given satisfaction.*'

News that her sentence would not be commuted was relayed to Minnie by the Reverend George Lindsay of St Paul's Presbyterian Church, Invercargill, who had attended her daily since her conviction. She responded, as always, with composure. She said she hoped she would not be a coward, but would face the end like a brave woman. She even remained calm when the sheriff informed her, on 7 August, that he had fixed the time of execution for 8 am on Monday 12 August. Only when he brought her the news that she would not be buried in the gaol yard like a common criminal, because her husband's request to take her body to Winton for burial had been granted, did she sob briefly.

Throughout her three months in the Invercargill gaol, Mr Bratby the gaoler and his wife the matron did their best to make Minnie comfortable. They provided her 10 foot x 12 foot gas-lit prison cell with a neat wooden bedstead, a table, two wooden stools, a strip of carpet, a Bible, a fire in the grate and a vase of spring flowers on the mantelpiece. Minnie wrote:

*From the gaoler and the matron I have received every care, attention and kindness that was in their power to bestow. From the matron I have received the affectionate consideration of a sister and she has tried in every way to alleviate and lighten the heavy burden that has been laid on me. May God's blessing rest on both of them, may they live to a ripe old age and may their end be peace.*

Charles Dean visited his wife for the last time on Saturday 10 August. After that Minnie spent her time praying, reading the Bible, writing the statement that she was never allowed to make in court, preparing herself for her fate and asking repeatedly to see the little children from The Larches:

*The one yearning wish of my heart has to remain ungratified – I have been refused to be let see the children. The thought and hope of being able to see them only once has sustained me in all my bitter trouble. And surely I have been punished enough without inflicting this worst of all troubles on me. What is to become of them now? Who is to love and care for them as I have done? Oh it is cruel to have to go to the grave with the only ray of comfort denied me, a fond last look at the faces of my little ones.*

The evening before her execution Minnie sat up late finishing her statement and writing letters. She slept from 11.30 pm until 3.00 am, then rose and again engaged in writing. She refused breakfast but accepted a few sips of tea. She also cut a lock from her fine, soft iron-grey hair, tied it with a ribbon, and left it on the mantelpiece beside the small vase of snowdrops and violets.

Shortly before 7.30 am the Reverend Lindsay came to pray with Minnie and hold her hand. Dr Macleod also called, and on learning that Minnie had taken no breakfast he ordered a glass of whisky and water for her. 'For goodness sake doctor,' she said. 'Get it over quickly.' But she left the whisky untouched.

At three minutes to eight the gaoler, the sheriff, the doctor and the executioner entered her cell. The sheriff formally demanded from the gaoler the body of Minnie Dean. Then he turned to the hangman and said, 'Executioner, do your duty.' Minnie stood quietly as the hangman strapped her upper arms to her sides, bent her arms forward, crossed her wrists and pinioned them to a strap around her waist.

The gaol bell tolled slowly as the procession to the scaffold began. At the head walked the gaoler and the doctor, then came the Reverend Lindsay, reading from the Presbyterian burial service. Behind him walked Minnie, erect and dignified, with a prison warder on either side. Next came the hangman followed by the sheriff. At the foot of the broad sloping stairs Minnie dropped one hand, lifted her skirt and ascended gracefully to the gallows. While the hangman pinioned her ankles, adjusted the noose around her neck and placed the white calico cap over her head and face, she held tightly to the hand of the warder beside her and took a few deep breaths.

'Do you wish to say anything before you leave this world?' asked the sheriff.

'I have nothing to say,' said Minnie. 'Except that I am innocent.'

As the warder beside her released his hand she swayed a little and seemed about to fall. Then she straightened herself and murmured, 'Oh God let me not suffer.' At that moment the sheriff gave the signal. The hangman drew the trapdoor bolt. Minnie Dean dropped from sight. The rope jerked taut. Minnie Dean was dead.

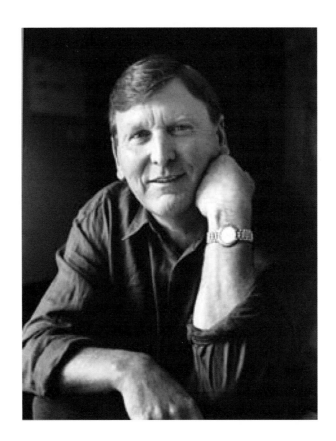

# OWEN MARSHALL 1992

*Owen Marshall has published eleven collections of short stories, three novels, a collection of poems, and contributed to Timeless Land. He has also edited a book of poems and five collections of short stories.*

OWEN Marshall was already an established master of the short story when he assumed the Burns Fellowship in 1992, as shown when his sixth collection, *Tomorrow We Save the Orphans*, was published early in that year. He took the opportunity offered by the Burns Fellowship to write a draft of what became his first published novel, *A Many Coated Man* (1995), which was shortlisted for the Montana Book Award for Fiction. The work was a considerable change in scale and mode from the mostly realistic short stories that had preceded it – a dark, 280-page novel set in the future with an obtrusive postmodern narrator.

The two excerpts below are from the novel. The first takes place early in the book, when the main character, the dentist Aldous Slaven, is in hospital because of severe electrical shock he has received in an accident, a shock that transforms him into a charismatic speaker with a social mission. He is visited by his wife Kellie. The second, which comes halfway through the book, is one of a series of lyrical and precise 'there is a place' descriptions of mostly South Island locations.

## FROM *A Many Coated Man*

*(Two excerpts)*

Norman Proctor has died before we have come round to telling his story. Let's just say that he had a good match temperament did Proctor. It used to be a treat to see him cope with the pressure at provincial, even national, tournaments. Oh yes, it's easy advice to treat each ball on its merits irrespective of the state of the game, but Proctor actually managed to do so on occasions which seemed important at the time. Had we started at the bed furthest from the door there would have been more of him and less of Montgomery and young Vincent I dare say.

Norman Proctor was dying anyway, but Kellie was the occasion of it, if not the cause, as the scholars say. Norman had very little movement and no woman. He had no enjoyment from watching Montgomery's wife when she came to call, but he admired Kellie's energy and sense of purpose. He made a considerable effort to watch Kellie inspecting the gladioli she had placed on his table the day before. Kellie's shoulder was brown and well-muscled by gardening. Unfortunately the strain brought on a cramp in Proctor's neck and he suffocated in silence there as Kellie talked to Vincent of the Mount Cook lily she had seen below the Hooker Glacier.

It is a Thursday, with a heat cloud pressing down on the city. The first trees and buildings from the hospital windows can be seen and then the white-grey uniformity of cloud like a well-used sheet. The nurses wheel Proctor's bed into the corridor and close the swing doors to the small ward so that the others don't have to see Proctor being tidied away. For some reason there is a good deal of birdsong on such a day and in his room Miles can hear the throaty whistles of the thrushes as well as the voices of the nurses outside his door.

'And I've just spent an age changing the dressings,' says Elaine.

'Ssh. Mr Kitson will hear you,' whispers Jan. What happens to such an instant, Miles wonders, what record is there of the momentary coincidence of all the elements that are there. Proctor cooling in his transported bed, Elaine and Jan on the shift together only because Nicola is to be a bridesmaid in Dargaville, the white gladioli stems with five buds still to open, the slight vibrato whistle of the birds in the heat mist underscored for Miles alone from the faint orchestra pit of his tinnitus. Often after such a day there comes in the evening a welcome drizzle which drifts and trembles in the failing light without ever leaving any trace of itself as rain.

Miles presses a key and begins to dictate the corporate structure that he wants for his new business in Indonesia. He wishes to carry his Board on the principle that stand-alone financial accountability is the best yardstick for measuring executive potential. Also he wants to be doing something unless the owl decides that it might be as well to take him while in the neighbourhood.

The orderly has arrived and Proctor is transferred to a trolley which squeaks cheerfully away down the corridor. 'Leave it to me, darling,' the orderly says. It won't hurt to follow him just a little, not to depress ourselves with the aftermath of Proctor's death, but rather see the misted grounds outside the corridor he travels. The corridor is long and narrow with many uniform windows on both sides, rather like a gutted railway carriage, and links ward seven with the main block. On the orderly's left – Proctor's too if you wish to be reminded – there are the dwarf conifers in the quartz pebble garden and on the right mainly *Scoliopius bigelovii* and ranunculus, which Kellie would tell us are prone to fungal blight after just such days as this. In the branches of a sycamore, just out of sight in the warm, gathering mist, is a canary which escaped from Mrs Wicks when she was cleaning the cage an hour ago. It adds nothing to the songs that Miles hears and Proctor is still relaxed enough about his death for his chin to quiver whenever the trolley jars over the joins in the flooring, almost as if he is attempting to join the orderly in a line or two of the Hoihos' hit of the moment – *Sure, all our friends are waiting in good old Half Moon Bay.*

Kellie is walking back to her car through the mist. Slaven goes in to see Miles. 'Fancy that,' he says. 'Kellie had just been arranging the flowers on his table and the next thing he was gone.' Jan stays a while in the ward to talk to Vincent and Mr Montgomery. Off-stage Mrs Wicks is weeping, because somewhere marooned in all the soft, massed vapour moving in from the sea, is her poor canary.

'Kellie came in before she left,' says Miles hoarsely.

'She finds you particularly interesting because of your money.'

'Is that it.'

'That's not quite how I meant it. To be fair, she hasn't any envious, or trivial, motive. It's psychological effects she finds fascinating; how it might influence a personality, a view of the world.'

'It means I don't have to be so accommodating, rather as some of those who have nothing decide they won't flatter, or appease anyone. At the two ends of the scale you see that, while the bulk of people are in between, oh, so very conscious of what and who can be to their advantage. To retain a conviction of freedom you should have nothing to lose, or so much that you don't believe it could ever happen.'

'That's what she senses, I think,' says Slaven.

'She brought me in two arum lilies and laughed when I said they had the stench of the funeral parlour. She said they weren't true lilies at all. I never knew that.' The two lily stems are on the bedside table, their great fluted, sari flowers

more arrogantly white than anything the hospital itself can provide, their yellow, parrot tongues upraised and the scent indeed crass and heavy.

Miles Kitson begins to revise his opinion of Slaven. He has begun to look forward to their talks and not just because there are so few he would choose for company within the hospital. Almost anyone would come in at his request. He realises that he is seeing a man in the process of metamorphosis, a change of priority and intention, although Slaven's commonplace exterior remains just the same. Well, almost the same. More and more there are times when his long, dentist's face loses its expression of habitual professional caution, becoming animated with the intensity of new ideas. There are times also when Miles is aware of a greenish haze, an emanation, around his friend's head, incongruous as a background to Slaven's black, pig-bristle hair, as you recall. Miles can't decide if this is some illusion arising from his own illness, an aura, or the lingering consequence of all that electricity suddenly surging through Slaven's middle-aged brain cells. 'When do you go home?' he asks him.

'Within a week I think. Dr Dunne said that I would have to keep on making out-patient visits for a while of course, but there's no need for me to be taking up a bed here for much longer.'

'I'm going myself soon, at least for a time. You won't be able to return to your practice though. Not with your hands.'

'No. I'll have an enforced lay-off for some time I suppose.' The old Slaven would have been very concerned about that; not just for selfish reasons, but from a reluctance to let down the many people he regularly cared for. But now there is a new willingness to let go of some responsibilities and so allow other opportunities to come within his grasp. 'I want to find out a lot more about people.'

'You want to save them, perhaps,' says Miles gravely and his eyelids fall closed in his delight at Slaven's ingenuous ambition.

'Come off it. What I think is that we've got to revitalise social action, have some concept of ourselves that's clear enough for us to charge the politicians with its accomplishment. We spend far too much time proving to each other that the process is tainted, rather than ensuring that the aim is pure.'

'So this is what you're going to tell people?'

'Government is just a process, not an end,' says Slaven. It is in time to become the first Slavenism.

'I like it,' says Miles. It isn't quite worthy of the energy to laugh aloud, but his breath comes more quickly and commensurate with that the scent of Kellie's arum lilies more strongly, so that for a moment he feels unpleasantly overpowered. 'Do you mind if I rest for a while now?' he asks Slaven and as his fellow patient is at the door, 'Is it still foggy? Is it raining?'

Through the window behind the bed, Slaven watches the mist unwind and stretch in the hospital gardens. Some billows are thicker than others so that there

are sudden scene changes, the grey forms of trees and buildings standing out for a moment and then so utterly erased. Where is the sycamore and the canary within it? Where in this drifting fiction, has the trolley borne our Proctor away?

When Slaven goes, Miles cannot sleep. Instead he activates his computer and begins a letter to Georgina – 'Aldous Slaven, the dentist, has decided to save the country.'

Φ

There is a place in the hills where no one wins farmer of the year; high up where the road is still unsealed and has bulges on its length occasionally so that if you're unlucky enough to meet something coming the other way it can be decided by eye contact and gross tonnage who will back down – and then back up. Much of the land has beaten its proprietors and so is given over to pine forest and if the stands are immature the pruned branches are rust filigree beneath the velvet green of the firs. The farm houses are weatherboard and the sheds mainly shot. The dogs are kennelled in a gully head where the mutton bones go to die and the white leghorns flap up into nooks of the equipment shed to roost, where they mute on the harnesses and the post-hole digger which have no other use. There are boxes and bags of apparently unused seed, but the birds and the mice have long since been in and all can be winnowed away. There's a tractor seat cover made from possum pelts and stirrup pumps that have never worked and refuse to start doing so now. In the shearing shed the wood is richly stained with fleece oil and dags and a little blood and sweat. A track winds over the gorse-covered top of the gully to the manuka country beyond and slopes of pigfern rooted over by the namesake, and screes of serpentine rock which make a cheap fence because the sheep will hardly cross and a high pond or two which you'd never know were there, but the stock tracks wind their way to them and the mallards which can be covered with a couple of guns. Pretty much dry country most of the time and the hack still better than the farm bike, but there are days when the cloud comes in, the gorse and briar glisten almost as much as the serpentine, the manuka stems gradually darken as the rain seeps through, the pigfern is bowed down by the weight of the drops it bears.

There are ridges and faces and gullies and spurs that don't appear on maps. They're given names by the family who have to climb them and when the people go they take away the names. There's a place where beech were sledded down to make their first houses and there's a place in the creek, a small falls, where the biggest boar was stuck whose tusks hang over the shearing shed and glint in the evening sun. No matter who does the muster, no matter how keen the dogs, there are a few old woollies on every place that never come down to the yards. But you know all that.

# Stuart Hoar 1993

*Stuart Hoar (b. 1957) has had eleven full-length stage plays produced, one of which has been published, and has written a number of radio plays and shorter stage plays. He has also published one novel.*

**IN** 1993 when he arrived in Dunedin to take up the Burns Fellowship, Stuart Hoar had established himself as an important new writer for the stage, having had four full-length stage plays produced in the previous six years after having previously written a number of radio plays. In his Burns year he wrote two new plays, both produced that year: *Not So Poor*, produced at Allen Hall Theatre in Dunedin, and *Yo Banfa*, a play about Rewi Alley in China.

The following excerpt is from the final scene in *Yo Banfa*, when Alley meets Mao Zedong for the first time and begins to see something of the nature of the man whose cause he has so long served.

## from *Yo Banfa*

(Later entitled *Gung Ho*)

Scene Twelve – Arrival and Departure.

REWI *and* AI-LING *enter, singing*:
We have come to Yan'an,
Having walked a thousand miles,
And seen much evil and greed.
Oh Singer of Songs,
Sing of the gallant dead,
Sing of those who fought
To change a corrupt society
With no thought of cost to themselves.
We live in such bitter times.
Oh Singer of Songs,
Record our despair,
Record our hope.
We have come to Yan'an.

*They stop.*

AI-LING: I have to say I'm not impressed. Yellow dust everywhere, and caves for houses. It doesn't look like the promised land to me.
REWI: This is a special valley, Ai-ling. You'll see.
AI-LING: I'm nervous. I've never met a lord before.
REWI: What lord?
AI-LING: The one you keep talking about. Lord Mao.
REWI: He's not a lord. He's just like you or me.
AI-LING: How can a master be like his servants? It doesn't make sense.
REWI: You don't understand. Things are different here. There are no more masters or servants.
AI-LING: Tell me then, who gives the orders in Yan'an? Who decides what the people do or don't do?
REWI: The party committees make the guiding decisions.
AI-LING: Ah ha. Then they are the masters here.
REWI: It is different here. You'll see.
AI-LING: I want to believe you, but everything seems just as it should be. I can see flies buzzing round a distant latrine. Yan'an shit smells like any other shit. This isn't a magic valley. (ZEDONG *enters*)
ZEDONG: Hello, hello, hello. You must be Rewi Alley. We need to talk of many

things, of your journeys in my old stamping ground of Jiangxi, your Indusco Co-ops, and the great and glorious cause of our shared ideas. You are welcome here, Rewi Alley.

REWI: Mao Zedong. I am greatly honoured to meet you.

ZEDONG: (Of AI-LING) And this good soul? Your wife, perhaps.

REWI: Oh no. This is my ideological companion and fellow traveller, Wang Ai-ling. Ai-ling, this is Mao Zedong.

AI-LING: This is the Lord Mao? (*She prostrates herself instantly*)

REWI: No Ai-ling, not –

ZEDONG: Ideological companion, eh?

REWI: Not necessary, Ai-ling. Truly.

AI-LING: This is correct form in my village.

ZEDONG: (*Bends down*) Up, up, Comrade Wang. I don't expect or want these forms.

AI-LING: (*Gets up*) But sir, you are the lord here.

ZEDONG: I represent a group of like-minded people, that's all. You two have obviously come a long way. Will you join me for a refreshing cup of tea?

AI-LING: I thank you for your kindness, sir.

ZEDONG: Comrade.

AI-LING: But you and Rewi will do all the talking.

ZEDONG: That's true but –

AI-LING: I would be embarrassed and bored.

ZEDONG: Nonetheless, I want you to drink my tea.

AI-LING: If that is your wish, sir –

ZEDONG: No, dammit! (*Controls himself*) That is my request.

REWI: Ai-ling would like to look around the town, Comrade Mao. She has walked half of China in search of her daughter.

ZEDONG: I won't expect your company, Comrade Wang, if you feel you have better things to do than take tea with Mao Zedong.

AI-LING: You are indeed a gracious lord, Lord Mao.

ZEDONG: (*Tightly*) Off you go then, Comrade Wang. We will have to have a serious chat – but not now. Off you go.

AI-LING: Thank you sir. (*She bows and goes*)

ZEDONG: There, you see, Rewi? A good person infected with a light dose of petit bourgeois immorality. What does her daughter look like?

REWI: Young. Dark eyes. Black hair.

ZEDONG: Could be anyone. (*Takes his arm*) We must talk, Rewi Alley. You interest me. You are English, I believe?

REWI: I'm from New Zealand.

ZEDONG: Dutch?

REWI: English dependency in the South Pacific.

ZEDONG: Of course. I recall now. A pleasant place, I've read.

REWI: Not particularly.

ZEDONG: No? I thought –

REWI: It's a trader's world built on nothing but considerations of immediate profit. I went back a few years ago. It was like going to Mars. The people there consider their affluence a virtue, their virtue as a people is that shallow.

ZEDONG: Sad.

REWI: I'm possibly being unfair. But those were my feelings.

ZEDONG: So, so. You make a career out of your unfair feelings here in China. I'm interested in your Gung Ho co-ops. I want some started here in Yan'an.

REWI: Yes, I'm here to –

ZEDONG: I want to see how far they grow before they self-destruct.

REWI: What?

ZEDONG: Come, come, don't be offended.

REWI: Gung Ho is working.

ZEDONG: It's a good idea built on sand. War refugees and capitalist-sanctioned loans. For the real good co-ops to germinate they will all wither and die.

REWI: Gung Ho is inspired by the Red Army!

ZEDONG: Inspired and supported by us all. It is all most interesting.

REWI: But –

ZEDONG: Come, come, you are a realist. Some people, the people you precisely attempt to reform, will not be reformed.

REWI: I can't believe you say this.

ZEDONG: I don't mean to offend you, Comrade.

REWI: As from a great height you stand there and piss warmly on my life's work in China.

ZEDONG: I respect your work. I don't eulogise it. I see contradictions in Gung Ho.

REWI: I know what you see. A white man doing good. That is your contradiction.

ZEDONG: No, Rewi, a good man doing bad.

REWI: I don't accept this.

ZEDONG: That's your choice.

REWI: No! This is my right. I am working with the people –

ZEDONG: Gung Ho is like a play on stage. The actors are working hard and the audience is straining to repay the work with good will. But the theatre is patrolled by government guards, anxious to ensure that, whatever happens on stage, no harm will come to the theatre. The guards pay the actors to demonstrate the reality of the play-acting. They don't pay the actors to burn down the theatre.

REWI: The play is still real.

ZEDONG: We must remake the theatre. Reality, economic reality is not objective. It is in our hands to remake it.

REWI: We have changed the lives of thousands of people.

ZEDONG: And it is your work alone, Rewi Alley. The solitary effort of your

passionate New Zealand fairness. I love you for it. What more can I say? It just isn't enough. (REWI *turns away, deeply hurt*) Please, I don't say this to hurt you intentionally.

REWI: I've heard you are a man of great qualities. I didn't expect great cynicism however.

ZEDONG: I resent that!

REWI: Good. I said it to hurt you intentionally.

ZEDONG: Fool. We are slipping into personal invective. Goddammit, I'm not cynical! (*He sings*)

So much work to do
For a man, for many people.
The world turns ceaselessly,
Oceans clash and continents move
With irresistible force.
We have no time, no time.
We can't wait a thousand years.
Seize the day, seize the hour.
Let us rid the world of pests!

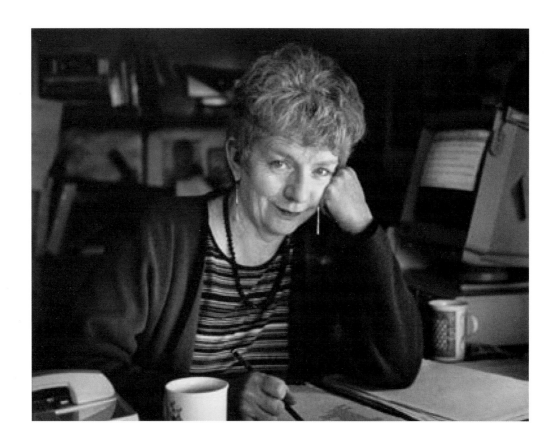

# CHRISTINE JOHNSTON 1994

**CHRISTINE** Johnston, after having some short stories broadcast and published, made a striking debut as a novelist with *Blessed Art Thou Among Women* (1991), which won the Heinemann Reed Fiction Award. In her Burns year she wrote a second novel, 'Settlers', but it remains unpublished. That year she also wrote some short stories, some of which were broadcast and/or collected in *The End of the Century* in 1999, and an autobiographical essay for an anthology of essays by Catholic writers. An excerpt from the first part of this essay follows.

*Christine Johnston (b. 1950) has published two novels for adults, three novels for adolescents and a collection of short stories. She has also edited an anthology of writing about Dunedin.*

# FROM **First Words**

*Scenes from a Catholic Girlhood 1*

*Do you renounce Satan?* asks the priest.

*We do renounce him*, we answer without hesitation.

*And all his works?*

*We do renounce them.*

*And all his pomps?*

*We do renounce them.*

At the back of the cathedral Satan lurks, riffling through the pamphlets, as if he might be about to purchase an encyclical or a monograph on the evils of communism. As if.

He is crestfallen. His tail protrudes dejectedly from under his coat – a black gabardine, nicely cut but a little shiny, not too unlike those worn by clerics. Renounced again. Evidently he had entertained hopes, expectations of this bunch of little Coughlins, Caseys and O'Sheas, Flanagans and Finnegans. Were they not, some of them, children of mixed marriages, and was it not a fact that their faith was consequently diluted?

Realistically, though, the chances were slim that one of them would stand up and say no, I do not renounce him, I embrace the horned one, I take him to my heart. Satan knows he has time on his side, but can't help feeling miffed. Renounced again. And all his works. And all his pomps. Out of sheer spite he spirits the meagre 1/6 from out of the poor box and pockets it without so much as a screwdriver. To hell with the lot of them!

*Scenes from a Catholic Girlhood 2*

It is almost midnight. Outside on the porch of the cathedral a brazier burns. Close by stand the bishop and his priests, dressed extravagantly – on this chilly autumn night in 1950s Dunedin – in vestments, embroidered with letters of the Greek alphabet and other symbols, worn over long white surplices. The traffic on Rattray Street is not heavy. Latterly the cable cars have been replaced by trolley buses, but at this hour there is only the occasional car.

(What those motorists thought or said if they glanced up at the spectacle outside the Catholic cathedral is not known to the writer at the time of writing. It may have been something to the effect that those crazy micks were at it again, dressing up and running around with candles. Or it may have seemed that the Roman Church was indeed The Antichrist, alive and well and living in Dunedin, under the very noses of Presbyterian elders, practising some hocus-pocus (from the Latin – the most sacred words of the Mass – *hoc est enim corpus meum*),

quasi-satanic rites right there on Rattray Street. More likely the scene elicited a shrug of incomprehension. In this day and age, Mrs Dunedin might have commented, I'm amazed they can be bothered.)

The oversized candle, blessed and decorated on Holy Thursday, is lit. Members of the congregation are gathered at a respectful distance. In the background the choir of skirted seminarians intones a Gregorian chant. There is an organised movement towards the large wooden doors and into the darkened cathedral where the congregation fills up the seats at the back.

The Singer Priest enters carrying the lighted Easter candle.

*Ecce lumen Christi*, he chants, moving slowly up the aisle towards the altar. The only light comes from the flickering flame.

*Ecce lumen Christi* (Behold the light of Christ), again on the higher note.

*Ecce lumen Christi* for the third time.

The parishioners' candles are illuminated from the Easter candle, the flame passing from man to woman to child along the rows. The celebration of the resurrection continues.

*Scenes from a Catholic Girlhood 3*

We were to form a 'guard of honour' on the steps of the cathedral after the funeral. The phrase was baffling. Hitherto, 'guards' had been associated with prisons, cowboys and Indians and the anti-German war games that had persisted in the playground.

We had lost a classmate, one of the Lebanese boys, who had been run over. I think he was hit by a car backing out of a driveway on the main street, but I can't be sure. It may be that I had been warned so often to be vigilant about those narrow driveways that I assumed he had died in that way. Or perhaps the story of his fatal accident was subsequently told as a cautionary tale. I was not entirely sure of his identity. (The boy I thought was him – a cousin perhaps – returned to school the following week, which was disconcerting.) We must have been about eight years old.

So we stand on the steps as the little coffin is brought out and carried down to the hearse. We have been singing. The pallbearers are prominent members of the Lebanese community, their swarthy complexions an unwelcome reminder that not all the world looks like us. As the coffin is eased into the hearse, the boy's mother begins to wail. She calls out for her baby to be brought back. We all turn to stare at the woman who is being restrained by relatives, but who continues to demand the return of her child.

It is for me a supremely terrible moment, the like of which I have never experienced. Never before have I seen an adult in the throes of grief and I will never forget the mother of the Lebanese boy. Later I will come to realise that it

is not at all common to witness such paroxysms. It is an education to see love so profoundly felt, to see a grown-up person so forget herself in front of people who know her and those who are perfect strangers. It inspires respect – for the boy whose face I cannot recall, for the woman whose name I do not know.

*Scenes from a Catholic Girlhood 4*

Priests come to visit us from time to time. To see them up close and without the vestments, the white surplice with the lacework and the long black cassock, is interesting. Some dress quite elegantly, their suits and coats tailor-made. Father X who is tall with delicate features wears a cream tasselled silk scarf which I covet as I hang it on a hook in the hallway. Although somewhat severe and otherworldly in church, he can laugh in a girlish way. Once he calls when my mother is baking. He comments on the biscuits which are waiting on the oven tray, the uncooked mixture neatly pressed down with a fork.

She asks him if he likes the raw mixture and he replies, doesn't everybody? She offers him the tray and he takes one and eats it. She presses him and he takes another. Father laughs and we all laugh, although to us children it is the most extraordinary thing, a kind of holy communion in reverse.

*Scenes from a Catholic Girlhood 5*

*Remember, man, that thou art dust and unto dust thou shalt return.*

The priest makes a smudge on my forehead with his thumb. It is not dust but ashes of macrocarpa from Mrs W's hedge, substituted for palm fronds and used during the Palm Sunday ceremony of the previous year. (Our climate does not afford us palm trees.)

We wear the mark all day even if we go down town. It is Ash Wednesday and Lent has begun. The plaster Virgin and Saint Joseph are shrouded in purple, as blank as Easter Island faces. Adults endure a regime of fasting which prohibits morning and afternoon teas and we give up sweets till Easter Sunday.

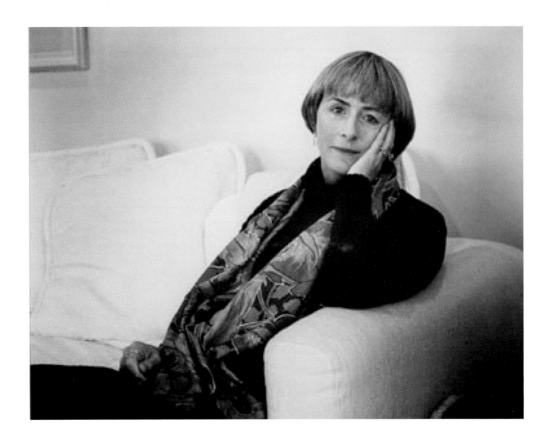

# ELSPETH SANDYS 1995

*Elspeth Sandys (b. 1940) has published eight novels and two collections of short stories. She has also written a number of dramatic works for stage, film, radio and television, and regularly writes for BBC Radio.*

**WHEN** she assumed the Burns Fellowship in 1995, Elspeth Sandys had been a full-time writer-editor for more than twenty years, in England and since 1989 in New Zealand. She had published four novels and a collection of short stories and had also written for stage, radio, television and film. During her Burns year, her fifth novel *River Lines* was published, but it had been written earlier. She has described her Burns year as a fruitful one: 'Looking back I have to say 1995 was the most productive year of my writing life, seeding a number of works that were published in the years that followed. Oh to have another year like that!'[63] She wrote a final draft of her sixth

novel, *Riding to Jerusalem* (1996), and worked on her seventh, *Enemy Territory* (1997), as well as some of the short stories that were to go into her second collection, *Standing in Line*, which won the Elena Garro PEN International Prize in 2003 and was published in 2006. The following story is from that collection.

## Swimming Away

It was a place where we'd been happy before: a beach, shaded by bowing pohutakawas, bordered at either end by domesticated hills. Close to the shore, but too far away to swim to, was an island that seemed, like the hills, to represent tranquil domesticity. You could see the solitary farmhouse, with its fringe of trees, and the wooden jetty carving its modest path through the water. And you could see, behind the farmhouse, snaking over the hills, the neat, confining fences. Perhaps it was the sense of order that drew us there that day: the visible proof that the terror of the bush, the unpredictable violence of the sea, could be contained. Other places were darker, wilder; more suited to our restless imaginations. But the beach, which I shall call Serenity Bay, though that is not its name, was where we'd agreed – how rare it was by then to agree – to spend the day.

'Shall I make sandwiches, or shall we …?'

My question petered out. Decisions had become like high jumps, the bar placed higher each time the need to confer arose. Neither of us, by that time, could express a preference for fear of offending – or, worse, provoking – the other. We couldn't even decide when to go to the supermarket anymore. 'There's fish in the freezer,' Harold would say. 'We can last another day.' The fact that the fish in the freezer was mullet, which he had caught and inadequately gutted, lay between us like the memory of a quarrel. He knew I disliked mullet, especially when it came with bits of gut still attached. *I* knew if I suggested an alternative, he would act as if he hadn't heard me; as if I were a whining child to be ignored.

Harold was convinced he was dying. He had had pains; there had been tests; but the results were inconclusive. All we had to go on was advice; medical advice. Harold should stop smoking. He should stop drinking. He should try to relax.

The third piece of advice was why we were here, at Serenity Bay, an icebox packed with beer and sandwiches (I had made *that* decision unilaterally!) on the sand beside us.

I reached for Harold's hand. I could feel his fear through his skin. In his mind he was already staring death in the face, and as he looked – glanced – at me, I could sense his hatred. I was younger. I didn't smoke. I drank only in moderation. I knew how to relax. How could I, with all those advantages, possibly understand?

There was so much I wanted to say to him. The fact that I could remember how it was when we were in love surely meant love was there still: that it could be revived. But words need breath to speak them, breath to get over that high jump, and I didn't have that much breath in my body.

'It's beautiful here,' I said instead. And for a moment it seemed my words had been the right ones. Harold raised himself on one elbow, looked at the island, and in a gush of words, as unexpected as it was welcome, said, 'There was a murder committed on that island. Over a hundred years ago now. A Maori worker killed his boss. It was a sensation at the time. The Maori was backward, or said to be. In other versions of the story it was claimed he was in love with his boss's wife.'

Listening to him, squinting at the island whose shadow rimmed the water like lace, I fell into a familiar enchantment. A decade ago Harold had wooed and won me with the brilliance of his storytelling. But for the last year and a half the stories had stopped. I was no longer a fit audience. I could not take away his fear of death.

'Why haven't you told me this before?' I asked.

'It's an old story. Everyone knows it,' he answered.

'What happened to the Maori?'

'He was hung.'

'Was he guilty?'

'Oh yes. According to the prosecution he killed a man, a white man, who had shown him nothing but kindness, treated him as one of the family.'

'Is that what you believe?'

Harold's eyes held mine. I put my hand on his chest. In the past that would have been the moment when we ran into the water to make love in the waves. But what I saw in his eyes then was not desire, but a sorrow so profound it entered my soul like the knowledge of evil. Was he sad because he no longer loved me? Or was he sad because his life – lived, as I knew to my cost, at several removes from the people in it – was drawing to a close? Just as, perhaps, thinking of the passionate young Maori whose rage had cost him his life, he understood, too late for it to make a difference, how his life might have been lived.

I don't know what thoughts swam behind those eyes of his I only know what happened next.

'I think I'll go for a swim,' he said.

'I'll come with you.'

'No!' His voice was harsh. It dropped like a stone into the hollow he had opened in my heart. 'I won't be long,' he said, quietly, as if apologising.

I watched him walk into the timid waves. He was not a strong swimmer, but the sea that day was calm, the sand warm between our toes. He walked like a man under sentence of death; head down, feet turned inward as if to deny their progress towards oblivion. He didn't look back. I stood at the edge of the water and watched his flailing arms; his grey head twisting this way and that as he fought for breath.

He'd been swimming for about three minutes when I could stand it no longer. I dived into the silky water and set off in pursuit of him. I'm a strong swimmer. Within a matter of seconds I'd drawn abreast of him. At which point he

turned and gave me a look of such malevolence it took my breath away, literally. I slid under the water like a stone. When I emerged, coughing and spluttering, he was already on his way back to the shore, arms flailing, grey head twisting this way and that.

Three days later he left me. There was no note, no explanation. He was there, and then he was gone. Like a stone tossed into the water.

# BERNADETTE HALL 1996

*Bernadette Hall (b. 1945) has published seven collections of poetry, co-edited an anthology of Canterbury poems, edited a selection of poems by Joanna Margaret Paul, and written several unpublished radio and stage plays.*

**BERNADETTE** Hall did not begin publishing poetry until she was in her forties, but she had had three collections published by the time she was appointed Burns Fellow late in 1995. She describes her Burns year as follows:

My mother, who had lived with our family in Christchurch for her last twenty years, died on Christmas Eve, her eighty-fifth birthday, in 1995 just before I took up the Burns Fellowship in 1996, I took her ashes to Dunedin with me and laid them to rest in my father's grave in the Southern Cemetery. The poems in

Still Talking are a record of the conversation I continued to have with my mother throughout the Fellowship year. They are songs of loss and argument and, of course, of love. 'Duck' was recognised as a love poem by Lauris Edmond, who included it in her anthology *New Zealand Love Poems*.[64]

Hall selected for this book two poems from *Still Talking*:

# Duck

there's a duck on the road
its head sticking out of the shiny dark
twisting like a tap turned on turned off

it's hurt, it's stuck
on the thin white line that divides
four lanes of manic traffic

why did the duck cross the road?
because she thought she had to
because her mother had done it before
because she didn't think
because she didn't think she had to think
because she was hungry

onoff onoff onoff

consider for a moment
the domestic situation of the duck:
the rough nip on the neck the bluster
the headshove under water
the fluster and wing flap indignant
the flash of an indigo armband

why did she fall for it this time?
the fat wibble wobble of a batty criss cross trundle
on the Main South Road, ten little Speights babies
left tweedling on the thick brown skin of the river
she didn't know / oh yes she did
oh no she didn't / too right she did
she knew damned well and she should have known better

onoff onoff onoff

someone's got to do something
oh yeah! she's made her bed and now she'll have to lie in it
you'd be far better off to whack her on the head
and put her out of her misery
just how much can you afford to invest in a duck anyway?

this is a classic film noir
one of us is the femme fatale
one is the chap's best friend
I just wish I could remember the ending!

I'm a gymnast on a narrow beam
I ride the slipstream of hot metal
it's wet, the road is slippery
people are in a hurry to get home
I'm a collapsing Z

I grab the duck

      the twiggy cretonne feathers scissorslip
      a bit I dig harder into her hot gut the way
      I would if I was stuffing her before basting

I wrench her off the road

      dumb demure dappling     her neck wobbling
      away from me     her open beak     her dribble

I hold up the duck like a trophy

WOMAN KILLED IN RUSH HOUR TRAFFIC
SHE WAS TAKING HER LIFE IN HER HANDS
SHE WAS HOLDING A DUCK IN HER HANDS
SHE WAS OLD ENOUGH TO KNOW BETTER

all the way home I crash the gears crying
and I rush into the house to get a blanket
and the others say what's wrong
and I say I've got a runover duck in the car
and I need a blanket and they all start to laugh
and make helpful suggestions like

it won't make any difference
I've got more to worry about than a bloody duck
it'll be dead by now anyway and there's no room
left in the garden to bury things, god almighty,
we've already got two dogs, three mice, five goldfish
and the rabbit buried there, what more do you want?

and they're right of course
when I go out to bring her in
she's dead

*aue! aue!* what will I do with you, *my own aisling?*

Queen of Spades in a brown tweed coat,
rocky skimmer in scungy water, corky decoy,
topsy turvy lady of dibble and dabble, mud shoveller,
funny puddler, silly quack quack

## Poem in the Matukituki Valley

I know some things
like you'd rather have seen a rotary
clothesline in my garden than roses

and when I dedicated my book of poems
to you, you hammed it up, mock horror,
with 'Jesus, what next!'

So coming down from the mountains,
when Rae asked me what you would have thought
of it all, the grandeur, the excess,

the jade water, the yellow starred flats,
the black peaks with snow like orca leaping,
I had to say that I didn't have a clue,

perhaps something like *what a fuss about nothing!*

and now at night, as the comet works its way
across the greybright sky, I see no sign
that you like Caesar have become a god,

you are far too reliable to be a god,

but rather the gauzy face of a woman,
hair streaming, running with a baby in her arms,
saving me again and again from the burning house.

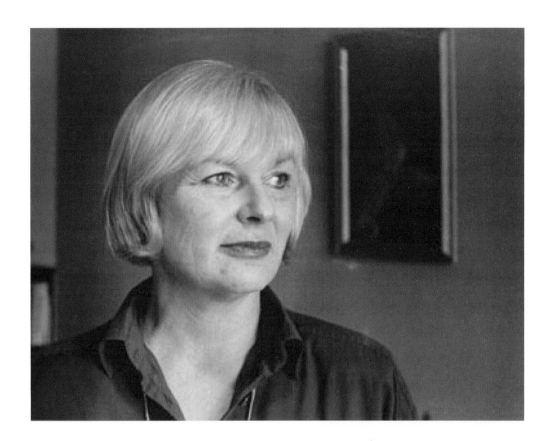

PADDY
RICHARDSON 1997

**PADDY** Richardson had published a short-story collection, *Choices* (1986), when she was appointed Burns Fellow. During the year she wrote the title story and others for her 2003 collection, *If We Were Lebanese*. However her focus was her novel, *The Company of a Daughter* (2000), represented below by an extract with her contextualisation:

*Paddy Richardson (b. 1950) has published one novel and two collections of stories and has a second novel appearing in 2008.*

*The Company of a Daughter* depicts both a physical journey where the major character, Zoe, travels back to her grandmother's house in Northland and an inner journey wherein she recalls her family's stories. In the extract below she first reaches the Hokianga.[65]

# FROM *The Company of a Daughter*

*5*

Hokianga. The returning place.

'At the first glimpse of those heads from the sea, one is white, the other black.'

I stand on the beach looking across at the contrast of light and shade and think of Augustus Earle's description, made as they sailed across the bar into the harbour, as he first caught sight of this land.

This is not only the returning place but a place of beginning since this is where Kupe, our first settler landed. There at the entrance to this vast harbour are the South and North Heads, Kupe's mokaikai, his pets, the taniwha, Araiteuru and Niua, left behind to protect this place for him and to guide other travellers in. There across the water are the ridged slabs of rock forming a dark verge between sea and land. When Kupe landed here he sent his slaves across the hills for these rocks so that mussels would grow on them and be harvested by his people. Here in Hokianga, Kupe left his footmarks on the coast near to the Heads, the bailer of his canoe at Kohukohu, the anchor near to the narrows at Rangiora, his canoe at Rangi Point, the resting place, where it was dragged into a secret stone cave. Here he left his child, Tuputupuwhenua.

These are the stories.

And I am overcome by this storehouse of myth and beauty. By the resplendent sea, brazen in its cloak of sapphire, sad grey-blue and shadings of dark and pale jade. By the sun-slashed sky, by the soar of cloud at the far end of the harbour. By the sandhills, those vast stretches of tawdry copper with their shaded pockets of cinnamon and taupe.

In the evening the sea is slate, the sandhills almond. I watch a woman with a plait down her back fishing from the jetty and listen to the sea slap against the sand. I feel the wind coming in from the harbour soft on my face, smell the salt and taste it in my mouth.

'Aunty. I'm goin' in the pub, Aunty.'

He is standing beside the shop, calling at the door.

She comes outside and stands over him.

'You 'lowed?'

'Cos I've been in there before, Aunty.'

I watch him run across the carpark, push in through the doors.

It's all that is left here now: the store, the pub, the school, the sea, sky and hills, the people and the stories.

At one time there could be thirty sailing ships in the harbour coming in over the bar from the ocean. They came for whale-oil, for loads of timber. Sailed up mangrove-fringed rivers, with the rise of bush so thick on either side the sun could scarcely pierce through. And then, when the kauri was gone they burned

the land, blazing away the bush so that the ridges were exposed like bones, the soil burnt the colour of dried blood. This is a place of fortune and misfortune, beauty and grandeur and ugliness and loss. Across the harbour, buried in the sandhills are the bones of the ancestors, scattered in the hills are the ruins of houses and churches, forgotten settlements. The land has been fought and cheated for, burned and pillaged and abandoned. The settlers' vision was the potential wealth to be mined from the land and the sea. The missionaries' concern was with the mining of souls.

I watch the sky streak pink scarlet and yellow. Listen to the silence, the slapping of the waves. See the creeping dark, wonder at the anguish over land and souls, gardens built then abandoned. The births, battles and death.

Now there's a battle over at the pub. They spill out, shouting from the bar and huddle closely at the top of the steps underneath the lights. I see three men scuffle, trying to hold somebody. A woman is screaming.

'Bloody wanker.'

'Leave him alone. Bastards. Fucking leave him alone.'

It all comes to nothing. The held man is shoved down the steps and the others yell at him to piss off, just piss off home. He stands, swaying at the bottom of the steps, moves forward to go back in, thinks better of it then turns and walks down towards the sea, slumps there on a bench.

A woman comes from the pub. She stands beside him.

'I told you. Told you to leave it.'

His head is bent and ashamed.

'I told you. I told you. Stupid bastard.'

He is silent and she stands over him watching.

'What're you doing?'

He looks up at her, 'Just sitting here. Just watching the harbour.'

She stares down, then sits beside him. Her body is upright, removed from his. They are both silent, watching. He takes her hand.

I also watch this stretch of sea. I think of Eliza, five months on ship then journeying, seven months pregnant, through mud and scrub and bush. To save souls.

I think of my own life of desires and loves and losses, of nurturing and neglect.

*I have done those things I ought not to have done and left undone those things I ought to have done.*

*And there is no health in me.*

It is a sentiment which fascinated me during my brief sojourn into the premises of Sunday School and the church. I liked to say it, that pleasingly resonant assonance of the not, ought and done. I liked the complicated syntax, liked the idea of myself pleading for mercy, eyes closed, hands devoutly clasped. The small sinner in the beribboned sailor hat.

But the words return to me. The things I have done. The things I have not done.

And there is no health in me.

I'm preoccupied by waste. By the waste of discarded aspirations, forgotten desires, loves. Lost gardens and lost battles. I try to comfort myself with the idea that it's the living of it, the doing, that is most important, but still it's the end product I find myself most concerned with. What am I? Where do I belong? What have I achieved?

Still, I sleep with the mutter of sea beneath my window. Sleep held, warmed and enclosed by Eliza's hills, rocked, lulled by her ocean.

I am the only guest at breakfast. As I eat, the woman who manages the hotel asks if I've been disturbed by noise from the bar.

'No, it's not too bad,' I say.

'It might be bad tonight,' she warns, 'It's Thursday. Benefit day. They come to celebrate. It gets pretty rowdy. We could move you to one of the units around the back if you like.'

But I like my room at the front of the hotel, close to the road and looking out to the sea. The night sounds, sea sounds, the birds.

'No. It'll be okay. If it gets too bad I'll just turn up the TV.'

She looks doubtful, 'Don't say I didn't warn you. You look a bit, uh, refined for the kind of row we have on Thursday night. On holiday are you?'

'Yes. And a bit of research as well.'

She's worried, 'You going to write something about staying here? About the hotel?'

'No. My family came from around here. I just wanted to come back. Find out what I could.'

She looks relieved, 'There's the information place just down the road. They've got quite a lot about the history of the place.' She laughs, 'Thought you might be writing about us. Or about all those marijuana plantations we've got hidden around here.'

'I've heard about those,' I say. 'Is it true people are making their fortunes up here?'

'If they are I haven't heard about them. Seen anyone around here who looks like they might've got a fortune stashed away?'

I think of the rusted cars, the old motorbikes filling the carpark, the modest little houses and shacks lining the road and I shake my head and laugh with her.

'Oh it's there,' she said. 'It's there all right. But nobody from around here makes anything out of it. Nobody I know. They might sell a bit but mostly they just smoke it. I won't let them have it here, though. I warned someone just last week. He was sitting out in the beer garden smoking it and I warned him but the silly bugger wouldn't listen to me so I threw a bucket of water over him.'

She is small, Pakeha. I'm amazed by her daring. The men I've seen around the

pub are huge, tattooed, dressed in leather.

'My God, weren't you afraid of starting a riot?'

'Nuh. They respect us. Have to. Nothing worse around here than being banned from the pub. And if there's any trouble the locals support us.'

It's hot again. I take a book and walk along the beach, lie on a stretch of sand and feel it heating my bare arms and legs. I stretch out on my stomach, digging with my toes into the sand, resting my head on my hands and close my eyes.

I came here once with Evie, in a bus jolting endlessly, it seemed to me, over narrow gravel roads. It was hot and the dust rose in clouds from the wheels, filling my mouth. Evie had to ask the driver to stop so I could be sick in the ditch.

We stayed at the old hotel. The imposing old wooden one with the balconies and verandahs that burned down.

Every day we went down to the beach. Evie would spread out a blanket near the edge of the water in the shade of the pines. She sat there reading while I swam and built sandcastles. Most days she came swimming with me – *A dip in the tide* she called it. She wore an old knitted black bathing suit. When it was wet it sagged over her bony shoulders and ribs, around her straight skinny hips. She swam silently and methodically, arms perfectly curved and legs straight, the way she taught me. When she'd swum out to the buoy and back she would turn over and lie motionless with her eyes closed, her hair billowing around her head. I would swim and dive and burrow around her.

# 1998– 1999

## MICHAEL KING

*Michael King (1945–2004) published thirty-nine books of non-fiction, mostly as sole writer, sometimes as editor.*

**BY** the time Michael King became a Burns Fellow he was already a national institution, the author of over thirty books of New Zealand biography, history, current affairs, landscape, Maori and Pakeha culture, and autobiography. He had entered a new area of research with his literary biography of Frank Sargeson in 1995, and this moved Janet Frame to agree for him to write her biography. King received the Burns Fellowship in 1998 and the first half of 1999 specifically to write the biography after almost three years of research. His book duly appeared to great acclaim (and some controversy) in 2000 as *Wrestling with the Angel: A Life of Janet Frame*, winning the Deutz Medal for Non-

fiction at the Montana New Zealand Book Awards. It was followed by a condensed and photo-centred brief life, *An Inward Sun: The World of Janet Frame,* in 2002.

The following extract from chapter six of *Wrestling with the Angel* is the editor's choice for personal reasons that need explanation. In 1998 I was writing an entry on the Janet Frame story 'Swans' for an American reference book, and, in making photocopies of a draft of the article, accidentally left the original in the photocopier. Someone found it, assumed it was Michael King's (since it was not signed) and put it in his Burns Fellow mailbox. He recognised it as mine and returned it to me along with a note and a page or so of his draft of chapter six dealing with the origins of 'Swans'. I had assumed that, like most of the other stories in the volume *The Lagoon,* it had been written in 1946. However, as the extract shows, it had been written two years later, a year after the death of Isabel Frame in February 1947. I had written that the story was built on the implicit contrast between the innocent and timeless world of the children and the world of time and death of which they were not yet aware, but I had not related it to the death of Isabel. Michael King let me use the material he had on the story's origins if I would let him adapt a phrase or two from my reading of it.

The extract with its footnotes illustrates clearly how King used the great asset he had in Janet Frame's unpublished letters. He combined this material with information gained from other sources – in this case the hospital notes – to tell a story that no one, including Janet Frame herself, had seen in its entirety before, an achievement of creative selection and synthesis.

FROM *Wrestling with the Angel*

'Dostoevsky and Rilke are dear friends,' she told [John] Money by letter in August 1948, 'though I do puzzle. When I read them I become more acutely alive … I do not live here with these people, yet I do.'[i] Frame had Grete Christeller to thank for her new awareness of the German lyric poet Rainer Maria Rilke. Christeller had lent her volumes of Rilke's poetry in translation, which led Frame to buy her own copy of *Sonnets to Orpheus,* in which the poet had attempted to discover 'a satisfactory spiritual position amid the decay of reality'.[ii] Frame devoured the work greedily, recognising that its preoccupations were similar to her own, and that its expression was powerful and reverberative. She quoted to John Money:

*Be not afraid of suffering, render
heaviness back to the earth again;
mountains are heavy, and seas, and the tender
trees that in childhood you set in their places
have grown too heavy for you to sustain.
Ah, but the breezes … Ah, but the spaces ….*[iii]

Commenting on this stanza, she wrote: 'We are the children and we run about with worlds on our shoulders, little Atlases and not knowing, taking trees in our finger, saying stay there, tree, and the tree stays, even the giant fir and oak. Can one in childhood catch the other side of heaviness, seas flowing like light and mountains wavering delicate as shadows? … My friend, you see the struggle in me between body and mind.'[iv]

Part of that struggle was externalised in Frame's ambivalence about the happiness of her surviving sister. In May 1948 June Frame had married Wilson Gordon, whom she had met the previous year at Otago University. He was a gentle man, twelve years her senior, who had been interned for four years during the war as a conscientious objector. For the first four months of their married life the Gordons rented rooms in North Dunedin, then shifted to Auckland in September. 'I do not confide in my sister now, though she confides in me,' Frame wrote to John Money in August. '[She] and Wilson are very happy and I love them very much. But when she takes his hand or touches him, something, a despair strikes me for I know that I will never be able to touch the man that I think of … I want the sun, somebody warm to touch and know, and make me feel that I am a wanted plant, not one of the lost seeds sprouting by mistake in a desert of ice and snow.'[v]

Nor was she unmindful of that other sister, lost the previous year. In July she had sent Money another story, 'Swans', to be added to the collection that Caxton would publish. It arose from the death of one of the Eden Street cats and an early family visit to the beach.[vi] But like so many of the stories that would appear in her first book it was a suggestive exploration of innocence and experience, a juxtaposition of the timeless world of childhood with the adult world of time and death. In a subsequent letter to Money, in August 1948, Frame explained how 'Swans' came to be written:

*The last thing I ever want to be is literary. I write … because I am scared and haunted and lonely and in love and full of wonder …. I am not thinking of what I shall say, in fact I do not remember how I manage to say anything. I remember being haunted, and very often the original haunting is scarcely recognisable in what has been written – unless of course you … have the clues. In ['Swans'], the original haunting does not appear on the surface at all. I had been feeling a bit lonely for Isabel, and I kept seeing her as a child, outside a country store and lost. I do not consciously remember her ever having been lost in that way, but the vivid imagery persisted. There was the store, you know country stores, the fly-dirt on the window and a dead fat blow-fly lying just inside, and the empty packets of food and the sham chocolates …. And outside there was a little fair-haired girl crying because she was lost. Nobody in the street, and the grey telegraph poles eaten by borer. And the wind high-up, talking through the wires. I saw it vividly and I sat down and wrote, feeling sad because of Isabel's being lost, and my unconscious very kindly took us for a day at the beach, and sneaked in the sadness with the dead cat and the wrong sea, and the father away at work, not sharing and not knowing. And so on. That is how the story gets written. I am interested to see how … June's marriage will find its way on paper …. I have been rather haunted, change and all that, and I am interested to see what kind of literary bread is baked when the haunting goes pop pop.[vii]*

'Swans', which Money forwarded to Glover at Caxton, was the last of the stories to be written for Frame's first book. Nearly two months later, instead of more stories, Frame had disturbing news for her expatriate friend. Even though her brother had moved, temporarily, to Australia, she was still finding life at Willowglen wearing. So for some weeks she had been sleeping away from the house, in a tent under pine trees on the property. From there she had visited the monthly mental clinic at Oamaru Hospital, which she had agreed to do at the time she left Sunnyside. She told Money what occurred early in October:

*I was scared of course and didn't say much and got in a bit of a panic. This doctor has communicated with Sunnyside and they have decided that I should not be free, that I should have some further kind of treatment. The doctor has told my parents that my mental state is serious, that I am not well enough to be admitted to Seacliff as a voluntary boarder, and that my parents should commit me without delay …. I don't care where I go or what happens to me for I am sane, I am terribly sane, so much so that it looks to other people like insanity …. [So] they are taking me away to Seacliff. How strange … I do not feel that I shall lose any freedom there, for I have discovered that my freedom is within me and nothing can destroy it, and I remember Pierre in Tolstoy's* War and Peace, *how he was a prisoner and looked out of the window and laughed and laughed because the world was inside him, his own ….*[viii]

It was dangerous to bandy about literary allusions in dealings with the mental hospital system. The following day, for the second time in her life, Frame was formally committed to Seacliff Hospital. And one of the general practitioners who signed the medical certificate noted gravely that 'she says she is a lot of people …. One of the persons is Pierre.'[ix] The other doctor identified her as a 'student' who was mentally ill because of 'competition and overwork for exams' – and this almost four years after she had sat her last examination. Such misunderstandings were possible because Frame did not cooperate with interrogation.[x] The second doctor went on to report that, when asked where she lived, the patient had replied, 'in the world'. When asked if this meant that she lived in China, she replied, 'at times'.[xi] Lottie Frame was persuaded to sign the application for committal and declared that she did so 'on advice of medical authorities and of Dr McLachlan … so that she will have to remain in Mental Hospital to have treatment completed'.[xii]

Frame arrived at Seacliff on the afternoon of 9 October. Admission notes state that she had been asked to return as a voluntary boarder but had been 'too mentally ill to appreciate her obligations …. When questioned she repeated … 'There's nothing to say, there's nothing to say' …. She recognised the Hospital as Seacliff and admitted that she had previously been here …. When asked about hallucinations patient replied, 'I'll be silly if I tell you what I hear. You would not let me go home.' When she finally talked freely, patient's conversation revealed

the extent of her illness. 'I am in all places and I am everywhere. I find every place interesting' …. Patient is suffering from Schizophrenia and is in urgent need of treatment.'[xiii]

This time Frame was sent to Ward Four, which housed acute women patients. She was back in the monochrome world of hospital clothes and regimented routines of, 'rise, ladies', 'dayroom, ladies', 'dining room, ladies', 'lavatories, ladies'; and she was not allowed out of the ward for work therapy. Now all her days would be divided between the dormitory, the dayroom, the dining room and the treatment room. And the treatment, of which she was judged to be in 'urgent need', was to be a resumption of ECT. She was given daily shocks for the first fortnight, reducing to every two or three days for another month, then once or twice a week until mid-January 1949.

Lottie Frame, filled with anxiety, and perhaps too feeling some guilt, heard no news of Janet. And so, a fortnight after her daughter's admission, she wrote to Dr McLachlan, on whose pressing advice she had been persuaded to sign the committal application. The reply came from Malcolm Brown, still medical superintendent of Seacliff. 'Since admission Janet has had intensive electrical treatment …. Her prospects of complete recovery are not good. In future would you please address any letters of enquiry to me, and not to individual members of my staff.'[xiv]

Notes to Extract

i    Janet Frame to John Money, 26/8/48.
ii   *The Oxford Companion to English Literature*, 1985, p. 831.
iii  This version is from the J.B. Leishman translation of Rilke (1957). Frame had an earlier edition of this volume, either the 1936 or 1946 printing. Coincidentally *Landfall* published an elegy from Rilke's *Duino Elegies*, translated by James Bertram in *Landfall* 10 (June 1949): 109–11.
iv   Janet Frame to John Money, 26/8/48.
v    *Ibid.*, 26/8/48 & 10/8/48.
vi   See *The Lagoon*, pp. 44–53. The story was sent to Money on 2/7/48. Frame commented: 'I send a story, formless, technically poor, slushy. I can't remember when I wrote it.'
vii  Janet Frame to John Money, 10/8/48.
viii *Ibid.*, 3/10/48.
ix   Janet Frame hospital notes, 4/10/48.
x    *Ibid.*, 4/10/48.
xi   *Ibid.*, 4/10/48.
xii  *Ibid.*, 4/10/48.
xiii *Ibid.*, 9/10/48.
xiv  Malcolm Brown to Lottie Frame, 27/10/48, JF hospital notes.

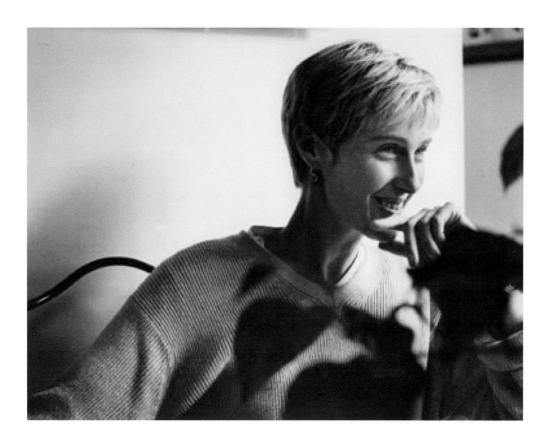

# PAULA BOOCK 1999

*Paula Boock (b.1964) has published five novels for younger readers and an essay. She is an award-winning scriptwriter of both adult and children's television drama.*

PRIOR to the Burns Fellowship in 1999, Paula Boock had published four novels for young adults, the last of which, *Dare Truth or Promise*, had won the NZ Post Children's Book of the Year. During the six-month tenure, she began work on a novel for adults set in Dunedin in 1929, loosely based on her father's early life growing up between the wars in Kaikorai. The book, provisionally titled *Boydi*, is still a work in progress.

An excerpt from *Boydi* follows, preceded by the author's contextualisation:

It's 1929, and Billy Boyd has just turned ten years old. He

comes from a large family and his twin died at birth, a fact that continues to disturb him. His older sister Ruth has just been sent out to work as a servant in the Mayor's house. Billy goes to school with the Mayor's son, Charlie Soper.[66]

FROM *Boydi*

It was early. A rooster crowed somewhere, and there was a line of light around the window. There was a tear in the blind too, and a beam shone through it like a teacher's pointer, landing on Eddie's sleeping shape. Ruth was getting dressed. She had a special black dress and I knew the white apron and hat she'd pressed last night were sitting on the kitchen table.

'What's it like?'

She spun, squinted at me across the room. 'Shhh, you'll wake him.' She meant Eddie. Nothing would wake him. 'What's what like?'

'The Sopers,' I said. 'Is it big?'

She turned away from me to put on a petticoat. Girls put things on differently. She poked her head through first, then one arm and the next. It would be better to put her arms in first and heave it over her head in one go.

'It's massive.'

Massive. Ruth liked words like that. She came over by my bed, tugging at her short hair with a brush.

'Eight bedrooms,' she whispered. 'Eight! And a drawing room, dining room, parlour, library, billiards room. You couldn't use them all in one day.' She leaned closer. 'They've got inside water closets. Two.'

'Two!' I thought about that. 'So they pee inside?'

She nodded, started to giggle. 'You can hear them. It's right through the wall from the kitchen.' Edith smothered her giggles, blurted, 'Mrs Soper farts like a horse,' and we both exploded. Our snorts sounded like farts so we laughed more until Edith squeaked 'Stop it!', crossed her legs and had to hobble out the door.

I lay there and thought about living in a house that big. You'd need so much stuff to fill it up. Tables and armchairs and settees (Mum called our couch a settee), rows of pictures on the walls in golden frames, long velvet drapes and fitted carpet throughout like in the movies. Maybe electric light chandeliers, massive chandeliers, and potted plants – yes, they always had potted plants. I closed my eyes. I closed my eyes and imagined that I was lying in a big feather bed all of my own. I was going to get up and walk down a wide staircase to the dining room table all set out for breakfast, a fire blazing in the hearth. Lambs fry and bacon and sausages and eggs and toast and tea … gee, imagine that. 'Tuck in, old man,' says Dad, clipping a white napkin onto his collar. 'You'll need to feed up for that cricket match this avo.' And then there's a wonka-wonk outside and the Buick is pulling up to take me to school.

My stomach was rumbling. I got up and went through to the kitchen. Mum

was poking the range to get the fire going. She was in her nightie and her dark hair hung like a fox-fur down her back. She looked different with her hair down, like someone she used to be, before Dad and us.

'What are you doing up? I hope you didn't wake the others.'

'No.'

Her face was pink and papery. It thinned out at night-time and I wanted to be close to her, have her pick me up and nuzzle me into her warm puffy neck while it was still sweet with sleep – and before she smelt of Ajax and onions and baby cack.

'Make yourself useful, Billy. Fill the kettle for me, there's a boy.'

Ruth was eating a piece and jiggling Dot to keep her quiet. She made a face at me. 'Don't start me off again,' she warned.

I filled the kettle. Pip waddled through in his nap, saw Ruth's bread and wailed, so she handed it to him. I cut us both a piece, trying to keep the bread straight, and she smeared them with dripping. It was dripping from the roast, salty and smooth. It wasn't lambs fry and bacon, but it was still great.

'Ruth?'

'Mm.'

'What about Charlie Soper?'

'What about him?'

'Do you see him?'

'Not much. Over breakfast, after school sometimes, that's all.'

'Does he talk to you?'

She snorted, then spoke through a mouthful of bread. 'No Billy, he doesn't talk to me.'

We were playing cricket against Morningside, which meant that standard five and six were allowed out to watch. When we played at Morningside their whole school came and clapped every ball. Davy Moss said Morningside had cheated with the scorebook last time. Paddy Harris said they couldn't have since one boy scores from each team, but Davy said our guy went away to get a pie and when he came back Morningside had made about seventy runs in ten overs. Paddy said he was pretty sure it was Davy Moss who did that when he scored against Kensington and that was why the Kensington boys did him over afterwards.

I was batting with Charlie Soper. He was hopeless. The Morningside bowler was bowling big donkey drops and Charlie would lurch forward too early, have a wild swing and miss it by a mile. All the Morningside lads would whistle and rub their hands together, as if their bowler was Clarrie Grimmett or someone.

I walked down the wicket, poking the ground with my bat.

'Keep your eye on it,' I said.

'I am. It's all right, I'll smash it.' Charlie was waving his bat around to demonstrate.

'You're playing too early. You have to wait for it.'

'Shut up.'

'Shut up yourself.'

'Boys,' said Mr Henshaw, umpiring. We walked back to our places.

Charlie had a new bat and proper cricket shoes like Fly. He brought his own pads, and wouldn't share them. I hated him.

'Play,' said Henshaw.

The donkey dropper floated the ball up like a big red pudding. Charlie's eyes ballooned and he flailed the bat across the line, nearly falling over. The ball hit his back pad right in front of middle stump.

'Howwwzat!!!' screamed the Morningside boys.

We all looked at Henshaw. He twisted his mouth and gave a short sniff. 'Not out.'

They wailed and dropped their arms, disbelieving. The donkey dropper put his hands on his hips and stared down the wicket at Soper.

'Play on,' said Henshaw.

Charlie lifted his chin and faced up again. This time he nicked it and the wicket-keeper leapt in the air with the ball in his glove. 'Howwww-zat!'

'Not out,' said Henshaw, and I saw his eyes flick to the right. I followed them, and saw Mayor Soper standing on the sideline, hands hooked into his waistcoat. The Buick was parked right up on the grass behind our team.

'Aww, come on!' said one boy.

'That's enough,' said Henshaw.

The captain threw his cap on the grass.

'Bloody cheats,' muttered a close-in fielder. I looked at the ground, felt my neck prickling.

'Play on, Morningside.'

Charlie managed to get a bit of pad on the last ball and it trickled down fine leg.

'Yes!!!' he screamed, and took off down the wicket, as if he were being chased by the Hun. I ran through for the single and the over ended.

The field changed, the new bowler was Larkins, an inswinger, and Mr Frew walked up from square leg to umpire. He nodded at me and I noticed he had two pink spots high on his cheeks.

Larkins jogged into the wicket, delivered a ball outside off-stump which bent in the air like a bow. It slid through Charlie's attempted cover drive and belted him on the front pad.

'Howwww-zat!!!'

'Out,' said Frew. His finger shot into the air before Charlie even had time to look up, register the decision, and drop his jaw. The Morningside players whooped and clapped and I watched Charlie Soper walk back to the sideline with his head down, stabbing the ground with his new bat all the way. He didn't even

talk to Fly as he walked past. Mayor Soper had disappeared, and by the time Fly was taking guard the Buick was already rolling away down the road.

I made 37 and Fly made 60 not out in double-quick time. We creamed them, without Davy Moss's help on the scorebook.

Paddy and Fly's dad had a wooden leg. It was funny because he used to bowl leggies and I had a great joke about him bowling one too many. Mum said it wasn't anything to joke about, a war injury, the poor man. It got shot off in the war, at the Somme. He wouldn't talk about it. He said he couldn't remember anything, but Paddy reckoned he woke up screaming in the night sometimes and Mrs Harris had to tell him where he was.

'He gets pains,' said Paddy. 'Like he's still got a leg. Phantom pains. Sometimes he goes mad thinking he can feel his leg itching and there's nothing to scratch.'

I thought about that. About dreaming you were running only to wake up and realise you didn't have a leg. To jump out of bed shouting like Mr Harris did once and fall on the floor because there was nothing there to hold you up.

I thought about being able to feel something that wasn't there. A phantom leg, like a ghost that didn't want to let go.

My twin wasn't dead. He'd got lost and was living somewhere. Men were lost all over the world from the war. They were reported missing in action but some were in prisoner of war camps and some were living secretly in Germany until the war ended and some had gone bush and didn't know the war had ended. Last week there was a fellow from Caversham whose wife and children had given up for dead and then, all of a sudden, there was a knock at the door and there he was. 'Gidday,' he'd say. 'Gidday,' just like that.

THE **2000s**

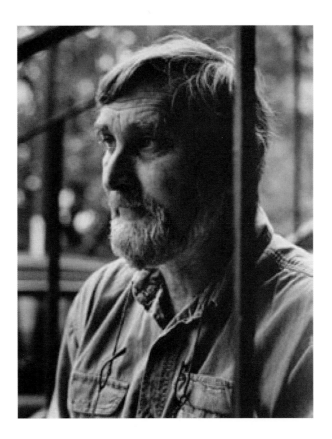

# James Norcliffe 2000

*James Norcliffe (b. 1946) has published six volumes of poetry, a collection of short stories, and five novels for young readers,*

**JAMES** Norcliffe was an established author in several genres when he took up his Burns Fellowship in 2000. He had published four books of poetry, one collection of short stories, and four novels for younger readers. Norcliffe had a very productive Burns year, completing his fifth collection, *Along Blueskin Road* (2005), and some of his sixth, *Villon in Millerton* (2007), as well as *The Assassin of Gleam* (2006), which won the 2007 Sir Julius Vogel Award for the best science fiction/fantasy novel, 'Yewfire', a fantasy novel being considered for publication, and the first draft of a novel, 'Nodding Donkeys'. Below are three poems from *Along Blueskin Road*, with Norcliffe's notes.

## a sense of direction

coming out of the theatre
I always follow the horses

the yellow dust they kick up
billows about me like talcum

later there will be silhouettes
of cactus and a circle of stars

and in the distance the mesa
a tableland under a purple sky

in some narrow gulch that way
lies the one I should rescue

hands roped behind her back
teeth biting into a red bandana

wriggling like a gingham rattlesnake
towards the muddy waterhole

the other way is cold and grey
with dark harmonies of meters

four squares and new worlds
damp footpaths and angle parking

no one at all to rescue
just a reflection in plate glass

not much choice really
but to follow that corona of stars

the clip clop of dreams

# planchette

at night the rats
are bigger than rats

they race back and forth
like typewriters
across the lath and plaster

like good little rats
they have taken their poison
and now they grow large with thirst

where are their pretty girlfriends
or love, the magician?

can not one of these
offer them solace or slake?

oh qwerty they clatter
oh qwerty qwerty

as the night grows hard around them
desperate in their scrabble

and the stars
set like teeth

Note: A planchette is a kind of ouija board. The scrabbling from beyond is no doubt telling somebody's fortune. Almost certainly in this case, the rats. This particular scrabbling I heard coming from above the ceiling in my room in the Ryeburn Wing, Knox College where I stayed (most enjoyably) during the time on the Burns.

# Yippee!

When the podiatrists escaped we immediately set up roadblocks. But they were apparently wise to us and kept to the footpaths. Somewhat unfairly, too, they must have been wearing orthotics with rich crepes soles, which allowed them, well after dark, to ripple right past our defences in a distinctly crepuscular manner and make for the safety of the park.

In this way the podiatrists taught us the meaning of frustration.

There was no way, especially in the darkness, that we could retrieve the podiatrists from the park. The powerful sequoias hid and comforted even the bravest of them in a scent of turpentine, made sharp by the moonlight, whereas the more timid lay pressed into the gaultheria where they were wrapped about with wintergreen.

We could do nothing. We did joke that the iron railings around the park meant that the podiatrists had simply caged themselves in, but we were equally aware that the railings with their fearsome spikes kept us out just as effectively.

In this way the podiatrists taught us the meaning of irony.

All night the podiatrists hid there, out of sight, out of reach, but not out of hearing, and eventually safety overcame them and they grew cocky and footloose and, realising our powerlessness, began to cry, Yippee! Yippee!

Thus the podiatrists taught us the meaning of scorn.

We could almost have tolerated this had it not been for the uncomfortable realisation that somehow in the night tinea had been set loose. We could feel it burning and insinuating itself all over our feet, between our toes. Burning and burning. Itching fearsomely.

And all the while the podiatrists, behind the iron rails and hidden in the dangling embrace of the redwoods, cried, Yippee! Yippee!

As the burning sensation all but overcame us it seemed almost as though we could hear the tinea joining in the chorus: Yippee! Yippee! in tiny subsonic harmonies.

When dawn broke we were in a really bad way, jumping from foot to itchy foot. The light, perversely, had made the podiatrists even cockier, more sure of

themselves. They broke free of the shaggy trunks, the perfumed groundcover and sported, gambolled. They flaunted their tubes of fungicide. They played touch rugby with them, flinging the crème of our desire from player to player, coming at times infuriatingly close to the railings. Every so often one would cry, Yippee! as if unable to help it. Would leap into the air clapping his crepe soles.

In this way the podiatrists taught us the meaning of hate.

Note: This prose poem, which is always great fun to read aloud, was prompted by my daily walk through the Dunedin Botanical Gardens on my way to the university. No slight to any podiatrist, living or dead, is intended.[68]

# JO RANDERSON 2001

Jo Randerson has had over twenty plays and revues performed. She has published two of these, two collections of short fiction and a separate 'picture book', as well as a number of pieces in periodicals and anthologies.

BY 2001 Jo Randerson had begun to define herself in several related modes – as dramatist, writer of dramatic monologues, comedian, performer and producer of her own writings, and as a writer of short fictions (some of which were monologues). She had had a number of plays and shows produced, and published a collection of short fiction, *The Spit Children* (2000), as well as *The Knot*, 1998, a story in the format of a picture book for early readers. In her Burns year she continued in these modes. She wrote a new solo play, *Banging Cymbal and Clanging Gong*, which she performed at the Allen Hall Theatre in March 2001. This was published in 2003 in *Red Light Means Stop: Six*

*Super Solos for Aotearoa New Zealand*, edited by Vivienne Plumb. For the rest of her tenure, Randerson concentrated on the short fictions that were collected in *The Keys to Hell* (2004). The following brief short story is from that volume.

## Gazelles

In an inspired and never-repeated moment of brilliance, my husband had the foresight to ask me, 'What is your life like?'

I answered, 'The dark night perspires over my soul, the rot has set in and is devastating the cavernous flesh. Great tides of blood rush in sweeping away the fleet, while its men – prisoners without their memory – surrender to the waves. The four gazelles of grief trample across my savannah, and the flourishing tussock has been left a threadbare mat. I no longer separate night from day, I can no longer distinguish person from person. All experiences are alike to me, they bear no surprises, no challenges, merely a series of obstacles to be overcome. The process of waking is one of re-ordering alone – there is no sense of sudden life, simply categorisation, recognition, and description. This is a chair, I sit in it; this is a person, I talk to it. As with the sky, dark clouds pass across my spirit, sometimes visible from a distance, sometimes rising without warning, as a serpent, slowly from behind, with a dagger, come to take everything: worldly goods, intangible spiritual possessions, and the small ball tossed between the two. There is nothing new, no surprises, everything has already been seen or thought of. Long patches of glorious sun, dry spells, storms, deserts, droughts. There is no pattern, not a single theory, no technique to ascribe to, only the sure and steady passing of time. That is all. The clock will tick. The days will pass. The worm will turn. The tide will high. The moon will wane. The sun will shine. The colour will fade. The flesh will wither. The pulse will subside,' I said.

'Darling, what a wonderful thing to say!' he cried. 'How witty and clever you are. Once I touched a small gazelle, it made me frightened and introspective. Their fur is rough and oddly arranged.'

(This is what I mean when I say that the system has not been designed for me, which I will comment on again later once they let me out.)

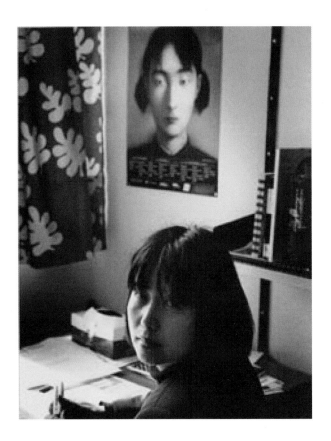

# ALISON WONG 2002

**ALISON** Wong, a founder of Porirua's Poetry Café, had published poetry and extracts from a novel in *Landfall*, *Sport*, and the *Listener* – but not yet a book – when she was awarded the Burns Fellowship in late 2001. During her Fellowship, she worked on her first collection of poetry, *Cup* (2006), and her first novel, which will be published by Picador in 2009. Below are extracts from the draft of the novel, with a contextualisation by the author.

*Alison Wong (b. 1960) has published one collection of poetry and has a novel forthcoming in 2009.*

The novel is set from the 1890s through to the 1920s in Wellington, Dunedin, Guangdong China and the Western Front during World War One. It follows the stories of

two brothers, Wong Chung-Shun and Wong Chung-Yung (Yung) and their families, and of Katherine McKechnie, her husband, Donald, and their children Robbie and Edie.

Mrs Mary Ann (Annie) Wong was the real-life widow of the Chinese Anglican Missioner, Daniel Wong, who is buried at Karori cemetery. The Chinese Anglican Mission Hall is situated next to the Murdochs vinegar and pickle factory, in Frederick St, Wellington, though neither are now used for their original purposes. The scene is completely fictional as are all of the other characters.[69]

The prologue remains in the finished novel, Edie's experience as a medical student during the 1918 flu pandemic is extracted from, and at least one of the other two chapters has fallen victim to narrative structure. To find out what *really* happens, you'll have to read the published version!

## Extracts

*Wong Chung-Shun, Wellington, 1896*
*Prologue*

It is a lonely place where the Jesus-ghosts preach. They preach about love, about a god who died of love, yet in the street the people sneer and call out and spit, then on Sundays sing in the Jesus-house.

Their god is a white ghost. You see the pictures. He has pale skin and a big nose and a glow of moonlight round his long brown hair. He has many names, just as we *Tong* people have many names. We have a milk name, a nickname, a scholar name, a married name. The Jesus-ghosts call their god Jesus and Father and Holy Ghost. Even they know he is a ghost. People are like their gods, just as they are like their animals. Here they even call him Father. We do not need to name them, these *gweilo*, because even they know they are ghosts.

We do not need to recognise their words; we do not need to interpret the raised syllable. It is there in a flicker of the eyes, the slight curl of a lip, in the muscles of the face, the way they set against us. Yung says, the body has its own language. He says, it can be as fluid as poetry or as coarse as polemic. Little brother has a way with words. He says, the language of the body can be used as a weapon.

Now that Yung is here, I do not have to pay a clansman. Now one of us can go to the market while the other keeps shop; one can sort bananas while the other trims vegetables. Now that my brother is here, I can save to bring to out a wife. It will take a good many years. To save the fare and the poll-tax. When Yung arrived, we did not recognise each other. We had not seen each other for over ten years. Now he is eighteen and books have affected his brain. He dreams big impossible dreams. He does not understand life, and he does not understand this land. He is full of too many feelings like wild animals caught and caged in a zoo. He likes to talk, and his words are quick, quicker than his understanding. He is young – twenty years younger. He is like a son, an only, foolish son.

*Edie McKechnie, Dunedin, 1918*
*Black November*

The hospital's overflowing, so too Stuart Hall, and the Hanover Street Baptist hall is filling steadily. So many doctors still overseas, and now we're all coming down with the 'flu like an avalanche – Dr Falconer, four of the five house surgeons, thirty-odd nurses …. Just a few days and we've suddenly been plunged into the real world. Twenty-five of us students here at the hospital, and thirty-five V.A.D.s. We follow Dr Bowie and Dr Fitchett, whatever they do: quinine, aspirin, Eusol, mustard poultices, alcohol (some of them come in reeking of brandy), morphine, turpentine inhalations, bronchitis vaccine, even heroin. The nurses and V.A.D.s sponge the patients and try to keep up the fluids. But it's the pneumonia that gets them. They seem to drown in their own secretions. I've never seen anything like it. All my childhood imaginations never came to this. Fever, yes, headache, nasal congestion, coughing, vomiting and diarrhoea, joint and chest and stomach pain. Their airways close up. They spit pus and phlegm, greyish-white, bloody, then if they're getting better, greenish mucous that gradually disappears. Others go from sweating profusely to nothing – no sweating, no coughing, just this silent lapse into coma. Some of them lose their hair, their finger and toe-nails. Some decline into delirium. I've heard stories of people leaping from upstairs bedrooms, shooting themselves, drowning themselves in the sea. I can't get used to all the young people. Usually it's the very young or the very old that are most susceptible to infection. But here it's all these great strapping lads and men in their prime, boys like George McAlister, the varsity wrestling champ, we're putting them in their coffins, while the likes of Tommy Brownlee, who couldn't lift a dumbbell if his life depended on it, it's some of the sickly ones who are pulling though. The worst thing, the thing I just can't get used to, is the cyanosis: the way they turn, the suddenness of it all, the skin translating to deep crimson, just one look away and they can turn, in an instant, jet-black.

I hear weird stories, there is nothing people will not try as prophylactic or as cure, such is the desperation. There was the woman who smeared her children all over with treacle. I suppose they spent all their time licking it off. One man came in unconscious, but it was a case of drunkenness rather than fever-induced coma. And now a package has arrived from home. (They've sent me back for a few hours sleep. On my feet forty-one hours. Started dropping things: syringes, surgical dressings, memories …). I'm supposed to boil these sticks and leaves and things and then drink the stuff down. Mother says it's foul but Mrs Wong brought it round and she apparently swears by it. Everyone wants a miracle. I just need some sleep. Then I'll be right ….

*Dunedin, 1919*
*First Church*

Katherine did not know why she turned through the iron gates that day. This was a building that represented everything she did not believe in. Its spire reached into the sky as if to strike the fear of God into the city. Even its name, First Church, spoke of the One and Only, unyielding God. She walked up the path, past the manicured lawn, the quiet trees, up the bluestone steps, then let the limestone swallow her.

In the foyer, she walked past shelves of red hymn books, through the open door, into the belly of God.

She had come between services, when the church was empty, only the distant sound of horse carts, the occasional motor-car. Late afternoon sun fell through the stained glass windows, leaving golden highlights on the western pews and across the straight-backed seats of the choir. She sat in the last row looking over the lines of wooden pews to the front of the church where the long pipes of God like silent cannons reached upwards. Two British flags hung from the wooden archway, one on the east, the other on the west, overhanging the altar. She sat alone with only the tall windows peopled with Christ and his followers, fragments of coloured light – blue, purple, red, orange, green, gold – streaking across the ivory-white walls. In the silence words resonated, words like forgiveness. Redemption. But she had no words to speak, no words to share. She looked down. On the back of the pew in front of her, someone had scratched, in angular letters, GOD IS. What? she wondered. She had heard many words. Righteousness. Justice. A consuming fire. And words like love, which could slip off the tongue too easily. A word spoken with the tongue or the eyes, with small acts of sacrifice or large. A word with many facets, capable of great clarity and great misunderstanding.

Katherine sat in the back of the church and realised two things: that Donald had taken away her words and that Yung had given them back. The little orange phrase book had been the beginning of her voice.

Now he was gone and what did she have left? A quiet still voice. Words that could never be silenced. This belly of God with slivers of light streaming in.

*Wellington, 1920s*
*As Vinegar to the Teeth*

How can we worship with the stink of pickle in our nostrils? Oh for a prophet who could have proclaimed, *Thou shalt not build the sanctuary of the Lord at that place for it is a place of desecration. Yea, in ten years and more there shall be lamentation for they shall come as a plague out of the hills and they shall build a factory and it shall be shoulder to mighty shoulder with the Mission Hall, and day*

*and night it shall spew forth vinegar and pickle and other such abominations. Thou shalt kneel to pray and thou shalt rise to praise and the mighty name of Murdoch's, the stink of Te Aro, shall never depart thy nostrils.*

Annie Wong stands in the kitchen beating eggs and sugar, beating and beating in air, if onlys, exclamations. She lifts the metal spoon to fold in the flour. Sighs. Calm down. Breathe. The Lord made a scourge of cords and drove the money-changers out of the temple and overthrew the tables, but he wasn't folding flour into sponge mixture. Ten eggs, sugar, a little flour, cornflour, oil, milk …. No vinegar ….

*They gave him vinegar to drink mingled with gall: and when he tasted thereof, he would not drink … My God, my God why hast thou forsaken me …. And straightaway one of them ran, and took a sponge and filled it with vinegar, and put it on a reed, and gave it to him to drink … and Jesus, when he had cried again with a loud voice, yielded up the ghost.* God and man; wine and vinegar. This is the double-edged sword: the Son of God and the Son of Man. Allejuia!

Tonight there will be another service, and the Missioner shall officiate. Annie sees him lifting the cup in the cool darkness, the only natural light falling softly from the small windows high in the clerestory and chancel, *And he took the cup, and gave thanks, and gave it to them, saying, Drink ye all of it; For this is my blood of the new testament …*, she sees him in the shadowy light, in the coolness of an imperial tomb, raising the cup to his lips, the taste of wine and vinegar on his tongue. She sucks in her cheeks, the taste of vinegar grating against her teeth. She is pouring the sponge mixture into the steamer (white egg cake for supper after the service) when she hears a knock, loud, urgent. She puts the bowl down on the bench and opens the door. For a moment she thinks it is Chung-Yung, but young and strong again, Yung breathing hard, small beads of sweat on the bridge of his long, straight nose, under his eyes and across his cheekbones, Yung catching ragged little breaths, breathing, and then she remembers.

# NICK ASCROFT 2003

PRIOR to receiving a one-semester Burns
Fellowship in 2003, Nick Ascroft had published one
collection of poems with another to be released that
year. He had also placed poetry widely in New Zealand
and international journals. During his tenure he worked
on poems for his yet-to-be-published third collection,
*Anonymous Phenomena*, and the draft of a novel. The work
included below is a haibun series which will appear in that
collection. Ascroft has written of 'Old Wives' Lives':

*Nick Ascroft (b. 1973) has published two
collections of poetry, has a third forthcoming,
and has completed a science-fiction novel.*

The haibun series was written for the art school ball at
which I performed between sets by the Chills. It had a

1950s theme, the ball. I was really looking forward to it, but in the end got shouted off the stage by a bunch of hell-pissed art dicks, most too gaga to realise it might be appropriate to be quieter for a small moment. Some horror of an art tutor pulled her dress up and down to expose her underwear, while running up to beneath the stage screaming, then popped a balloon at me, while Kate [Wanwimolruk] and Kushana [Bush] looked on in disgust. I cut the poem short, and loped off a little humiliated. Martin Phillipps wished me some small condolence, shaking his head. So, it's nice the poem has a life beyond the Caesarean.[70]

## Old Wives' Lives

i. *False Teeth*

It was common practice in the middle part of the last century to have your daughter's teeth knocked out prior to marriage, thus lessening the financial burden on a prospective husband. At least, particularly among rural families. The logic being that they'd all rot out soon enough, & filling work was a fortune in gold – now less necessary, as daughter A had netted herself a husband & the work of her pearly teeth was done. The denture manufacturers encouraged it of course; World War Two had seen them waltzing to the bank, the Armed Forces having a similar rationale, & most soldiers forcedly going to war in their gums. Now they needed to keep their profit-wheels a-rotoring. Brochures were sent around the farming communities of the fifties. It became an easy sign, cheaper than the flash of an engagement ring: a mouthful of nothing. Others, forced into the series of extractions, let alone into the wedding itself, would remember weeping themselves to sleep, pausing only to exchange a piece of bloodied gauze in a mouth of scabs.

> She holds her breath to
> Kiss. The veil smells. Consumed,
> The wedding sours.

ii. *Vicaring*

Homosexuality among the clergy was generally more accepted in fifties New Zealand than we would perhaps think. Covertly, to a degree, of course. But then as now, many of those who felt the call to ministry felt a calling to quite the other brotherhood. A number of parishes delighted in the camp jokes & double entendres that laced their sermons, the older members of the women's choirs tittering into their handkerchiefs. The prevalence of openly gay Anglican priests especially led to the slang term for queer of the period – 'vicar'. It was also the term for married husbands who strayed for nights of drunken homosexual

adultery – 'vicaring'. *She caught him red-handed vicaring Thursday last.* The gay vicar was often the centre of parish gossip & intrigue. Not only did it enhance one's reputation inordinately to be a favourite wife on his visiting list, one was feared for the knowledge inherent in the arrangement. Seeing a young curate sauntering in a leather jacket & dog-collar at the dockside, cigarette between thumb & index like a Frenchman, one would throw him a knowing smile, feeling devilish & modern.

> The minister twists
> Out of his alb, sugary
> Skin, like shrove Tuesday.

### iii. *Experimental Agricultural*

Genetic Engineering is, as we know, nothing new. Every domesticated plant & animal has been carefully bred, its genes skilfully interwoven over many generations, to make such atrocities as the brussels sprout & the chihuahua. Dogs in their multitude of generally distasteful forms are the best example of the wide-ranging palette available to human gene-engineers. In the 1950s there was another creation New Zealand farmers could not get enough of: the breed of sheep known as Romney. From the plumpness of its hindquarters over its particularly curly back to that fat-headed expression of permanent surprise, it was beloved, a burgeoning cash-cow the cow wasn't. One wily agriculturist of the MacKenzie country, a Mr James Godby, noted that a ewe was twice as profitable if she lambed twins. He put himself to work trying to breed a Romney that could be relied upon to always do so. At first he had limited success, twins bred with twins seemed just as likely to produce a single offspring as any other coupling. One mutated form, however, produced a reliable twin-machine. Godby made easy money selling the extra lambs, but, in interbreeding the mutant with its own lineage, managed to produce many more twin-makers which he hawked off at stock auctions for very tidy sums. The new sub-breed became known in the unpolished back-sheds of the trade as a two-twot-Romney. At the end of the boom, the breed drifted out of circulation.

> A field of her
> Own, subjects crowd her fence, queen
> Of uteruses.

iv. *Schism*

The Protestant girl peered around the corner into the vestibule of St Patrick's Greymouth. Seeing no one, she steadied herself on her crutches, & swung inside. The sensation was one of bravery – symptomatically identical, as that is, to fear: knee-sweat, quasi-palpitative heart, asthma – & also the elation of revenge. Perhaps there was a lesser, less conscious thrill, simply in the awfulness, the illicit mischief of it, but revenge was what they called it, her & her friends waiting around the corner in the bushes; this was the late fifties, & Catholic-Protestant relations seethed in the small towns & neighbourhoods of the country, an underbelly of civil war. In the Yugoslavia of Greymouth the week preceding, some kids from St Patrick's school had ambushed them with stones. The Protestant girl still had an azalea of a bruise on the left of her semifunctional legs. She had managed to clip one of the dools around the back of the head with a crutch, before they'd scuttled off cackling, but it was clearly a Catholic victory. The sound of hymnsingers dirged from within the double doors leading to the nave of the church: it was still safe – tone-deaf basses & screechy sopranos lisped their heresies into the empty air of the basilica. The jar she clutched awkwardly under one wing had made the crutch-work up the steps difficult. One of her friends should have made the trip, but something in her condition outranked them in terms of bravery, audacity, commitment. She plucked it from under her arm & unscrewed the lid. On the previous night, from her lavatory, the Protestant girl had fished out part of a turd, & they had mixed it with warm water in a jar. The contents trickled into the birdbath, as her father called it, that held the holy water by the exit.

> The Catholics file
> Out, crosses of shit, twinkle-
> Stink on their foreheads.

# SARAH QUIGLEY 2003

*Sarah Quigley (b. 1967) has published three novels, a collection of short stories, a collection of poems and a guide to creative writing.*

SARAH Quigley has a D.Phil. from the University of Oxford, where she studied under the supervision of Professor Jon Stallworthy. Her doctoral thesis was based on the life and works of Charles Brasch, whose personal papers were then under a thirty-year embargo in the Hocken Library. Their release in May 2003 meant that Quigley could spend a six-month period as Burns Fellow, in the second half of 2003, researching these documents towards a full-scale biography of Brasch.

Aside from her academic work, Quigley is a published novelist, poet, columnist, and critic. Her books include a collection of short fiction, two collections of poetry, three

novels, and a creative writing manual. Her most recent novel is *Fifty Days* (2004), published by Virago. Since 2000, when she held the Inaugural Creative New Zealand Berlin Writers' Residency, she has divided her time between New Zealand and Germany.

Below is a short story that was published at the end of Quigley's tenure.

## Donkeys are Introverts

I was lying in bed beside you one day when suddenly I knew what it was to be a gopher. I wasn't actually in bed with you – more on the bed, because it was only six o'clock and we were resting. Why were we tired? Because we had carried heavy root vegetables from one side of the city to the other. Potatoes in our backpacks: that was why.

So there I was lying on the bed with you, feeling the movement of the red duvet at my back. And suddenly it came over me. Gopherness came over me. Why, I couldn't say.

It started at my mouth as I lay looking at the ceiling. My front teeth emerged and, when I turned to look at you, my mouth was a gopher's. A small pointy mouth, pointed at you. When I laughed the gopher mouth disappeared. But when I became serious it rushed back again.

Then the gopher qualities spread to my nose. My nose had burned all winter afternoon from the cold, but it forgot this now and became the nose of a gentle gopher. It twitched. In all seriousness, it twitched of its own accord.

The eyes. They had taken in the face of every vendor at the frozen marketplace, they had eyed up many bargains in a wholly human way. But now, in the dim red light of the six o'clock duvet, they began to run into the side of my face. They narrowed and became beady. They were gopher eyes.

Why, I couldn't say. We were resting, that was all, we were tired and we had soup to make and suddenly I was a gopher.

This sort of thing had happened once before, remember. A long time ago, but, still, it happened. All that time ago I became a hen.

We had been walking over some hills, if you cast your mind back. The hills were foreign to us. They were domed like the head of an old man, and just as grey and crumpled. We stopped in a stale farmyard to look at some hens.

Then I knew it. I could run like a hen. So I ran, around and around the yard. My straight legs flew out in front of me like banners, my arms were wings. There was something unearthly about it. I was silent and hen-like, but you stood and screamed.

When we were asked by Customs some weeks later if we had been on a farm – have you recently been on agricultural land? – I could only say no. My feet had

no memory of mud: they had barely touched the ground. The talons of a hen rise and fall so fast, its legs are so brittle and weightless, that it leaves no tracks.

There is a painting that hangs in the National Gallery. It is of a chestnut horse and it was painted by Stubbs in 1762. You can stand flat-footed in front of this painting and still know the hardness of the horse's shoulder. If Stubbs had lived three centuries later he might have been a photographer.

Jeff Wall is a photographer. He is highly respected. He is so highly respected that on his first day at a German university someone pointed a gun at him and he had to fly home, instantly.

Jeff Wall admires Stubbs's rich chestnut horse. He knows how difficult it is to record skin: thin fine skin like the back of an old woman's hand, and threaded with veins. But he prefers donkeys. He likes their enigmatic qualities.

When Jeff Wall finds Champion on a Blackpool beach, he takes her back to the studio. There he spends a long time – as long as we lie on a bed, longer than the land – waiting for Champion's ears to move towards the shutter.

Donkeys are obsolete introverts.
Hens are unintelligent long-distance runners.
Gophers can't carry root vegetables over long distances on their backs.
But we – we can rest and record and remember. Occasionally, we can leave.

# KATE DUIGNAN 2004

KATE Duignan had published one novel and some short fiction in periodicals when she took up the Burns Fellowship in 2004. During her Burns year she worked on a second novel, 'The New Ships', as yet unpublished. An extract from the manuscript follows.

The novel is set in Rome, where the narrator, Peter, is on an art history tour with his mother-in-law, Claudia.

*Kate Duignan (b. 1974) has published one novel*
*and has a second in process.*

## FROM The New Ships

Outside the Colosseum, a range of shabby gladiators pose for tourists. I pass one who is taking a break from the work, sweaty lipped, drinking from his plastic water bottle and rubbing at the indent the helmet has made in his forehead. A queue winds around the coil of the stadium, and suddenly the wide ruin appears banal, a place for rabid, salivating crowds; what pulls at me are the broken blocks of the Forum with their narrative of law, of language triumphant over violence. I want to walk through the valley where they built it, word by word, the old men, white-haired, rheumy-eyed patricians; their protective veil, a constitution to keep the ambitious from one another's throats for almost five hundred years, one generation graciously giving way to the next, until it frayed and was ripped apart in the brute onrush of power.

On the way up the Via Sacra, it begins to rain. There are bay trees and shrubby yews, but the best shelter on offer is beneath the span of Titus' arch. A French man is there, and also the remnant of a Japanese bus tour, young couples who huddle in excitement, the girls forming a nucleus in the centre, the men pitching umbrellas around the edges. The French man consults his guide book, flicking the pages back and forth and murmuring. He points up to the frieze running along one side of the arch which shows legionnaires sacking the Temple in Jerusalem. The menorah they strain to carry stands out in relief, the faces of the soldiers a vague suggestion, melted back into the stone.

One of the Japanese women struggles with her camera. Her husband takes it from her. He shoots a number of photos of the frieze, and then turns around and takes one of her. She holds her blue umbrella aloft and offers an insubstantial smile. As the rain thickens and pelts, she squeals and darts inwards. I check my watch.

'Excuse me,' the French man says, tapping my shoulder. 'You have a familiar look. Perhaps a movie star?'

'Paul McCartney,' I say.

He raises both hands in astonishment. 'Yes!'

'Uncanny, isn't it?' I shrug.

'*Mais c'est incroyable!*' He blushes a deep, violent red and starts to fumble in his leather satchel, presenting me, his hand trembling, with a pen and the blank page of a notebook. 'Would you?'

'Oh,' I say, 'no, I'm not Paul McCartney. I just look like him. So I've been told.'

'Please,' the French man is saying, jabbing the page, pressing the pen upon me. 'Please. I am a particular fan. My first wish is always to see the Beatles play, but this is impossible you understand, because I have only thirty-two years and already it is finished.'

'*Je n'étais pas –* ' I say, fishing in the recesses of memory, '*je ne suis pas –* '

But already, from nowhere the whispering has begun, *Beetle, Beetle*. Several cameras flash, and the Japanese are bowing low to me, and one woman starts to cry, and I'm shaking my head, *no, not I, I am not the one you seek*, but more sheets of paper are thrust into my hand, and giving up, I sign several, and touch those who reach for me, and stand still for photographs amongst the umbrellas. In the end, I raise my hands like an exhausted Christ and walk away into the weather.

At the church, the group is below, clustered into a dim subterranean vault where subdued lights are trained on half-vanished frescos. The sound of running water rises up from some deeper part of the structure; Marsha is holding forth.

'The miracle of the Sea of Azov,' she says, tipping her white pointer towards a square of strange forms in tones of red and brown, 'is apocryphal. Saint Clement was banished to the Crimea, where he slaked the thirst of two thousand newly converted soldiers with miraculously produced freshwater. In revenge, the Emperor Trajan had him bound and thrown into the sea with an iron anchor. You see the anchor, here.'

I peer in, and indeed, it emerges from the gloom, without the upturned barbed ends, but certainly, a recognisable anchor. As I look, there is more to see: etchings of fish and sea creatures around the central scene become apparent. Claudia, standing on the far side, is waving at me, and I wander around to her.

'What happened?' she asks.

'It's raining,' I say. 'And I was mobbed.'

'You what?' she hisses. Her expression is one of pure alarm. 'You were robbed?'

The woman in front of us turns around.

'No, no,' I say, whispering. 'Nothing. I'll tell you later.'

'You've missed an awful lot,' she whispers back, clutching onto my arm, and pointing to her feet. 'There's a pre-historic temple down there. Terrible smell.'

Her daughter shared the same wildly inaccurate sense of time. I fold my hands together and concentrate on Marsha.

'Some time later the sea receded to reveal an underwater tomb built by the angels, from which the saint's body was recovered, and moved, onto a nearby island. In fact, Clement's alleged remains were to have a long journey, finally coming to this church in the ninth century.'

'We're thinking of pizza for lunch,' Claudia says, somewhat too loudly. 'Marsha knows a good place nearby.'

'Excellent,' I say. 'I'm famished.'

'From that day on the waters drew back once a year to reveal the tomb. A festival grew up around it. But on one occasion, a child was swept away as the sea flowed back, and drowned.'

The Professor has wandered off again, and is examining a sarcophogus. I suspect he has a particularly low boredom threshold, although it is equally possible, I suppose, that his hearing is no longer what it once was.

'The miracle, after which this fresco is named, occurred when the tide ebbed one year later, the child found safe and well. The scene depicted here is the happy reunion, the child slipping out from the tomb and embracing its mother.'

An underwater tomb where time and rot have no hold, constructed of wood and tiles, with a canopy of white curtains drawn back like elephant tusks, and yes, I suppose it could be a woman, that figure with the astonished mouth, swooping to her knees and reaching out for the small body in a blue dress, drawing it back to safety.

'I prefer the ones upstairs,' Claudia says to me. 'Much more colourful.'

'Are there any questions?'

Marsha is a competent leader. The group is tired now, ready for refreshments and toilets and idle chatter, wanting to be released from the strictures of forming a single entity, itching to separate into twenty independent bodies again. She doesn't draw the process out.

'Have lunch wherever you choose. We'll meet at three o'clock by the obelisk at St John Lateran.'

'How do we find that?'

This from Tanya, the anxious woman with the dyed auburn hair. She wears all her valuables against her body in a series of pouches, buttoned beneath her raincoat. I fear this is not as safe as she thinks it is, as the unidentifiable bulk rather gives her the profile of a suicide bomber.

'It's at the end of the street,' Marsha answers. 'A pillar of stone one hundred and fifty foot tall.'

# CATHERINE CHIDGEY

# 2005 –2006

*Catherine Chidgey (b. 1970) has published three novels and a number of short stories and has translated two children's books.*

**CATHERINE** Chidgey entered her Burns Fellowship in 2005 having published three much-acclaimed novels for which she has received several prizes, bursaries and fellowships. In her Burns tenure – all of 2005 and the first half of 2006 – she worked on a fourth novel, still in process. She also translated two children's stories from the German for publication in the Gecko series, and wrote a short story for the anthology *Are Angels OK? The Parallel Universes of New Zealand Writers and Scientists* (2006), an excerpt from which follows. The stories for the anthology were intended to deal with scientific concepts and be written in consultation with scientists.

Chidgey consulted with scientists David Wiltshire and David Hutchinson, and then made several false starts, finding that her 'biggest problem was to make the leap from theory to a believable, breathing character'.[71] She comments on her solution:

When I settled on the (very broad) topic of gravity … I realised that I could take many of the terms metaphorically as well as literally, and the story grew from there. Pressure, load, weight, force, how much a person can bear – thinking about the different meanings of these terms told me about my main character's nature and relationships as well as about his physical talent.[72]

## FROM The Deadlift

There was a time when I was the strongest boy in the world. I have sashes emblazoned with that title; I have trophies and certificates and shields. I remember the way my body felt: hard, defined, a carapace of muscle. At the lab, the calipers scrabbled at my skin like chopsticks and found not a morsel too much, but even then, I saw room for improvement. I knew all the places a body could hide its flaws. My mother told me that before I was born I punched and stretched and kicked until she was bruised inside, until her heart was black and blue. I crawled at six months and walked at nine. And at this time, when I was a creature without words, when the top of my skull was still soft and open to suggestion, she began to exercise me. She lay me on the bunny blanket and moved my little limbs up and down, up and down, pumping my arms as if saving my life. As soon as I could crawl, she tied weighted bags to my wrists and ankles so that every movement was useful, every random action part of my instruction. She calculated how much I could bear, and then encouraged me to bear more. Dr Sime is quite correct when she notes that I did not initiate this regimen, but she overlooks the fact that by the time I could talk, I never once refused a training session. On the contrary, I looked forward to those hours, when my mother and I worked as one body again, as if we had never been parted. She wanted me to be happy, and she was always checking my mood, as if the slightest change might signal cause for concern. She always said I must tell her if I was no longer enjoying myself.

After two years of entering the smaller, local competitions, I won my first title at the age of four, and from then on we took things seriously. Baby Atlas, Junior Muscles, Little Mr Hercules: I won them all. My mother quit her job at the institute and became my manager and agent, and we were often away from home for weeks at a time while I competed all over the country. I loved travelling, watching my hometown drop away as the plane took off and rose above the clouds, where the sky was always perfect. I would settle into my seat and listen to music on my Walkman or play Pacman on my mother's calculator. I was good at that; I could gobble up legions of aliens as easily as vitamin pills.

I don't tan easily – I imagine this comes from my father – but for

competitions the skin must be as dark as teak, so that the muscles reveal themselves, so that they cast a shadow. My mother knew how to colour my skin so they stood out. Before each meet she applied the fake tan to my body, taking care to massage it into my hairline and to cover my palms and the soles of my feet. I became a different person, my pale eyes stark against my face. I learned not to flinch when she stroked the backs of my knees and under my arms; I was not ticklish, not like other children who shrieked and screamed and ran from their parents. When she rubbed the stain into my chest, I felt calmed, and when she did the whorls of my ears, I heard the ocean. In the shower the fake tan turned the water brackish. It pooled at my feet, spattered the white walls, as if there had been a storm inside. I scrubbed at my skin until the water ran clear, but even then a layer of colour lingered for a time, so I was never sure what my real complexion was. Every day, with my breakfast, my mother gave me vitamins from a bottle with no label.

I had my rivals, of course; the prizes were such that there were always new contenders. My mother taught me not to talk to them, but to concentrate instead on my stance and my lifts, running through my routine in my head so that when my name was called I could walk onto the stage and perform without thinking. *Smile*, she willed from the audience, stretching the sides of her mouth apart as wide as they would go, showing all her white teeth. The other mothers always made a space for her.

I was not like the other boys my age, and I was not like their elder brothers either. At breakfast I did not sit down to a plate of cereal or toast; I did not drink glasses of orange cordial or mugs of hot chocolate. My mother made me liquid meals in the blender instead: bananas and berries and milk, and of course the powdered protein supplements that always left a sandy residue in the bottom of the cup, as if someone had used it for sandcastles. In the school playground I danced across the monkey bars; I slipped like water through the cool concrete pipes. I twisted the chain handles of the swing, winding myself up then letting myself go so that I spun and spun, and the playground disappeared, and all the other, weaker children disappeared. When we were learning about the solar system Mr Mayhew took us outside late in the afternoon, just before the bell rang. He made us stand very still while he traced our shadows with chalk. I could smell the stones and the dirt and the stale sandwiches as I stood waiting for my turn. When he had finished there was a forest of bodies on the warm concrete, as if there had been a slaying. They were gone the next day, these chalk children, washed away by rain in the night, but I could not forget my stocky shadow, so different from the others.

My mother and I did well. I was invited to open gyms and health-food shops; my image sold breakfast cereals and long-life batteries and super-strength glue; a line of sportswear for children bore my name. We bought a much bigger house which had its own gym and swimming pool just for me. My mother let me

unlock the front door the day we moved in, as if it were another official opening, but I did not rush ahead of her. I turned and scooped her up in my arms and we entered together. She felt as light as a shadow to me.

I was happy in the new house. It had everything I wanted, and I imagined myself staying there forever, like the people who shut themselves in giant glass domes as experiments. There was a wall-sized TV in front of the treadmill and the rowing machine and the stationary bicycle, so that I could pretend that it was a picture window, and that I was outside as I trained, but of course, no matter what distance I covered on the machines, I never ended up anywhere different.

We met The Cougar soon after we moved there. I had seen him at the competitions, prowling about in the halls and auditoriums, a sleek figure with a powerful torso and the bowed, wishbone legs of a serious lifter. He watched the junior competitors as if he would like to devour them, now and then approaching close enough to hand over a business card. These days a man like that would be quietly taken aside and questioned, but back then the mothers were delighted if someone ran an assessing eye over their children; every stranger was a potential talent scout. (Josh Conroy had been spotted that way and now, despite the dyslexia, had a scholarship to one of the better universities; Cameron Hayden had been whisked from the locker room to children's television where he was granted his own weekly slot with Dr Woofs, a puppet dachshund who was an expert on pre-teen nutrition.) One day The Cougar took my forearm and examined it, nodding to himself, pursing his lips.

'You have the right bones,' he said, turning my arm over and looking underneath, pinching the skin to check for fat, assessing the width of my wrist against his own. It was simple physics, he said, addressing my mother now but still holding my forearm. 'The shorter the bones, the easier the lift.'

When he gave his card to my mother, she slipped it inside one of the secret inner pockets of her purse, as if it were a winning ticket.

Within a week The Cougar had started training me and my sessions with my mother had stopped. I had thought she might be sad about that, perhaps even refuse to step down, but on the contrary, she seemed glad of the time to herself, and whenever I saw her she was painting her nails, or trying her hair in a different style, or hanging new clothes in her walk-in wardrobe. Sometimes she sat in on our sessions, but even then she offered none of her usual advice or commands, and I had the feeling that although she was watching closely, it was not me she was observing.

If I wanted to make any real progress, The Cougar told me, I would need a name – something that made people think of strength, potency. Animals were good. Did I have any favourite animals?

'I like fish,' I said.

The Cougar laughed, but not in a friendly way.

'Um … I had an ant farm once. Ants are pretty strong.'

The Cougar ran his eyes over my pale arms and legs, my milky chest. 'The White Rhino,' he said. 'Very rare and very strong.'

I wasn't sure I wanted to be a rhino. They bathed in mud and had horns on their noses and little stumps for legs. I looked at my legs.

'We'll have some T-shirts made up for you,' said The Cougar. 'You can give them to your friends at school. Your mother and I will wear them too.'

I wanted to tell him that I couldn't think of anyone to give a T-shirt to at school. It was bad enough that I was so much bigger than everyone else; the boys were intimidated by my bulk, and the girls just thought I was a freak.

'I'll have another think about a name,' I said, and for the rest of that week I tried to find something that fitted. The problem was, all the ones I could come up with were already taken: The Bomb, T-Rex, The Hammer. Besides, my mother and I had been very successful up until then without using a nickname, a fake ID; why change what worked? I could not rid myself of the feeling that The Cougar wished to remake me entirely, and that I was expected to go along with the christening of this new being, this giving of a name to a child who was not quite human.

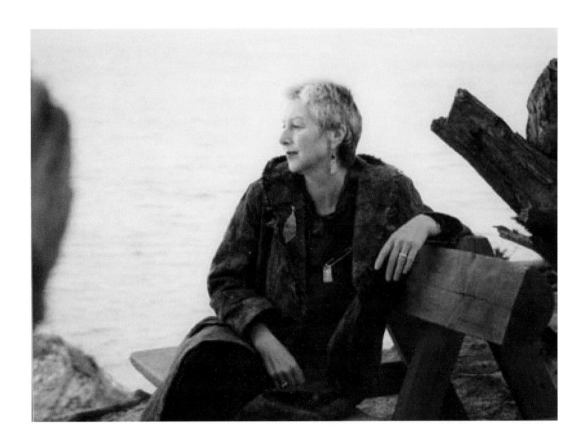

# DIANNE (RUTH) PETTIS 2006

Dianne (Ruth) Pettis (1955–2008) published
one novel. A second novel has been accepted
by Penguin Group (NZ) to be published in
March 2009.

**DIANNE** (Ruth) Pettis, prior to taking up a Burns Fellowship in the second half of 2006, had published poetry and short stories in *Sport*, *Landfall* and other literary periodicals as well as one novel. During her tenure she edited her second novel, *The First Touch of Light*, which she sent out for consideration, and began work on a third, described by the author as follows, from an email sent three months before her death from cancer in May 2008:

It is, in part, set in a small New Zealand seaside town, and also on one of the Aran Islands, off the coast of Galway. The novel, as yet unnamed, explores the theme of identity

– both the loss of it and the importance of belonging. It looks at the phenomena of something I will call 'racial memory', or that feeling of familiarity with a place and a people we have never come across before. The memory is laid down in our bones by our ancestors and when it surfaces in our lives, it is a feeling akin to 'coming home.' I had written 50,000 words by the end of the tenure, and am currently working towards finishing the first draft. I have included the prologue to this novel as a sample of my writing from that time.[73]

The 2008 Burns Fellow Sue Wootton's poem about her friend Dianne's last weeks, 'Fall Sonata', is the final selection in this volume.

# Prologue

Katherine was born into a pool – not of water – but of grief so dark she had to fight her way spluttering to the surface. And it took a good deal many more years to tap the last of those black droplets out of the myriad of tiny elbows inside her body. Her mother lay flat and lifeless on the narrow bed as if the baby she had just given birth to took her last breath. She didn't even have the strength to cry any more, not even for the one before, the one that had been lost to her just months earlier. Her boy.

Next day the nurse brought her a fat, grinning baby with a fuzz of red hair, the colour of her own, and she couldn't help herself. She cradled that child and stroked its forehead to the tip of its nose, marvelling over its likeness to her first-born, another daughter. They lay together with the sun spilling through the one window on to the bed, dozing in and out of sleep. Until the same nurse broke in on them, her rubber heels sucking the lino, and snatched the sleeping baby out of her arms.

I'm sorry Mrs O'Reilly, there's been a mistake. I've given you the wrong baby.

And she jammed a tight bundle into the empty crook of her arm. A black shock of hair sprouted from the top and beneath it, a tiny dark face, eyes blinking at the new brightness. Before Mary O'Reilly could say 'Are you sure?' the nurse had slammed out of the room with the 'wrong' baby under her arm.

Her mother stared at her, trying to see a likeness, but the crumpled face looked back at her as different and as strange as a creature from another planet. She couldn't even see a resemblance to her husband, as dark as he was. This one had a look about her that denied any possible connection. Her mother sighed deeply and tucked the bundle under the bedclothes so she could sleep. She didn't have the energy to get out of bed and put the baby in her bassinette.

Mary slept the sleep of the dead – its heaviness weighing her down in the hospital bed. She woke briefly as it was getting dark, noticed the baby was gone, and closed her eyes. She couldn't imagine ever getting up again. It took all her strength to

ring the bell for the bed pan. The nurse who came gave her a good ticking off for going to sleep with the baby in her bed.

What if she had slipped out onto the floor?

Mary looked blankly at the nurse.

If you can't manage, just ring the bell and we'll take her to the nursery. Do you want to try feeding her now?

I suppose I … I could try.

I'll just go and get her then. Don't go back to sleep again, mind. You'll need to prop yourself up with a few pillows. I'll be right back.

And the nurse sailed out of the room, closing the door behind her with such force that the bed shook. Katherine's mother eased herself up and tried unsuccessfully to position the pillows behind her back. She ached all over and sitting was particularly uncomfortable. The baby had been in such a hurry she had ripped her way into the world and her mother was now suffering the consequences of that rapid entry. Coupled with the fact that this baby seemed not to have come from her own body, she couldn't imagine how she would put the creature to her breast.

Before she had time to ring the bell and put off, for at least another day, what was bound to be an unpleasant experience, the nurse was pushing open the door with her free elbow and plonking the baby in her lap.

There you go Mrs O'Reilly. See if you can get her to latch on.

I'm not sure … I don't think my milk's come in ….

There's only one way to find out.

And she lifted the baby to Mary's breast, pulling open the unwilling nightgown with her other hand. Katherine's mother sat with her hands, palm up, beside her on the bed. When the baby nuzzled around her nipple, she remained still, as if she had no idea what to do next. With one swift movement, the nurse grabbed her breast and rammed it in the baby's mouth.

You have to show them you mean business Mrs O'Reilly. Now here, you hold her.

It hurts. She's sucking too hard.

Nonsense. It's supposed to feel like that. You'll get used to it. Now make sure you swap to the other side before she's had her fill. I'll be back in a while to see how you're getting on.

This baby was greedy for milk but her mother's breast was empty. It did not even oblige with an oozing of creamy-coloured colostrum to whet her appetite. But she sucked hard as if she would, with the strength of her gums, bully the milk into coming in. Her mother grimaced in pain and tried to slip her finger under Katherine's lip to break the suction. When she finally succeeded, the baby clamped her finger between her gums and kept on sucking. Her mother was

crying now, softly at first, the tears dripping off her cheeks onto the baby's face. Then she gave in to full-blown sobs that shook her shoulders. Katherine's mother sobbed for all that she had ever lost and most of all for her darling boy, taken from her by a cruel disease that struck out of nowhere and made him pale and floppy before it stopped his breath completely. She had loved him so much there was nothing left. She was dry as her breast.

# LAURENCE FEARNLEY 2007

*Laurence Fearnley (b. 1963) has published six novels.*

**WHEN** she took up the Burns Fellowship early in 2007, Laurence Fearnley had already published five novels in nine years. During 2007 a sixth novel came out, written before she came to the Fellowship. During her Burns year she finished the draft of a seventh novel, 'Mothers' Day', which will join *Butler's Ringlet* (2004) and *Edwin and Matilda* (2007) to finish a rural Otago-Southland trilogy about love – looking for it, finding it, and losing it. The extract below is from the unedited first draft of 'Mother's Day' and is preceded by Laurence Fearnley's contextualisation.

The novel is set in Invercargill and centres on Maggie, a woman who is a caregiver employed in her sister's agency. Forty years old, Maggie lives with two of her three children as well as her young grandson, Storm.

This piece describes a competition for a car her teenage son, Bevan, has entered. The idea is that the person who can keep one hand on the car the longest wins it.[74]

### FROM **Mother's Day**

A small group clustered around a vehicle parked at the edge of the car yard. As Maggie approached her eye was caught by a wind torn banner which twisted and flapped from a single rope tied to a pole. A second length of rope, hanging from the banner's bottom corner, flicked with each gust of wind so that the image overall reminded Maggie of a recently caught fish thrashing on a jetty.

Seated on a white plastic chair towards the rear of the car was Bevan. By his feet was a tartan thermos which rolled on the ground, blown back and forth across the short distance separating the hem of Bevan's blanket and the rear wheel. The palm of one gloved hand placed on the car, Bevan raised the other in a weak wave of acknowledgement as Maggie and Storm approached. He appeared to be half frozen and tired.

Running ahead, Storm clambered onto Bevan's knee. Oblivious to Bevan's panicked, 'Get off! You'll knock me over!' Storm began questioning him, his words tumbling ahead of his thoughts as he tried to ascertain how close to winning the car his uncle was. Looking around, Maggie could see three other people, all with gloved palms pressed firmly against the car. They, too, appeared bleary eyed and chilled to the bone, but, like Bevan, their faces seemed set with determination. Seeing them, Maggie felt sick. It was all she could do not to drag her son away. Instead, however, she pulled Storm to one side before placing a small carton of Kentucky Fried Chicken on her son's knee. 'You need to eat something warm,' she muttered, her eyes glancing over the faces of the other contestants as they watched her carefully. 'There's soup, too but I left it in the car.'

She stood back and watched as her son fumbled with one hand in an attempt to open the box. A sense of irritation took hold of her. Snapping, 'You look like you've had a stroke, or something!' she snatched the box from him and ripped it open, before returning it to her son's knee with a curt, 'There you go, grandpa.'

With nothing more to say, she stepped back and, holding Storm by the hand, watched as Bevan carefully tore at the chicken, ripping chunks of flesh and skin from the bone as small pieces fell away, dropping to the ground by his feet. Hearing a whisper, she glanced down and catching sight of Storm she followed the direction of his hand which was pointing towards a clear plastic bottle quarter filled with yellow liquid. 'What's that?' she heard her grandson ask. 'It looks like pee,' he added, giggling.

'It is pee,' muttered Maggie, catching Bevan's eye as she spoke. She stared hard at her son but, her gaze returned, she turned back to Storm, asking, 'Are you hungry?'

Pushing him forward, she told him to take a piece of Bevan's chicken and then looked around once more, shuffling uneasily as she did so. 'Well …' she began but then, thinking of nothing to say, fell silent, before beginning again, 'Looks like you're having fun.'

Bevan scowled, 'It's not meant to be fun,' he grunted, 'It's a competition.'

Nodding, Maggie fell silent, then, for the first time looking closely at the car, commented, 'It's very yellow, isn't it? Is it any good?'

As expected, her son only frowned, sneering, 'What do you think? It's a 1996 Mitsubishi Evo4 ….'

Maggie shrugged, 'Carol told me they were offering a BMW soft top ….'

'What would she know?' interrupted Bevan, 'Her head's so far up her arse, she wouldn't have a clue.'

Shocked by what he had said, Maggie was about to reprimand him when she heard a voice from the other side of the car suddenly announce, 'Shit, I've had enough of this.' Following the sound, she saw a plump woman get stiffly to her feet and stretch. As Maggie watched, the woman took off her woollen beanie and turned towards her. It was a face Maggie recognised immediately as belonging to Justine's old friend, Amber. Years had passed since she'd last seen her but even so Maggie was surprised by her appearance. Though no older than twenty three or four, Amber's face was weathered and blotchy, dark shadows encircling her eyes. Not wishing to be recognised, Maggie quickly looked away, catching sight of a familiar red car pulling up behind hers as she did so. Her heart sunk. 'Todd,' she muttered, before facing her son, asking, 'What's he doing here? I thought I asked you to stay away from him.'

Turning back, she saw the door of the car slowly open, loud music preceding Todd as he emerged. Catching sight of her, however, he hung back, leaning against the bonnet as he pulled a packet of cigarettes from his pocket which he tapped absently against his leg. To her surprise, Bevan didn't appear particularly pleased to see him. Mumbling, 'I didn't tell him to come,' he neither smiled nor waved in the direction of his acquaintance. Frowning, he simply continued to eat, ignoring the older boy who was now trying to light his cigarette in the shelter of his cupped palm. Sensing that something had changed in her son's relationship with the boy, Maggie began to relax. Perhaps, she thought, things weren't as bad as she'd imagined. Trying to be helpful, she offered, 'I'll tell him to clear off, if you like.' A pained look crossed Bevan's face but he said nothing.

Several seconds passed, neither of them speaking and then a bell rang. 'Toilet break,' muttered Bevan, standing up. 'I'm allowed five minutes.' Stretching and rubbing his legs, he added, 'Hand me that bottle, Storm.' Then for the first time since she had arrived, Maggie saw her son smile, a foolish grin crossing his face

as he explained how, during the night, he had been caught short between official breaks and that with only one hand he had had to wrestle the bottle under his blanket, and, without anyone seeing, try and pee into it. Still smiling, though looking somewhat embarrassed, he explained that he had pretty much missed most of the time and had got his trousers all but soaked in the process. Then, indicating a boy not much older than himself who was also competing for the car, he added that he should have just done like him and peed against the car. 'If you come back later,' he finished, 'can you bring me some clean trousers and undies otherwise I'm going to wind up smelling like one of your piss in the pants clients.'

He wandered away and Maggie watched as Todd trailed after him, catching him just as he disappeared into a nearby port-a-loo. She'd intended to remind him that he had school in the morning but it didn't matter, she'd call back later. Glancing down at Storm, who was munching away on a drumstick, she recognised a look of admiration on his face. Looking up at her, he whispered, 'It's a really cool car, eh? It looks just like one of those boy racer cars.' He sounded so impressed that Maggie had to smile, then leading him back to her own worn out vehicle she warned, 'I don't want you ever taking part in a competition like that.' She could see that Storm didn't understand. He was too young to realise that competitions like that one were humiliating, that their success depended on their appeal to those with nothing to lose. She didn't want Storm to be dragged down to that level. It was bad enough that Bevan had been sucked in. Watching her son stoop that low filled her with anger – but, he was old enough to make his own decisions. In any case, there was no way she could have stopped him.

# SUE WOOTTON 2008

*Sue Wootton (b. 1961) has published two collections of poetry, had short stories published and broadcast, and has a children's book appearing in 2008.*

**THE** incumbent Burns Fellow Sue Wootton, when appointed late in 2007, had published one collection of poetry, *Hourglass*, in 2005, with a second, *Magnetic South*, forthcoming. The second collection was launched at the end of February 2008. At the time of writing (April 2008), Wootton has outlined ambitious plans for her tenure, including a collection of short stories, essays and poems for a third collection. Wootton also plans to complete work on an illustrated children's story to be published in 2008.

The following poem is a personal response to the terminal cancer of her friend, the 2006 Burns Fellow Dianne Pettis.

# Fall Sonata

*Adagio*

i
All week the house is keening and adjusting.
Joists creak and whisper as the sun contracts:

secrets being transferred between seasons.
This is the week you turn to your dying,

embarking as if newly blind upon
unwrapping what has landed in your lap –

this last exquisite gift bestowed by life –
intent on transforming fumbling to grace

as piece by piece the wrappings fall.

ii
                                             As you
almost fell, yesterday, swaying on stick legs –

no, not even that: card cut-outs, fake stilts.
Paper woman, thin and crisp, and drifting

sideways in some slight current that eddied
through the room – I thought I might not catch you,

that you were going to slip between my fingers
to the floor. Another near catastrophe

endured, survived.

iii
                              And somehow you abide.
An hour before, your sudden giggling

at being asked your preference in tea:
trim milk or blue? That set you off, a maraca

shaking laughter into my arm; my arm
on your back where I had laid it to absorb

your sobs. Full-fat mirth – we both drank deep
and just as well. You couldn't touch the tea

for nausea.

iv
           Each breath in its tortuous
tracheal kiss is intimate and precious

and plays through the pipes and cavities
of you like harsh revving, like an engine

turning over, turning over, like the sound
of imminent departure. You are down

to wicker ribs, inadequate to cart
each inhalation. Every load of air's

so heavy.

v
      Storm clouds bank up, high stalled wall
on the horizon. A southerly blast

is due, but idles. Meanwhile, full-fat heat
stupefies the kereru undulating

on its twig in the Green Belt. It is all
so improbable. Then, a soft leaf-rattle

as a breeze goes through, where there was (I'm sure)
no breeze. Angel wings, perhaps. I think you

   hear them.

   vi
              I listen harder. Just a breeze,
   just clicks and flicks and ticks that punctuate

the waiting air. Just this shimmering planet
afloat in its membranes. Just an unwanted

forecast, and useless hands, that can only
dangle round your suffering. Yet … the house

cracks its knuckles, so gentle. So alert.
This vigil is full of hands. The world has

other ways of holding.

vii

                                        And other ways
of letting go. The leaves now definitely

working loose, all grips loosening. From hand
to hand you fall away from us towards

an inward cave, dark haven rich with bones.
A place to bite the tail of zero, count

yourself immeasurable. Null season.
Season replete. Season beyond deepest

fall.

1  Charles Brasch, 'Notes', *Landfall* (March 1959): 3

2  Ian Cross, report to the Burns Fellowship Committee, 6 April 1960, University of Otago Registry archives, Burns Fellowship file, 00-156/52, Hocken Library.

3  Ian Cross, *Such Absolute Beginners: A Memoir* (Auckland: David Ling, 2007), p, 90.

4  *Ibid.*, p. 96.

5  Ian Cross, 'Writers in New Zealand: A Questionnaire', *Landfall* 53 (March 1960): 44.

6  Maurice Duggan, 'Beginnings', *Landfall* 80 (December 1966): 337.

7  Maurice Duggan, 'The Burns Fellowship', *Landfall* 87 (September 1968): 238.

8  Maurice Duggan, letter to Frank Sargeson, 16 August 1960, quoted in Ian Richards, *To Bed at Noon: The Life and Art of Maurice Duggan* (Auckland: University of Auckland Press, 1997), p. 271.

9  Maurice Duggan, letter to Keith Sinclair of 17 August 1960, quoted in C.K. Stead, 'Introduction', *The Collected Stories of Maurice Duggan* (Auckland: Auckland University Press, 1981), p. 16.

10  See 'Burns Fellowship Shows Literature has Value in Our Society', *Critic* 7 April 1960: 8; and 'Maurice Duggan on Art and Form in Fiction', *Critic* 28 April 1960: 8.

11  Maurice Duggan, letters to Frank Sargeson, 17 August 1960, 18 October 1960, quoted in Richards, *To Bed at Noon*, pp. 274, 275.

12  Maurice Duggan, letter to Keith Sinclair, 3 April 1960, quoted in Richards, *To Bed at Noon*, p. 261.

13  Maurice Duggan, letter to Charles Brasch, 6 November 1960, quoted in Richards, *To Bed at Noon*, p. 276.

14  Charles Brasch, letter to Maurice Duggan of 13 August 1961, quoted in Richards, *To Bed at Noon*, p. 290.

15  See Duggan, 'Writer's Problem of Ordering his Experience for the Purposes of Prose Described by Burns Fellow', *Critic* 28 April 1960: 8; and *Ibid.*, 'Only Connect (a Presumptuous Note on the Teaching of English Literature)', *Manuka* (1960): 5–8.

16  John Caselberg, letter to Charles Brasch, 29 October 1960, quoted in Peter Simpson, *Answering Hark: McCahon/ Caselberg Painter/Poet* (Nelson: Craig Potton, 2001), p. 84.

17  John Caselberg, Report to the Burns Fellowship Committee, 17 January 1962, University of Otago Registry archives, Burns Fellowship File, 00-156/52, Hocken Library.

18  Registrar, University of Otago, letter to Brash, Thompson and Millar, 19 October 1961, University of Otago Registry Archives, Burns Fellowship File 00-156/52.

19  R.A.K. Mason, 'Writers in New Zealand: A Questionnaire', *Landfall* 53 (March 1960): 59.

20  R.A.K. Mason, letter to the Registrar, University of Otago, 17 October 1961, quoted in Rachel Barrowman, *Mason: The Life of R.A.K. Mason* (Wellington: Victoria University Press, 2003), p. 348.

21  R.A.K. Mason, quoted in *Evening Star* (Dunedin) 22 January 1962: 1.

22  R.A.K. Mason, letter to the Registrar, University of Otago, 26 August 1961, University of Otago Registry Archives, Burns Fellowship file 00-156/52, Hocken Library. See also *Evening Star* (Dunedin) 22 January 1962: 1; *Otago Daily Times* 26 January 1962: 6; *Press* (Christchurch) 17 January 1962: 13.

23  R.A.K. Mason, letter to the Registrar, University of Otago, 31 August 1962, University of Otago Registry Archives, Burns Fellowship file 00-156/52, Hocken Library; for the plays and poems see 'Asclepius' (John Caselberg), *Poet Triumphant: The Life and Writings of R.A.K. Mason (1905–1971)* (Wellington: Steele Roberts, 2004), pp. 247–8, 256–9.

24  R.A.K. Mason, letter to Douglas Lilburn, 23 June 1970, quoted in Barrowman, *Mason*, p. 376.

25  R.A.K. Mason, letter to John Weir, 8 June 1970, quoted in Barrowman, *Mason*, p. 393. For the identification of Szasy, see *Mason* p. 357 and endnote 41, p. 428.

26  See Geoff Adams. 'Breathing Space for a Writer', *Otago Daily Times* 13 April 1963: 7.

27  Janet Frame, letter to the Burns Fellowship Committee,

21 October 1966, in the Burns Fellowship file 00-156/52, University of Otago Registry Archives, Hocken Library.

28 Fellowship Committee, Letter to Brash, Thompson and Millar, Barristers and Solicitors, 11 November 1966, University of Otago Registry Archives, Burns Fellowship file, 00-156/52, Hocken Library.

29 James K. Baxter, letter to the Registrar, 27 August 1966, University of Otago Registry Archives, Burns Fellowship file 00-156/52, Hocken Library.

30 Ruth Dallas, letter to Professor E.A. Horsman, 4 December 1968, from a copy from the author.

31 According to Dibble, 'from a review by "R.B."...' from either the *Dominion* or *Evening Post*.

32 Nola Millar, 'Universities Drama', *Landfall* 91 (September 1969): 290, 292.

33 George Webby, 'Review of Lines to M', *ACT* 10 (Summer 1970): 7.

34 Warren Dibble, Introduction included with letter to Lawrence Jones, 10 April 2008.

35 Warren Dibble, letter to Lawrence Jones, 10 April 2008.

36 *Ibid.*

37 O.E. Middleton, email to Lawrence Jones, 15 February 2008.

38 Ian Wedde, letter to Lawrence Jones, 11 February 2008.

39 Graham Billing, report to Burns Fellowship Committee, November 1973, University of Otago Registry Archives, Burns Fellowship File, 00-152/56, Hocken Library.

40 Denis Welch, 'the spiral ascent of Graham Billing', *Listener* 23 October 1993: 26.

41 Witi Ihimaera, letter to Lawrence Jones, 12 February 2008.

42 Witi Ihimaera, 'Deep South/Impressions of Another Country', *Review* 75: 13, 15.

43 Ihimaera, letter to Lawrence Jones, 12 February 2008.

44 *Ibid.*

45 Witi Ihimaera, 'Maori life and literature: a sensory perception', in *New Zealand through the Arts: Past and Present* (The Turnbull Winter Lectures 1981) (Wellington: The Friends of the Turnbull Library, 1982), pp. 50, 53.

46 Ihimaera, letter to Lawrence Jones, 12 February 2008.

47 Keri Hulme, letter to the Registrar, July 1976, University of Otago Registry Archives, Burns Fellowship File 00-156/52, Hocken Library.

48 Keri Hulme, email to Lawrence Jones, 4 March 2008.

49 *Ibid.*

50 *Ibid.*

51 Roger Hall, email to Lawrence Jones, 23 January 2008.

52 Peter Olds, letter to Lawrence Jones, 1 April 2008.

53 *Ibid.*

54 Philip Temple, email to Lawrence Jones, 16 January 2008.

55 Brian Turner, email to Lawrence Jones, 16 February 2008.

56 Robert Lord, 'Playwright: Robert Lord talks with Rowena Cullen', videotape, Audiovisual Learning Centre, University of Otago, 1987.

57 *Ibid.*

58 John Dickson, *Sleeper* (Auckland: Auckland University Press, 1998). Back cover.

59 *Ibid.*, Acknowledgements.

60 John Dickson, letter to Lawrence Jones, 14 February 2008.

61 Renée, email to Lawrence Jones, 11 February 2008.

62 David Eggleton, letter to Lawrence Jones, 22 February 2008.

63 Elspeth Sandys, email to Lawrence Jones, 7 January 2008.

64 Bernadette Hall, email to Lawrence Jones, 23 January 2008.

65 Paddy Richardson, letter to Lawrence Jones, 17 February 2008.

66 Paula Boock, email to Lawrence Jones, 20 March 2008.

67 James Norcliffe, email to Lawrence Jones, 14 February 2008.

68 *Ibid.*

69 Alison Wong, email to Lawrence Jones, 14 February 2008.

70 Nick Ascroft, email to Richard Reeve (Otago University Press), 19 May 2008.

71 Catherine Chidgey, 'Notes on Contributors and Collaborations', *Are Angels OK? The Parallel Universes of New Zealand Writers and Scientists*, ed. Paul Callaghan and Bill Manhire (Wellington: Victoria University Press, 2006), p. 305.

72 *Ibid.*

73 Dianne Pettis, email to Lawrence Jones, 14 February 2008.

74 Laurence Fearnley, email to Lawrence Jones, 29 January 2008.

# ACKNOWLEDGEMENTS

**THANKS** are due to the University of Otago's Department of English, the University of Otago Registry Archives, the Hocken Collections, and Otago University Press for making sources available and/or their support for this publication. For portraits of the Burns Fellows, we are especially grateful to the University's Central Library and to Judith and the late Reg Graham. Dr Lisa Marr's work in obtaining copies of the portraits has been invaluable. The families and estates of contributors, and of course the Fellows themselves, have helped with the preparation of this anthology. We owe them our thanks and gratefully acknowledge the following sources:

**Nick Ascroft**, 'Old Wives' Lives', typescript.
**James K. Baxter**, 'The Burns Fellowship', *Landfall* 87 (September 1968): 243–7; 'On Possessing the Burns Fellowship 1966', *The Man on the Horse* (Dunedin: University of Otago Press, 1967), pp. 14–5; 'At Kuri Bush', *Runes* (London: Oxford University Press, 1973), pp. 37–8; 'Words to Lay a Strong Ghost: The Rock', *Runes*, p. 15; *A Small Ode on Mixed Flatting* (Christchurch: Caxton Press, 1967).
**Graham Billing**, excerpt from *The Primal Therapy of Tom Purslane* (Dunedin: Caveman Press, 1981), pp. 12–5.
**Paula Boock**, excerpt from an unfinished draft of 'Boydi', typescript.
**John Caselberg**, 'William Wilberforce to Everyman' (Dunedin: Otago Bibliography Room, 1972).
**Catherine Chidgey**, excerpt from 'The Deadlift', in *Are Angels OK?: The Parallel Universes of New Zealand Writers and Scientists*, ed. Paul Callaghan and Bill Manhire (Wellington: Victoria University Press, 2006), pp. 87–91.
**Ian Cross**, from 'The Girl', *After Anzac Day* (London: Andre Deutsch, 1961), pp. 187–91.
**Ruth Dallas**, 'Night Piece', *Experiment in Form* (Dunedin:

Press Room, University of Otago, 1964); excerpt from *Ragamuffin Scarecrow* (Dunedin: Bibliography Room, University of Otago, 1969), pp. 3–5; 'In Central Otago', *Walking on the Snow* (Christchurch: Caxton Press, 1976), p. 9; 'In the University Library', *Walking on the Snow*, p. 23.
**Warren Dibble**, excerpt from 'A Marriage', typescript.
**John Dickson**, 'The Assumption of Mr Dickson into the Order of Domestic Cats', *Sleeper* (Auckland: Auckland University Press, 1991), pp. 13–6.
**Maurice Duggan**, from 'Riley's Handbook', *Collected Stories*, ed. C.K. Stead (Auckland: Auckland University Press, 1981), pp. 310–2; excerpt from 'Along Rideout Road that Summer', *Collected Stories*, pp. 196–7.
**Kate Duignan**, excerpt from a draft of 'New Ships', typescript.
**David Eggleton**, 'Top Dollar', typescript.
**Laurence Fearnley**, excerpt from a first draft of 'Mother's Day', typescript.
**Janet Frame**, 'The Burns Fellowship', *Landfall* 87 (September 1968): 241–2; excerpt from *The Rainbirds* (Christchurch: Pegasus, 1969), pp. 163–4; 'The New Building', *The Pocket Mirror* (New York: Braziller, 1967), p. 6.
**Maurice Gee**, excerpt from *A Special Flower* (London: Hutchinson, 1965), pp. 71–5.
**Bernadette Hall**, 'Duck', *Still Talking* (Wellington: Victoria University Press, 1997), pp. 21–4; 'Poem in the Matukituki Valley', *Still Talking*, p. 51.
**Roger Hall**, excerpt from *Middle-Age Spread* (Wellington: Victoria University Press, 1978), pp. 55–9.
**Noel Hilliard**, excerpt from 'Encounter', *Landfall* 99 (September 1971): 271–6.
**Stuart Hoar**, excerpt from *Yo Banfa* (*Gung Ho*), typescript.
**Lynley Hood**, excerpt from *Minnie Dean: Her Life &*

*Crimes* (Auckland: Penguin, 1994), pp. 192–7.

**Keri Hulme**, 'Moeraki Conversations: 2 He Wahi Tapu', *The Silences Between (Moeraki Conversations)* (Auckland: Auckland University Press, 1982), pp. 15–7; 'Moeraki Conversations: 3', *The Silences Between*, pp. 22–4.

**Sam Hunt**, 'Liz', *Drunkard's Garden* (Wellington: Hampson Hunt, 1977), p. 2; 'Two Winter Settings', *Drunkard's Garden*, p. 7; 'Those Eyes: Such Mist', Drunkard's Garden, p. 12; 'My Father Today', *Drunkard's Garden*, p. 30.

**Witi Ihimaera**, 'Masques and Roses', *The New Net Goes Fishing* (London: Heinemann, 1977; rpt Auckland: Heinemann, 1978), pp. 165–71.

**Christine Johnston**, 'Scenes from a Catholic Girlhood', from 'First Words', in *The Source of the Song: New Zealand Writers on Catholicism*, ed. Mark Williams (Wellington: Victoria University Press, 1995), pp. 91–95.

**Michael King**, excerpt from *Wrestling with the Angel: A Life of Janet Frame* (Auckland: Viking, 2000), pp. 98–101.

**Robert Lord**, excerpt from *The Affair*, July 1987 typescript.

**Cilla McQueen**, 'Crikey', *Wild Sweets* (Dunedin: John McIndoe, 1986), p. 22–3; 'Otherwise', *Wild Sweets*, p. 17; 'Axis', *Wild Sweets*, p. 16; 'Recipe for One', *Benzina* (Dunedin: John McIndoe, 1988), p. 48; 'Synaesthesia', *Benzina*, p. 17.

**Owen Marshall**, excerpts from *A Many Coated Man*, (Dunedin: Longacre, 1995), pp. 20–4, 147–8.

**R.A.K. Mason**, 'Tria Carmina Ad Miram', *OUSA Literary Review* 1962, pp. 6–9; 'Song for Dunedin', *Otago Daily Times* 27 July 1963: 7.

**O.E. Middleton**, excerpt from 'The Loners', *The Loners* (Wellington: Square and Circle, 1972), pp. 97–101.

**Michael Noonan**, 'Three Soldiers – Notes on New Zealand Historical Writing', *OUSA Literary Review* 1979, pp. 18–21.

**James Norcliffe**, 'A Sense of Direction', *Along Blueskin Road* (Christchurch: Canterbury University Press, 2005), p. 17; 'Yippee!', *Along Blueskin Road*, pp. 52–3; 'Planchette', *Along Blueskin Road*, p. 65.

**Peter Olds**, 'The Green Gate in Ward 10', *Beethoven's Guitar* (Dunedin: Caveman Press, 1980), pp. 25–6.

**Rawiri Paretene**, 'Untitled', 'Dunedin Wake up…', 'To US…', 'To Robin', typescript.

**Dianne Pettis**, excerpt from an untitled draft, typescript.

**Sarah Quigley**, 'Donkeys are Introverts', *Listener* 3 January 2004: 39.

**Renée**, excerpt from *Jeannie Once* (Wellington: Victoria University Press, 1991), pp. 21–4.

**Jo Randerson**, 'Gazelles', *The Keys to Hell* (Wellington: Victoria University Press, 2004), pp. 56–7.

**Paddy Richardson**, excerpt from *In the Company of a Daughter* (Wellington: Steele Roberts, 2005), pp. 34–7.

**Elspeth Sandys**, 'Swimming Away', typescript.

**Bill Sewell**, 'Pearse at Mount Erebus', *Solo Flight* (Dunedin: University of Otago Press, 1982), p. 21; 'Spain', *Wheels Within Wheels* (Dunedin: University of Otago Press, 1983), p. 26.

**Maurice Shadbolt**, 'The Burns Fellowship', *Landfall* 87 (September 1968): 239–41; excerpt from *Among the Cinders* (Christchurch: Whitcombe and Tombs, 1965), pp. 259–61.

**Philip Temple**, excerpt from 'Strongbeak's Dreaming', *Beak of the Moon* (Auckland: Collins, 1981), pp. 250–3.

**Brian Turner**; 'Listening to the Mountain', *Bones* (Dunedin: John McIndoe, 1985), pp. 48–50; 'Photograph at the Caledonian Games', *Bones*, p. 12.

**Hone Tuwhare**, 'Rain', *Come Rain Come Hail: Poems by Hone Tuwhare* (Dunedin: Bibliography Room, University of Otago, 1970), p. 6; 'Hotere', *Come Rain Come Hail*, p. 17; 'Child Coming Home in the Rain from the Store', *Come Rain Come Hail*, p. 21; 'Reign Rain', *Making a Fist of It* (Dunedin: Jackstraw Press,1978), p. 11.

**Ian Wedde**, 'In Clover', *The Shirt Factory and Other Stories* (Wellington: Victoria University Press, 1981), pp. 26–30.

**Alison Wong**, excerpt from an untitled draft, typescript.

**Sue Wootton**, 'Fall Sonata', typescript.

# Illustration Sources

*Also published by Otago University Press*

**KA TAOKA HAKENA**
TREASURES FROM THE HOCKEN COLLECTIONS
EDITED BY STUART STRACHAN AND LINDA TYLER

This book marks the centenary of the Hocken Collections' Deed of Trust in 1907. In that year Dr T.M. Hocken of Dunedin – historian, bibliographer and collector – undertook to gift to the University of Otago his magnificent collection of books, manuscripts, paintings and other historical documents relating to New Zealand and the Pacific, in trust for the people of New Zealand.

*Treasures from the Hocken Collections* documents almost 200 items, dating from the seventeenth century to the present day, photographed by Bill Nichol. These include historical and modern paintings, photographs and drawings, maps and plans, books, newspapers and posters, sheet music and sound recordings, and of course early New Zealand manuscripts. Many items relate to Maori history. Together they comprise an album in which the reader may browse the origins, obsessions and accomplishments of New Zealand and New Zealanders. Letters, diaries, a jigsaw puzzle, suffragette badges, a skirt embroidered whilst on an Amazonian bicycle ride, a facial tattoo used as a personal signature, leaves employed as writing paper … an ever-changing array of interesting material awaits the reader.

Introductory essays by Rachel Barrowman and Stuart Strachan on Dr Hocken and the development of the Hocken Collections from 1910, along with short essays by curatorial staff, provide the necessary background. Taken as a whole, the book stands as a tribute to the generosity of the Hocken Collections' many benefactors.

ISBN 978 1 877372 40 7, $65.00